The Writer's Essential Desk Reference

THE Writer's ESSENTIAL DESK REFERENCE

Edited by Glenda Tennant Neff

Writer's Digest Books

Cincinnati, Ohio

The Writer's Essential Desk Reference. Copyright 1991 by Writer's Digest Books. Printed and bound in the United States of America. All rights reserved. No part of this book may be reproduced in any form or by electronic or mechanical means including information storage and retrieval systems without permission in writing from the publisher, except in a review. Published by Writer's Digest Books, an imprint of F&W Publications, Inc., 1507 Dana Ave., Cincinnati, Ohio 45207. 1-800-289-0963. First edition.

This hardcover edition of *The Writer's Essential Desk Reference* features a "self-jacket" that eliminates the need for a separate dust jacket. It provides sturdy protection for your book while it saves paper, trees and energy.

98 97 96 95 94   7 6 5 4

Library of Congress Cataloging-in-Publication Data

The Writer's essential desk reference / edited by Glenda Tennant Neff. — 1st ed.
   p. cm.
Includes bibliographical references and index.
ISBN 0-89879-477-3
   1. Authorship. I. Neff, Glenda Tennant, 1961- . II. Writer's Digest Books (Firm)
PN151.W74   1991
808'.02 — dc20   91-12656
                                                                                  CIP

Designer: Carol Buchanan
Typesetter: Sharon Lee

Contents

About the Authors

MATTHEW JACKSON, author of "Living as a Writer," is a freelance writer based in Cincinnati who writes regularly on marketing, legal and financial issues for national business and trade publications. He's a former newspaper editor and a trained tax preparer who handles his own bookkeeping and tax returns. He started freelancing first as a newspaper stringer at age 16.

GLENDA TENNANT NEFF, author of "A Community of Writers," began her career as a newspaper reporter and editor at *The Clermont Sun* in Batavia, Ohio. She served as assistant editor for the 1987 editions of *Writer's Market* and *Fiction Writer's Market* and was editor of the 1988-1991 editions of *Writer's Market*. She currently is assistant managing editor of the market books department at F&W Publications.

PAULA DEIMLING, author of "Producing and Polishing It," edited the 1985 and 1986 editions of *Writer's Market* and wrote The Markets column for *Writer's Digest* magazine. She continues to study publishing trends and to teach writing and editing in addition to writing a novel. An adjunct assistant professor at the University of Cincinnati, she holds a master's degree in journalism from the E.W. Scripps School of Journalism.

CHRIS DODD, author of "Researching It," is a former editor of The Markets column for *Writer's Digest* magazine and has written freelance articles for magazines and newspapers for more than 20 years. Her work has appeared in *Health*, *Victoria*, *Boys' Life*, *St. Anthony Messenger*, and many other publications. She currently is a freelance writer and copyeditor in the Washington, D.C., area.

BONNIE GORDON, author of "Selling It," is a writer and editor with bases in Cincinnati and Philadelphia and has written for book, magazine and newspaper publication. As a freelancer, she has taken on assignments ranging from women's magazine quizzes to technical copy for trade journals. She is on equally familiar ground preparing collateral materials for corporate communications as with publishing her own fiction and producing literary magazines. She currently is writing for visual media as well and is at work on an independent video documentary.

FRED KERNER, author of "Writing and Selling in Canada," is an author, journalist, editor and publisher who has worked in Canada, the U.S. and Britain. Much of his spare time is spent helping writers and publishers, both as a volunteer and through his consulting firm, Publishing Projects Inc. in Toronto. He has been a news executive with The Associated Press and The Canadian Press, and a publishing executive with Prentice-Hall, Fawcett, Hawthorn Books, Reader's Digest and Harlequin Enterprises.

Editor's Note

The idea was simple enough: We wanted to pull together, in a single volume, the information and resources writers needed most.

Then we began the work, and we found out only the idea was simple.

From talking to a variety of writers we discovered they use — or need — a vast amount of information, ranging from advice on contracts to tips on finding out-of-print books. Writers sometimes find the sources they need, sometimes learn about them from other writers, and other times they simply do as well as they can without any help. They agreed, however, that putting background information and a list of these sources in one place would save them time and make their writing lives more efficient.

We organized this "most desired" information into five sections: Living as a Writer, A Community of Writers, Researching It, Producing and Polishing It, and Selling It. We designed the format with both text and listings to offer information and to guide writers to other books, directories, people and groups that could provide them with more specific information. For Canadian authors, whose needs are often overlooked in U.S.-published books, and those U.S. writers who want to know more about the specialties of the Canadian market, we included a chapter on Writing and Selling in Canada.

Although this is a reference book, we didn't want it to have a dry tone or textbook feel, so we asked six authors to gather and present information as though they were sharing tips from their experience with another writer. In distilling the information, we wanted to keep the writer's viewpoint in mind — and also the viewpoints of writers at different stages of their careers. Tax information is abundantly available, but if you want to know what is most likely to apply to you as a writer, this is the place to look first. It can save you hours paging through tax volumes of general information — whether you are making a little extra as a freelancer, planning to make it full-time or have been working that way for several years. And, depending on where you are in your career, you may want to take advantage of either the section on *choosing* a continuing education class or the section on *teaching* a continuing education class. We tried to look at each chapter this way to give you the information you need throughout your career.

You'll find, of course, that some information overlaps. Many resources can be used for both research and sales, for instance, and many groups offer services in more than one area covered in the book. For that reason, you'll want to make use of the extensive index and the references to other sections within the chapters.

The Writer's Essential Desk Reference isn't a substitute for your own research, bookkeeping or promotion efforts. But we hope it will be the *first* source you consult on writing-related matters, one that leads to other sources, provides you with tips you hadn't considered, and generally makes your searches less time-consuming. When valuable books, directories and other information sources are available, we've included the names of these sources. When a comprehensive directory is not available, we've included listings for those people who responded to our request for information. In most sections we also have a sampling of those sources for which we thought writers would be most likely to want information.

Both national and local resources are listed in the book, but you'll undoubtedly find many more on the local level. Be sure you explore these options; they often can provide you with the best value for your money, especially if most of your writing is on the local level.

As you use this book, and other reference books or directories, make it a habit to check information before acting on it. We've tried to include only those directories that are current, but all books with this type of information are subject to the constant changes of the publishing world. Book prices—as well as postage—increase, computer bulletin boards may no longer be available, computer software may be updated and contact people may change from the time we gathered this information until you use it.

Although we've tried to include as much information as possible, we'd also welcome your input about other sources you've found helpful in your writing life. Let us know about books, groups, directories and equipment you've found make your work more efficient and would make this book more useful to other writers.

No reference book could be compiled without the assistance of a number of people, and *The Writer's Essential Desk Reference* is no exception. The authors for each of the chapters brought abundant enthusiasm, expertise and a willingness to ask questions. Countless writers, librarians, lawyers, computer experts and other professionals were open to the questions and offered detailed answers, specifically designed for writers. In house, this book also owes its existence to Connie Achabal's advice, Mary Junewick's production guidance, Sharon Lee's wide-ranging expertise and Catherine Brohaugh's attention to detail.

Together we hope we've provided you with a book that gives you the everyday information you need, so you can get on with your writing.

Chapter 1

LIVING AS A WRITER

As you turn toward the path of freelance writing, you'll find the way strewn with the horror stories of those who gave up on it. They've scurried back to unpleasant jobs, begged for a place beneath the iron heels of the most imperious bosses. Anything but the poverty and insecurity of freelancing.

They probably didn't fail because they couldn't write well enough. They probably failed because they never grasped that writing is a business, too. The business side of freelancing may be as important to success as the creative side. But it's a lot less appealing. Tending to business seems greedy and pedestrian. It's certainly not what you became a writer for. So it's easy to shove business matters into the bottom drawer. There, they fester until one day they burst into your consciousness in a blaze of uncollected bills and overdue taxes.

Neglecting business can ruin even the most talented writer. But the chorus of moans from freelancers who've failed can drown out the fact that many freelancers make a decent living.

Nothing you've done to perfect your craft will prepare you to live as a freelance writer. The business side of writing is confusing. It takes time, hard work and talent. You don't have to consume yourself with business matters to keep them from eating away your livelihood. But you do need to adopt a businesslike approach and commit yourself to taking the time to handle the business chores.

FINANCES FOR WRITERS

As you launch a freelance business, setting up a simple budget will make your life easier. Like any budget, it's only a representation of what's going to happen, not the real thing. But it's important to have some idea of what you're going to spend and earn in the coming year and months.

Once you've been freelancing awhile, budgeting gets easier. You have last year's expenses as a basis for this year's planning. You also have some established markets and clients to make your income a little more predictable. But as a beginner, you'll have to try some educated guesswork.

Start by estimating your costs, because you'll need to plan your income based on these. Monthly overhead, or what you must pay whether you have any work or not, should be the first category you calculate. Overhead includes any payments on your computer or other business equipment, rent on any office space or equipment for the business, publications, answering service, an estimate of your out-of-pocket auto expenses, etc.

Some things that you can deduct from your taxable income you don't need to include in your overhead calculation. For instance, you may be able to deduct some of the interest and value of your house. But since you'd be paying it anyway, you need not consider it business overhead for budgeting purposes.

Conversely, there are some non-business expenses you should include in your overhead. These include the costs of your health and disability insurance. If you were an employee, they'd be part of your compensation. So as a freelancer, consider them part of your costs of doing business.

After figuring overhead, take a look at your household budget and calculate the minimum amount you'll need for living expenses. Include your rent, mortgage, car payments, other consumer debt, groceries and the like. Then, subtract from this amount any take-home pay from your spouse or other sources of steady income.

Financial planners recommend freelancers or any entrepreneurs have two to six months of overhead and living expenses available when they start business. Even if you start with as much work as you can handle, you should still count on two to three months for the checks to appear in your mailbox. A 1988 survey by the Editorial Freelancers Association in New York City found that freelancers waited anywhere from a week to a year to get paid, with one or two months being typical.

Ideally, your capital reserve will be in your savings account. If not, you may consider getting a personal line of credit from a bank. For a freelancer, one obvious obstacle to approval for such credit is not having any inventory or significant business assets as collateral. If you have a good credit record or other assets, such as a home with sufficient equity, you may get around this.

Even if you don't need the money at the outset, it may be a good idea to establish a small line of credit, says Robert J. Oberst, a Red Bank, N.J., financial planner. You can pay the line of credit back early. And even though the process may cost you some time and money, it will also help establish your credit rating in case you really do need money down the road.

To get a bank loan, you may need to develop a business plan. It's probably not a bad idea to develop one anyway, even if you're not applying for a loan. Your plan should include:

- Description of your business, including your background and why your services are unique and valuable to clients in the market.
- Analysis of the market, including the key characteristics of the publications and clients that will use your services and your competition.
- Your marketing or sales plan.
- An outline of your finances, which will include a balance sheet, cash-flow statement and break-even analysis.

If you're turned down for a loan—a distinct possibility—you may be eligible for a government-guaranteed loan through the Small Business Administration.

Even if the SBA doesn't give you a loan, it can give you something that may be more valuable. The Service Corps of Retired Executives (SCORE) is an SBA service that offers business advice to small businesses from retired executives who volunteer their services. They can help steer you through a business plan and other decisions you'll make in starting a business.

HEALTH INSURANCE

Unless you're a Canadian writer covered by national health insurance or fall under the umbrella of a spouse's medical plan, health insurance will be one of the biggest expenses you'll face as a freelancer. It will also be one of your fastest-growing expenses. Annual premium hikes of 20% have been common in recent years.

One option, if you're leaving a job with health benefits, is to continue that coverage. Terms of the Consolidated Omnibus Budget Reconciliation Act (COBRA) of 1985 require employers to continue coverage for at least 18 months at their cost plus a 2% administration charge.

The advantage of COBRA is that you can continue a high-quality group plan. One disadvantage is that a year and a half later, you could still have to hunt for your own plan. And if your employer's plan is generous, you can expect to pay a generous premium.

Writers may also have access to group medical plans through writers' or business organizations. Many national and local groups of writers and affiliated professionals offer access to group health insurance. Some offer several choices, including major medical plans with a range of deductibles and health maintenance organizations (HMOs), in which a group of doctors and hospitals provide services.

For organizations that offer health insurance, check the listings in Chapter 2. Your local chamber of commerce may also have a group plan available to members.

Group plans may offer a discount over getting coverage on your own. But membership in one of the organizations may not guarantee you'll be accepted for coverage. And because states and some cities regulate insurance companies separately, not all group plans are available in all states. You should check with the organization and its insurance carrier for details of the plan, its cost and your eligibility.

A third option is independent coverage. Such coverage isn't necessarily more expensive than a group plan, says Melanie Marsh, spokeswoman for the industry group Health Insurance Association of America in Washington, D.C. But she says an independent plan will probably offer lower benefits than an employer group plan.

The annual deductible for an employer plan is often $100, with up to 100% of major medical costs covered above that. Most independent plans have deductibles of $500 and copayments of 20% for costs above that.

With independent coverage, your premiums are also based more on your individual risk factors. "If you're younger and very healthy, chances are your prices might even be less than for comparable group health insurance," Marsh says. "If you're older and have specific health problems, it's more likely you'll be charged a higher price."

Most independent plans don't include frills like dental or optical coverage, Marsh adds. And they may cover less than employer group plans for mental health and chemical dependency treatment.

The reason for the no-frills approach in most independent plans is something the insurance industry calls "adverse selection." Dental and optical coverage are optional parts of such plans. So most of the people who opt for the coverages are those who need them. That drives the costs sky high, and convinces others who don't use the coverages very much to drop them.

Marsh suggests checking local HMOs for independent coverage. HMOs likely won't be cheaper than standard indemnity insurance, she says. But they may cover more of your expenses, including routine doctor visits and prescriptions with relatively small copayments.

One drawback to independent coverage is that, depending on your state's insurance regulations, you may be vulnerable to cancellation should you develop a lengthy, expensive-to-treat illness. Even if your policy isn't canceled, your premiums may rise precipitously.

Also, most independent coverage will have a waiting period of several months in which treatment for a pre-existing condition won't be covered, Marsh says. Whatever plan you choose, expect it to cost no less than $1,500 a year and possibly $6,000 or more, depending on whether it's an individual, two-person or family plan and on your age and health.

A minor tax break may provide some consolation. If you're not eligible for coverage under a spouse's plan, you can deduct 25% of your self-employed health insurance costs from your taxable income. If you don't qualify for this break, you may also be able to deduct insurance premiums and other medicals costs as an itemized deduction — but only when medical costs exceed 7.5% of your taxable income.

OTHER INSURANCE NEEDS

Leaving the ranks of employees also means leaving behind disability insurance in many cases. Unless you get coverage on your own, that could bring financial hardship on top of an extended illness or disabling injury.

"Disability insurance is really important for the self-employed, especially if they're supporting themselves and a family and no one else has an income coming in," says Elaine Bedel, an Indianapolis financial planner.

Oberst recommends the self-employed get a plan that covers the highest possible percentage of income for as long as possible. No insurance company will underwrite a policy that pays 100% of your income, because that would provide no incentive for you to go back to work once you become disabled, he says. But policies may go as high as 80% and as long as 10 years or age 65.

Cost of a disability plan is determined by your age, health, how long you must be disabled before you collect and how long the payout is, Bedel says.

Many writers' organizations offer group disability coverage. Check with your group's membership director and insurance carrier for details of the plan and whether you're eligible. The groups may also offer relatively inexpensive group life insurance that can cover such items as your mortgage and other obligations.

If you work from your home, you should also check with your home or renter's insurance carrier to make sure your business equipment is covered against casualty and loss. If not, you may need to purchase a rider to cover them. Professional liability is another coverage to consider. Unless you operate some kind of storefront operation, your exposure to being sued for "slips-and-falls" and other common business liability suits is fairly minor. Your largest liability exposure is for libel. If your work seems likely to involve you in libel litigation somewhere down the road, you may want to try taking out a separate libel policy through a business insurance agent.

PLANNING INCOME

The overhead calculation you did earlier is also important in figuring how much you should charge, or at least try to charge, for your services.

To calculate an hourly rate, figure the amount you hope to earn. That may be what you used to make at your old job, or what you'd dream of making at your new one. Then, add in your overhead expenses. Divide that figure by the number of "billable" hours you hope to work in a year. Even if you're a full-time freelancer, this won't be all the hours you work. Count on spending at least a quarter of your time doing your books, marketing your services and reading professional publications.

The hourly rate you arrive at is a starting point. Most magazines don't pay by the hour but by the word, inch or article. But you can analyze how long an assignment will take and multiply that by your hourly rate. That should be something resembling the fee you agree to for the article or project.

Remember to consider expenses, too. Try to estimate your costs for phone calls, mileage and other out-of-pocket expenses and add them to the fee you negotiate if you won't be reimbursed for them.

Freelance writers, like any independent business people, are subject to market forces. And what the market will bear should be part of your calculations. Check with other freelance writers in your area to find out what they charge. In some cities, groups of freelance writers have done surveys to judge the going rate for various kinds of work. Usually, there's a range in hourly rates from entry-level to experienced writers. Try to judge where in that range your services fall and charge accordingly.

Don't charge more than you can get. But don't underestimate yourself, either, even if you are just starting out. Lowball pricing may get you a few jobs. But it will hurt your image with clients and editors.

Once you've begun to establish yourself with some markets, try to estimate how much each one will pay you over the course of a year.

You'll also want to take a shorter-term view. Keep a sheet or a computer file that lists your assignments or jobs for this month and two months down the road. Estimate how much each one will pay you and total your estimate. Though you can't do much now about this month, you can at least look at your projections for the following months and start marketing to meet your income goals.

RECORDS AND ACCOUNTS

Nobody becomes a freelance writer to do bookkeeping. But freelancers quickly find it becomes an important part of their jobs.

Financial planners recommend you set up a separate checking account and credit for your business. That may help keep you from tapping business funds for personal needs. And it provides clearer documentation of your self-employment income and deductible expenses. The Internal Revenue Service doesn't require separate accounts, but it does require you keep basic records of your income and expenses.

The basis of your recordkeeping system should be a daily log of income and expenses. All you really need is a simple, single-entry recordkeeping system, as opposed to the more complicated double-entry acounting format used by larger businesses. In any business supply store, you can find a plain accountant's ledger or a bookkeeping record that will do a passable job.

If you're more comfortable keeping records on your personal computer, your local computer store should have a wide array of software that can do the job. Some more sophisticated programs will also help separate expenses according to client, track billable hours and bill clients. Depending on your level of computer knowhow, you can also customize a recordkeeping system using a spreadsheet program.

If you do keep business records on a computer, that's one more reason to make backup copies of the data on your computer daily. That will prevent a bad floppy disk or a hard disk crash from destroying the records that can't be replaced.

You'll also need to develop a system for saving your receipts. It can be a series of shoe boxes, envelopes or tin boxes. Receipts can be organized by week or month or by their category. For instance, you may want to keep one envelope or box for auto expenses, another for office supplies, etc. Any system can work. Just keep in mind that you may have to show these receipts to an IRS auditor—so you'll want to be able to find them easily.

You need some kind of documentation for every transaction you hope to deduct. That can be a canceled check, a credit card slip, or a cash receipt. Each receipt should also correspond to a dated entry in your records briefly describing what you bought, and, if it's not obvious, the business purpose. You may also want to write the business purpose for the transaction on your receipt, check or credit card slip.

Since you'll probably deduct auto expenses on your tax form, you'll need a mileage log to substantiate them. The log must show the date of each trip, the beginning and ending mileage, and the business purpose for the trip. You should keep the log in your car and transfer information from it to your general records regularly.

Entertainment expenses require particularly stringent documentation. Each entertainment entry for these must show who was entertained and the business purpose for the meeting.

If you use a computer or a portable phone, you may need to keep an additional set of documentation on the business use of those items. You'll also need additional documentation if you plan to deduct home-office expenses.

If you've got several clients, particularly national publications, long-distance phone calls can quickly become difficult to track come billing time. Even if you start marking up your phone bill as soon as it arrives, remembering why you called Pasadena five Mondays ago can be difficult.

Here are some ideas for making your job easier:

- If your phone company offers dial-one long-distance service, you can put different clients on different long distance services. Calls you make for one client can be on your main long-distance company. You can make calls for other clients on competing long-distance lines by dialing an access code instead of 1 before the number. Dialing 10222 instead of 1, for instance, puts you through to MCI's lines. That gives you a way to divide your calls four ways, by ATT, MCI, Sprint and Allnet.
- A slightly more expensive method is getting Call Accounting service for your business line. This allows you to dial a two-digit code that can separate your long-distance bill for up to 100 accounts.
- Keep a phone log, either on paper or on your computer, listing the number, person called, date, time and length of every call you make.

When calculating and billing your phone expenses, don't forget about taxes and directory assistance charges.

Federal, state and local excise taxes on long-distance phone service can increase your bill by as much as 10%, depending on where you live. To find out the tax rate in your area, call your local phone company or calculate it by dividing the tax line on your bill by the total long-distance charges.

Directory assistance charges, which are also taxed, can cost as much as 60¢ each and add up quickly. They aren't itemized on your phone bill like long-distance calls, but you can keep a log of directory assistance calls if you need to itemize them when you bill publishers or other clients.

You'll have to find a safe place to keep all these records you've accumulated for at least two years. The IRS strongly recommends you keep all records for as long as the period of limitations for audits. In most cases, that's three years from the date the return was filed or two years from when the tax was paid, whichever is later.

Keep records documenting income for six years after the return was filed. That's the period of limitations the IRS has for going after unreported income that's greater than 25% of the amount shown on the return.

You'll need records for the cost of your home or improvements for as long as you own the home if you take the home-office deduction. Also, you must keep records of items for which you claim depreciation, such as cars, for as long as you depreciate them, plus the three years after you file your return. For more on depreciation and home-office expense, see the tax section of this chapter.

TRACKING INCOME

Expenses are only half of what you'll be tracking. You'll also need to record income as you receive it and keep check stubs that support the income entries in your books.

Most publishers and other clients will report your earnings as an independent contractor to the IRS and send you a Form 1099 showing the amount. Your income records are important for comparing to the amounts reported on 1099s. And they will also document income not reported on a Form 1099 because you received too little from that source to qualify.

If you've been bartering with other businesses, receiving goods or services rather than cash in return for your services, you must also report what you receive in barter. The law requires you to report the fair market dollar value of what you receive. You can deduct from that amount any out-of-pocket expenses involved in your part of the transaction. But you can't deduct the cost of your labor.

Tax experts provide one additional word of caution. If you're self-employed and your bank account swells far beyond your reported income, that may pique the curiosity of the IRS. So you should also document any non-business income, such as gifts or savings or lottery winnings, that aren't part of your earnings. If you have cash or personal purchases that can't be accounted for from your earnings, and you don't have any record of legitimate sources for your windfall, you could end up paying additional taxes and penalties.

Try to keep your bookkeeping system simple. As long as your system clearly documents your income and your expenses, you don't need much else for tax purposes. Ideally, recordkeeping should take you no more than an hour or two a week, even if you're a full-time freelancer.

GOING WITH THE (CASH) FLOW

That first big check from your freelance efforts, or any check at all, will be a thrill. But don't get carried away. "We all have a tendency when that fat check comes in to think we're rich," Oberst says. "You're really not, because there's going to be a lean period."

Dealing with the choppy seas of cash flow takes a level head and a disciplined approach. Financial planners suggest putting yourself on a salary as one method that may help.

"It depends on the discipline of the individual," says Bedel. "Probably, a person should set a maximum that he or she will take out in any month. Of course, there should also be a minimum amount."

For tax purposes, it doesn't matter whether you hold the money in a personal account or a business account, unless you've incorporated. But it could have an important psychological effect.

"Some people, if they allow themselves free access to all that they bring in, end up spending it all," Bedel says.

ESTIMATED TAXES

Living from check to check can be particularly dangerous because it can leave you in an immense hole on April 15. Freelancers don't have any taxes withheld from their income. As a result, they can be in for a big shock the first time they tally their taxes.

The self-employed are liable for paying estimated taxes quarterly once their net earnings exceed $500. If you owe the IRS more than $500 when you file your return, you may be subject to a penalty for underpayment of estimated tax. To avoid this, track your income and expenses so that you can document exactly when you began turning a profit. And get a copy of Form 1040-ES from your library or the IRS to calculate and make your estimated payments.

The IRS expects you to make a good faith effort to estimate your annual income, even though you're estimating it early in the year. And in most cases, the IRS expects you to pay the tax due on your income in four equal payments. The IRS assumes earnings came in an even flow unless you can document otherwise.

You'll be safe from paying any penalties if you pay estimated taxes equal to at least 100% of your prior year's taxes or 90% of what you owe for this year. If you can't estimate this year's income accurately, a safe bet is to pay a sum equal to last year's tax liability in four installments.

Your state and city may also have rules requiring withholding. If your taxes exceed a certain amount when you file your return, you could also be forced to pay a penalty at this level, too. So you should also contact state and city tax officials to get appropriate tax forms.

To be safe, put aside 33% of your net earnings from self employment each month. That should cover your federal income and self-employment taxes plus state and local income taxes. Try to track when you reach the 28% federal income tax bracket and start putting aside 50% after that. Your tax return has a table near the back that shows the cutoff points.

While underpaying estimated taxes can bring an IRS penalty, overpaying brings another penalty. You lose interest on any money you pay the IRS before it's required. So pay the least allowed. For instance, if your income is up this year from last, just pay 100% of last year's tax liability and bank the rest until April 15. But if you're likely to spend any money you have, it's probably better to pay the IRS now. Otherwise, you may have to borrow to pay your taxes later.

LEVELING OUT CASH FLOW

Dealing with estimated taxes systematically is one of the best ways freelancers can avoid cash-flow problems. A few other strategies may also help.

Marketing is a crucial element. There's nothing like regular work to provide regular cash. Developing a few key accounts, preferably large and reliable enough to cover your overhead and basic living expenses, is important. It's all the better if these accounts provide assignments as well as fielding queries from you, so it's not always your burden to come up with ideas.

Once you have such accounts, however, don't become complacent. Nothing lasts forever, so don't let any one account become more than a third of your business. If you want to avoid cash flow problems down the road, keep working on developing new clients, large and small.

Incorporating a marketing strategy into your routine is also important. That means sending out queries or contacting potential clients even when you're busy. If you market only when things are slow, you may put yourself on a psychological and financial roller coaster — sending queries one month, getting assignments the next, and then waiting for the checks during another slow month. Try to set aside at least one day a month for marketing, even during the busiest times.

Once you're selling your work, you should meticulously track accounts receivable. That is, what publishers and other clients owe you. Unless you write a lot of low-paying articles or you've delved into a retail aspect of the business, such as résumé writing, this is a fairly easy task. You probably won't have more than 10 accounts at a time that owe you money. Find a way to record who owes you money, how much it is and when it's due on a weekly basis. To the extent possible, arrange payment on your terms. The norms vary widely depending on what you're doing. Book authors have the strong advantage of receiving advances, something article writers rarely enjoy. But you may be able to get some money up front for copywriting jobs, or even expense money up front from magazines.

For article writers, publications that pay on acceptance are obviously more desirable than those that pay on publication. If you're getting paid on publication, you could wait months for your article to be published, and at least a month after that to get paid. If paid on acceptance, you should get paid within a month of your final rewrite no matter when the article is published.

Some writers refuse to work for pay on publication. While this is a principled stand for writerdom, it can crimp your marketing prospects. Payment on publication isn't so bad if you can develop a long relationship with a publication that will publish your work regularly and pay promptly. A publisher who pays promptly after publication is always better than one that allegedly pays on acceptance but strings you along for months with niggling rewrites and excuses.

Whatever payment cycle you ride, fast action is the key to good cash flow. "The quicker you move to collect, the greater the chance it will not become a lengthy account receivable," Oberst says.

Some other billing and business practices that should improve your cash flow are:

- Incorporate billing into your weekly schedule.
- Bill as soon as payment is due, sending an invoice with your manuscript.
- Tabulate your phone and other expenses as soon as you can after the bill comes and send out expense bills to publishers.
- Send late notices or call when payment isn't received within 30 days.
- In most cases, you won't know how good a publisher's or client's payment practices are until they owe you money. So don't let a new, unproven account run up huge tabs before you get paid.

CREDIT-CHECKING TIPS

Dun & Bradstreet, virtually the only source for comprehensive credit reports on businesses, is probably too expensive for most writers. But there are some informal ways to get a feel for how creditworthy a publication is.

First, look at a sample copy, and preferably several, before you do any work. Editors routinely advise writers to do this anyway. Their goal is to help you to mold your work to their format. But you also should do it to protect yourself.

Editorial quality is one sign of business integrity. If a publication shortchanges its readers, what makes you think it won't shortchange its writers, too? Some danger signs are headlines that promise what articles don't deliver and articles that are misleading, over-hyped and under-researched. Look at the masthead, too. Who's the publisher? Does it list an address or just a post office box? Look also for contributing editors — freelancers who contribute regularly to the publication. Having contributing editors is one sign that a publication treats freelancers well enough to keep them coming back.

If still you have doubts, call and ask to be put in contact with one or more of the contributing editors. Ask them about the publication's payment practices.

Also look for bylines. Do writers seem to have bylines for several consecutive months and then drop out of sight? If so, it could be a sign they aren't getting paid. You may want to contact one of these writers to find out about the publication's payment practices.

Finally, count how many pages of advertising the publication has this month compared to preceding months and the same months the previous year. If the ad pages are slipping seriously, it could be a sign of a failing publication. Also check who advertises. Are the advertisers reputable companies, or are they mostly sleazy-looking get-rich-quick schemes?

These aren't scientific methods that will always keep you out of hock. But they are prudent steps that can steer you away from a few freelance sinkholes.

SAVING FOR THE FUTURE

Once the cash starts flowing, it's time to start thinking about your future. As a freelance writer, you won't have an employer-sponsored pension plan. Social Security may, at best, pay a third of what you'll need to maintain your standard of living in retirement. Sure, you'll still be able to write in your retirement years. But you still will need some other savings if you hope to maintain your standard of living.

Self-employed writers have options that allow tax-free accumulation of retirement income and current deductions from taxable income. Your options include an ordinary Individual Retirement Account, a Simplified Employee Pension (SEP)-IRA, or a Keough Plan.

You may not qualify to deduct your contributions to regular IRAs if your spouse is covered by a pension plan or your earnings exceed certain limits. But a SEP-IRA isn't so restricted and provides the same benefits. Even if you have a pension from another job, you can set up a SEP-IRA for your earnings from self-employment and deduct your contribution to the plan from your current taxable income.

Each year, you can deduct up to 15% of your taxable self-employment income through SEP-IRA contributions, but only after you subtract the SEP-IRA contribution from that amount. The maximum actually comes down to about 13%. Also, your yearly contribution can't exceed $30,000 (a ceiling most freelancers won't have to worry about).

Under a Keough Plan, you have two options. A money-purchase plan requires you to contribute a fixed percentage of your income every year — up to 25%. With a profit-sharing Keough you can put in as much or as little as you want each year. But you're limited to the same 13% of self-employment income as with a SEP-IRA. With either Keough setup, you're also subject to the $30,000 annual limit.

The major advantages of these plans is that you can both deduct your contributions from current taxable income and accumulate interest tax free. At 8% interest, a $2,000 investment you make this year becomes more than $20,000 in 30 years.

But there are, of course, drawbacks:

- If you withdraw money from the plan before you reach age 59½, you're subject to a 10% penalty as well as the tax due on what you withdraw. You can withdraw the money in small amounts calculated to last the rest of your life and not pay the penalty, but still pay tax on your annual withdrawal.
- All this money is taxable when you take it out. But if you're in a lower tax bracket then, you've come out ahead. Plus, tax-free interest accumulation has left you with a lot more money then you'd have had saving the money without the plan.
- You must start to withdraw the money and pay taxes once you're 70½, whether you need it or not.
- If you hire employees someday, you'll have to cover them with whatever plan you've established for yourself.
- You can't reduce self-employment tax with these plans, only federal income tax. You may not get any deduction from state and local taxes for your contribution, either.
- You may have to pay somebody fees or commissions to administer your plan, such as a bank, brokerage, insurance company or mutual fund.

SHOULD I INCORPORATE?

Once they're established, some freelance writers incorporate to protect their personal assets from creditors and litigants or for tax purposes.

Generally, when professionals form corporations, only the assets of the corporation are liable for seizure by creditors or potential litigants. For freelance writers, however, that may not be the case.

Libel is one of the largest litigation traps a freelance writer faces. But because libel may be considered a personal statement, the legal doctrine of "piercing the corporate veil" could come into play. That means a court could make an incorporated writer's personal assets available to a successful plaintiff.

Incorporating can also subject a writer to double taxation. Since you become an employee of your corporation, you become responsible for such payroll taxes as employer Social Security, worker's compensation and unemployment insurance. Also, any profits of the corporation may be taxed, and then if you take a dividend from the corporation, that is taxed again.

If you opt for S Corporation status with the IRS, you can overcome this problem. For the most part, S Corporation profits are only taxed as income to the shareholders of the corporation.

Whether you have an S Corporation or a standard corporation, the salary you pay yourself is only taxed once. But if you use a high salary or a year-end bonus to avoid double taxation, the IRS may construe that as a "constructive dividend," which would subject you to double taxation all over again.

Traditional corporations do have a benefit in terms of deducting health insurance and other benefits. If you're incorporated, you can deduct 100% of your benefit costs from corporate income. If you're unincorporated or have an S Corporation, you can only write 25% of that cost off your taxes and nothing for such benefits as disability.

Whether to incorporate is a tough question best handled with advice from an accountant and lawyer who knows about your situation.

Should you opt for incorporation, the state office that oversees corporations, such as the Secretary of State, will send you a packet of information detailing the steps you need to take.

FOR FURTHER INFORMATION

Support Services Alliance Inc.
P.O. Box 130
Schoharie NY 12157
(800)322-3920

This group administers health plans offered by many writers' and affiliated groups. For a small annual fee, SSA also offers the self-employed wellness programs, business newsletters, access to a credit union, discount pharmaceutical plan, group life insurance, etc.

Service Corps of Retired Executives (SCORE)
National Headquarters
409 3rd St. SW
Washington DC 20416
(202)653-6279

Safeware
2929 High St.
P.O. Box 02211

Columbus OH 43202
(800)848-3469

Sells insurance for computer equipment and property and liability insurance for small businesses.

St. Louis Volunteer Lawyers and Accountants for the Arts
3540 Washington
St. Louis MO 63103
(314)652-2410

Volunteer accountants will set up bookkeeping systems, prepare financial statements and tax returns and advise on budgeting, financial management and computers for writers and other artists in the St. Louis area. Income eligibility limit is $15,000 a year plus $2,000 for each family member.

Volunteer Lawyers and Accountants for the Arts
  % Cleveland Bar Association
113 St. Clair Ave.
Cleveland OH 44114-1253
(216)696-3525

Provides tax and recordkeeping help for artists who make less than $12,000.

Oklahoma Accountants and Lawyers for the Arts
3000 Pershing Blvd.
Oklahoma City OK 73107
(405)948-6404

Provides help with accounting problems such as taxes and bookkeeping for writers with household incomes under $15,000.

The following Texas organizations offer services for writers and other artists who make less than $15,000 a year:

Austin Lawyers and Accountants for the Arts
P.O. Box 2577
Austin TX 78768
(512)476-7573

Texas Accountants and Lawyers for the Arts
5151 Belt Line Road, No. 1005
Dallas TX 75240
(214)701-8275

1540 Sul Ross
Houston TX 77006
(713)526-4876

Volunteer Lawyers for the Arts
1285 Avenue of the Americas
Third Floor
New York NY 10019
(212)977-9270

Can make referrals to any Volunteer Lawyers for the Arts chapters in your area, some of which also offer accounting services or referrals to accountants.

TAXING MATTERS FOR FREELANCERS

Becoming a freelancer means saying good-bye to the days you spent 30 minutes filling out your annual tax return on Form 1040 EZ. As soon as you make any money freelancing, you'll have to fill out the long form 1040 and Schedule C for business profit or loss. If you plan to deduct car or equipment expenses, you'll have another even more complex form to fill out. You'll also need to keep records of any expenses you hope to write off against your income.

If you don't want to bother about taxes and records, you could just refuse to take deductions. That will greatly simplify your recordkeeping. But it will also cost you hundreds or thousands in additional taxes each year. Or you could hire someone to do your taxes and keep your books. But even if you do, you'll have to be responsible for keeping your receipts and some records.

The best strategy is to spend a little time learning the tax rules that affect you and adopt a simple system of keeping records. Even if you do hire an accountant or tax preparer, keeping good records will save them time and you fees. Expect to pay more if you dump a shoe box full of unsorted receipts on your accountant's or tax preparer's desk.

DEDUCTING EXPENSES

Freelancers can deduct from their taxable income virtually any legitimate expense they incur while doing business, provided they have a receipt or other documentation.

The IRS applies the "ordinary" and "necessary" rules in judging the validity of a business expense. That just means the expenses should be ordinary for your profession and necessary for carrying out your business.

Chances are one of your largest expense categories will be your car.

If you work from your home, you can deduct mileage from home and back to any interview, or trips to the library for research or travel for any business function. This is true even if you don't qualify for the home-office deduction, which will be discussed later. If you work from an office outside the home, however, you can't deduct mileage for commuting to the office.

You can calculate auto expenses using the standard mileage rate or the actual-cost method. Either way, you'll need to keep a mileage log. You'll also need to record your car's mileage at the beginning and end of the year.

To use the standard mileage rate, you'll merely multiply your annual mileage by the current year's mileage rate. It's the easiest method in terms of recordkeeping, but it may not yield the highest deduction.

As the name implies, the actual-cost method measures what it really costs you to operate your car, rather than using a rate that approximates the cost. For this method, you'll have to keep receipts for all automobile expenses, including gas, maintenance and repairs, insurance, taxes, loan interest and depreciation of the car's cost.

If you lease the car, you deduct the lease payments instead of the depreciation and interest.

If you use the car for both business and personal reasons, you calculate the percentage of business miles each year and deduct that percentage of your costs.

There are limits to how much of your car's value you may write off each year. For cars you placed in service for the first time after 1988, you can depreciate no more than $2,660 the first year, $4,200 the second year, $2,550 the third year and $1,475 in subsequent years. Those limits are reduced by the percentage of personal use. The IRS also limits how much you can deduct for leasing a car. For details of the exact amount you can depreciate, you'll need a current copy of IRS Publication 917.

You may not have a choice of methods in some circumstances. If you lease your car, or you use more than one vehicle in your business, you must use the actual-cost method. But if you only use a second car occasionally for business, you can still use the mileage rate. If you deduct actual costs the first year you use your car for business, you will have to stay with that method as long as you use that car. If you use the mileage rate the first year, however, you can switch to the actual-cost method in later years.

Keep in mind that switching methods involves some complicated calculations. Given the difficulty of switching methods later, it makes sense to work through an estimate of what your annual deductions will be over several years under both methods before you first put the car into service. If you wait until tax time to decide, you'll probably be stuck with the standard mileage rate, because it's too late to collect receipts.

Which method is better for you depends on several factors.

- The first year you buy a car is usually the most lucrative time to use the actual-cost method.
- If you plan to use the car less than 50% for business it will restrict how quickly you can write the car off. So you're probably better off using the standard mileage rate.
- If you drive a new $25,000 car to your interviews and use the car more than 50% for business, you should probably deduct actual costs. If you're driving a 1971 Gremlin, the mileage rate will probably give you the biggest deduction.
- Living in an area with high auto insurance rates or steep automobile taxes may tip the scales in favor of the actual-cost method.

Starting in 1990, the IRS threw out limitations that made the standard mileage rate less attractive. Those limits sharply reduced the mileage rate after the first 15,000 business miles deducted annually or first 60,000 miles deducted over the life of the car. Now, one rate applies to all business miles.

HOME-OFFICE EXPENSES

Qualifying for the home-office deduction means jumping through some regulatory hoops and increasing your risk of an audit. For these reasons, even freelancers who meet the requirements are reluctant to take the deductions. But the tax savings can be big and tempting. You may be able to deduct a percentage of your mortgage interest or rent, utilities, upkeep and value of your home each year.

To qualify for the deduction, you must use an area or room of your home regularly and exclusively for business.

"Regular use" is defined as use on a continuing basis. Occasional or incidental use of your home office won't cut it, even if you don't use the space for anything else.

"Exclusive use" means just that. If you use the office for any personal activity, it doesn't qualify. That means no games on your personal computer, no personal calls from the phone in your office, and no relatives rolling out sleeping bags there on the weekend. Some furnishings are off limits for your home office, too, like TVs and sofas. True, ordinary business offices may have these things. But in a home-office, the IRS sees them as a sign of personal use.

The most accurate way to calculate the business portion of your home is to divide the square feet in the office by the total square feet of your home. If the rooms in your home are of roughly equal size, you can also divide one by the number of rooms in your home to arrive at the percentage.

Expenses you can deduct include the business percentage of:

- Rent
- Mortgage interest
- Utilities and services, such as electricity, heat, trash removal, and cleaning services
- Depreciation of the value of your house
- Home security systems
- Repairs, maintenance and permanent improvement costs for your house.

You can deduct 100% for repairs, painting or modifications of your home office. Beyond that, figuring out what you can deduct and when you can deduct it gets tougher.

Generally if the work affects the whole house, such as a new coat of paint or a new roof, you can deduct the costs for the business percentage of your home. If the work only affects a non-business part of the house, don't deduct it at all.

In one of its amazingly murky distinctions, the IRS makes you treat "repairs" differently than "permanent improvements." Repairs you can write off the first year. Permanent improvements are considered capital expenditures and subject to depreciation over several years. What's the difference between the two? IRS Publication 587 says that if repairs are part of a general plan to improve the house, they must be considered permanent improvements.

Keep in mind, if you itemize deductions on your tax return, you can still deduct the non-business portion of your mortgage interest on Schedule A as you deduct the business portion on Schedule C.

Now for the disadvantages. The IRS believes the home-office deduction is widely abused, so it scrutinizes returns with home-office deductions more carefully.

Moreover, when you sell your home, you may have to pay income tax on the amount you depreciated through a home-office deduction. But you can get around this by officially converting your office to personal use the year you sell your home. Just make a personal call, and that exclusive use disappears — along with the home-office deduction.

One other word of caution — you can't use home-office expenses if they put you in the red. They can't be used to help create a tax loss.

Before you take home-office deductions, figure out what the tax savings will be. If the savings are minor, you may not want to bother. What you lose in taxes, you may gain in peace of mind.

COMPUTERS

Computer equipment is another major expense for most freelance writers. Deducting the cost of computers may also involve some extra paperwork. That's because personal computers and peripheral equipment fall under the heading of "listed" property that commonly has both business and personal use, along with cellular telephones, automobiles and entertainment equipment.

If your computer is used in a regular business establishment, including a qualified home office, it doesn't fall under the listed property category. Otherwise, you'll have to calculate the percentage of business use for your computer in Part V of Form 4562. Even if your computer is in a home office, it might be a good idea to document your computer use in case the IRS denies your home-office deduction in an audit someday.

Documenting the percentage of business use means keeping a log much like an auto mileage log. You should record the date and hours each time you use your computer, and whether that use is personal or business. For business use, also briefly describe the business purpose. Your entry should read something like, "2/10, 2:30 p.m. to 5 p.m., wrote article for *Redbook*."

If you use your computer less than 50% for business, you'll have to depreciate the business percentage of its cost in equal installments over 10 years. If you use the computer more than 50% for business, you can deduct the business percentage of its cost over seven years and up to 25% the first year. You may even be allowed to write off the entire cost the year you buy the computer system.

If you have a cellular phone you use in your business, you must keep a log similar to the log you use for a car or a computer—documenting every use of the equipment. The same listed property rules apply to cellular phones as to computers.

OFFICE EQUIPMENT

Desks, chairs, bookshelves, filing cabinets and other office furnishings are also deductible expenses if you use them in your business. They can be deducted even if you don't opt for the home-office deduction.

Like computers and other equipment with useful lives of more than a year, office equipment is subject to depreciation rules. You may deduct it over seven to 10 years, or, in some cases, deduct the full amount the year you buy it.

DEPRECIATION AND SECTION 179

Though most business equipment and property must be depreciated over several years, freelancers and other small businesses can take advantage of Section 179, which allows up to $10,000 of business equipment costs to be fully deducted the first year they buy it.

Things you can't write off fully the first year under Section 179 include vehicles, computer equipment, cellular phones and entertainment equipment used less than 50% for business and the business portion of your home.

But Section 179 can yield big tax savings in any year you make a capital expenditure, such as buying a computer system or car that you use more than 50% for business. Even if you don't use the equipment 100% for business, you can write off between 50% and 100% of the cost the first year rather than depreciating it over several years.

But if your business use of the car or computer equipment falls to less than 50% in later years, you may have to pay tax then on some of what you deduct now. Like the home-office deduction, Section 179 and other forms of depreciation can't be used to deduct more than you make from your business. But unlike home-office expenses, you can carry over Section 179 expenses to future years if you don't have income to deduct them from this year.

IRS Publication 534 provides more details on how to depreciate business property and use Section 179, including a full set of depreciation tables for various classes of property.

CONVERSION FROM PERSONAL TO BUSINESS USE

You probably won't go out and buy all the equipment you use as a freelancer. Some of it you may have already owned. But you can still deduct the value of the office furnishings, computer equipment or car you've put in service for your business.

To deduct items converted from personal to business use, first determine the fair market value. Essentially, that's what the item would command if you were to sell it instead of using it for business. That value can be depreciated over several years and deducted from your self-employment earnings. Property converted from personal to business use is not eligible for a Section 179 deduction.

OTHER EXPENSES

Besides the big-ticket items above, there are several other expenses freelancers frequently deduct.

Phone expenses are among the largest non-capital costs for freelancers. Since 1989, the IRS has prohibited deduction of any percentage of your personal phone line, even if you use it for business part of the time. But you can still deduct business long distance calls, even if they're from a personal line.

If you entertain sources or clients, you can deduct 80% of that expense. You must keep a log of the date, location, person entertained and business purpose of the entertainment for every item you deduct.

If you travel in connection with your writing, you can deduct travel expenses. Those include transportation, lodging and meals.

Other deductible expenses freelancers often incur include:

- Dues to professional organizations or unions;
- Costs of newspapers, magazines and other periodicals you use for your business (Note, most books are considered to have useful lives of more than a year, so they must be depreciated—probably not worth the trouble unless you're depreciating the value of an entire library you convert to business use.);
- Research costs, such as copying services and the cost of on-line databases;
- Office supplies;
- Postage for business use;
- Cleaning supplies for your office;
- Legal, accounting and other professional services;
- Fees for business licenses, etc.

If publishers or clients reimburse you for some of your expenses, remember to keep records of those payments and either report them as income or subtract them from the expenses you report.

SELF-EMPLOYMENT TAX

Besides ordinary income tax, freelancers must pay a self-employment tax for Social Security and Medicare. Employees pay Social Security tax too, as do their employers. But the self-employed pay roughly twice as much, because they're expected to cover both parts. When you look at your tax bill, you'll find that's one of the strongest motivations for taking every deduction you're allowed.

Keep in mind that the more you cut your self-employment tax, the lower your Social Security check will be once you retire. That considered, you'll still likely do better if you take some of your tax savings and put them in a tax-exempt retirement arrangement to be discussed later.

In 1990, calculating self-employment tax became more complex. You now deduct 7.65% of your income before you calculate the 15.3% self-employment tax. Half of what you pay in self-employment tax also can be deducted from income subject to federal income tax, whether you itemize your deductions or not. The self-employment tax deduction also may provide a tax break in some states.

These new deductions were meant to soften the blow when the self-employment tax rate increased in 1990. They reduce the effective self-employment tax rate to 13.07% for income in the 15% federal income tax bracket and 12.15% in the 28% bracket. The effective rate may be even lower, depending on how your state and city taxes work.

Perversely, these changes made one of the nation's most regressive taxes even more so. That's because people who make more money are taxed at a lower rate than those who make less.

CONTRACTOR OR EMPLOYEE?

A major reason publishers and other clients like using freelancers is that they don't have to pay the employer's share of Social Security taxes, not to mention unemployment, worker's compensation or benefits. These taxes are also a reason some companies treat freelancers as contractors even if they're really employees.

Here are some key points to consider in determining whether you're an employee or contractor.

- Contractors generally set their own hours, choose their work site as needed, use their own tools (such as computers and office supplies) and supervise their own work.
- Employees work during hours and at sites determined by and with tools supplied by the employer.
- Contractors generally submit bills or invoices for payment.

If you're being paid as a contractor but working as an employee, you're being cheated, and so is the government. That's because you're picking up the tab for the employer's Social Security taxes, and the employer is shirking some of its tax responsibility.

If the IRS finds out, the employer is more likely to get in trouble than you are—unless you haven't been reporting the income. But it's best to refuse to work under such conditions by asking to rearrange circumstances so you qualify as a contractor.

HOBBYIST OR BUSINESSPERSON?

Another tax distinction you may face is the one between hobby and business. Writing provides enjoyment as well as income. So the IRS is more likely to classify a self-employed writer as a hobbyist than it is, say, a plumber. Being classified as a hobbyist can have an important effect on your tax situation.

Income from a hobby is reported as miscellaneous income on Form 1040, not as business income on Schedule C. One plus is that you don't have to pay self-employment tax on hobby income. The down side is that you can't deduct as much of your expenses.

Hobby expenses, along with some other miscellaneous deductions, are only deductible to the extent they exceed 2% of your adjusted gross income. And you can't deduct losses from plying your hobby, though you can from a business. The IRS presumes you're in business if you make a profit in three of five consecutive years. The IRS also considers:

- Whether you operate in a businesslike manner, such as maintaining complete and accurate records;
- Your professional expertise;
- How much time you spend in the activity;
- Whether you've engaged in similar activity in the past for profit;
- Whether the activity is your sole source of income.

If you're audited over the hobby-business question, the IRS will look at the complete picture rather than any single factor.

SOME SCHEDULE C POINTERS

Schedule C is a catch-all form for businesses ranging from widget makers to people who write about widget makers, and everyone in between. As such, much of it can be meaningless and mysterious for a freelancer. Here are a few things to note if you fill out the form yourself:

- You'll probably be checking the "cash" box for accounting method. That just means you record income when you get the check and expenses when you pay them. Few freelancers will use the more complicated accrual method or any more exotic variety.
- Check the "does not apply" box for method used to value closing inventory. You don't have any inventory. Unpublished manuscripts don't count.
- Under the income section, such items as returns and allowances and cost of goods sold probably will not apply to you.
- In the expenses section, you can't write off any bad debts unless you use accrual accounting.

- The office expense category is a catch-all that includes office supplies, postage, etc.
- You only fill out the pension and profit-sharing portion if you have employees participating in a plan. Your own plan contribution, if any, is reported on Form 1040.
- Tax and license expenses you can deduct include real estate and personal property taxes on business assets, employee Social Security and federal unemployment taxes and federal highway use tax, or any business related state or local license.
- Long distance charges fall in the utilities line. Since long distance can be a big expense for freelancers, it may be wise to itemize the components of your utility expenses on a separate sheet and attach it to your return.
- A big total in the "other expenses" column can make the IRS very suspicious. Break these items down as much as you can in categories, using a separate piece of paper attached to your return if necessary.
- Ignore the "Cost of Goods Sold," section, because you're not a retailer or manufacturer.
- Your "Principal Business or Professional Activity Code" will be 7880 "Other Business Services," unless your freelance writing is primarily public relations (7260) or advertising (7716).

PROFESSIONAL HELP

As you've figured out by now, business tax forms are a lot more complicated than ordinary income tax forms, which aren't exactly easy. So you may want professional help with your taxes.

If so, your options include independent tax preparers and tax preparation services, accountants and enrolled agents. You may also get tax-preparer training offered by H&R Block or other services. That can save you money in the long run and even allow you to start a sideline preparing taxes for others.

If you're incorporated or face particularly complex business issues, you'll probably need help from a Certified Public Accountant. CPAs are generally the most expensive option for tax preparation. Small or medium-size firms are most likely to be familiar with issues that concern you.

For strictly tax issues, don't overlook enrolled agents, who are required to pass a two-day exam given by the U.S. Treasury Department and then attend tax courses 24 to 30 hours a year. Many are former IRS employees. Though they aren't all accountants, EAs should know at least as much as accountants do about taxes. They can provide year-round tax planning. And they usually charge less than CPAs.

Franchise tax services are the fast-food operators of tax preparation — good at providing a consistent, mass-produced product. They're the cheapest option. But they may be less familiar with some of the unusual situations of freelancers than CPAs or EAs. And they usually aren't around for year-round tax advice.

Ask your prospective tax pro how many of his or her customers are freelance writers, or at least self-employed. If you plan to take the home-office deduction, ask how many of your preparer's customers have home offices. See listings at the end of the finance section for information about volunteer services that may help you or may at least refer you to accountants versed in your area.

THE DREADED AUDIT

People tend to fear something in inverse proportion to their chance of experiencing it. Such is the case with audits. Though costly and time-consuming, audits are relatively rare. The IRS audits fewer than 1% of tax returns each year, down from more than 2% in 1970.

Even if you're audited, you won't necessarily owe money. In 1988, 21% of audit victims didn't owe any additional taxes, and 8% even got refunds. Unless you're a celebrity or you committed fraud, you're unlikely to be sent to jail.

If you're self-employed and file Schedule C, however, your odds of being audited can quadruple. But, even among the most audited group of taxpayers — Schedule C filers with gross receipts of $100,000 or more — the audit rate was only 4.2% in 1988. If your gross self-employment income is under $25,000, your odds declined to 1.45%.

Audits come in three forms. Mail audits are the least burdensome, requiring only an exchange of correspondence about specific points in your return. Office audits require you go to the nearest IRS outpost, receipts in hand, for that personal touch. The most intrusive form is a field audit, in which the IRS comes to you. The latter usually results in the biggest amounts of additional taxes, interest and penalties.

A properly calculated tax return with reasonable deductions is the best way to avoid an audit. The IRS analyzes returns according to average ranges of deductions for particular professions. The computer kicks out returns with deductions that are particularly high for taxpayers in particular professions. Then examiners can take a closer look. If you have an unusually large expense in relation to your income, such as $10,000 in travel expenses on $15,000 of income, you'd better have a good explanation. To avoid an audit, it's best to attach that explanation to your return.

YEAR-END TAX STRATEGIES

The end of the year presents some opportunities to minimize your taxes. "A tax delayed is a tax saved," goes the old accountant's adage. Well, at least it's a tax delayed for a year, during which you can earn interest on the money.

Among the things you can try:

- Bill late in December so checks won't arrive until after Dec. 31 and you won't owe taxes until next year.
- Buy equipment you're planning to use next year before Dec. 31, so you can take advantage of depreciation or a Section 179 deduction this year.
- Load up on office supplies and other essentials you'll need for the coming year before Jan. 1.
- Pay for next year's subscriptions and professional dues in advance in December.

Publishers and other clients have their own year-end strategies. That means you'll see checks dated in December that end up in your mailbox in January. You aren't liable for taxes on money until you receive it, so you don't have to report those checks as income until the year you receive them. But since your 1099s may not agree with the income you report, be sure to document when you received the checks. You may even want to attach a note of explanation to your tax return.

IRS PUBLICATIONS OF SPECIAL INTEREST TO WRITERS

    1 Your Rights as a Taxpayer
  17 Your Federal Income Tax (A digest of several key publications)
334 Tax Guide for Small Business
463 Travel, Entertainment and Gift Expenses
502 Medical and Dental Expenses
505 Tax Withholding and Estimated Tax
520 Scholarships and Fellowships
523 Tax Information on Selling Your Home
529 Miscellaneous Deductions (Particularly important if your writing is a hobby rather than a business)
533 Self-Employment Tax
534 Depreciation
544 Sales and Other Dispositions of Assets
551 Basis of Assets
552 Recordkeeping for Individuals
560 Self-Employed Retirement Plans

587 Business Use of Your Home
589 Tax Information on Subchapter S Corporations
590 Individual Retirement Arrangements (Including information on
Simplified Employee Pension IRAs that the self-employed can set up)
910 Guide to Free Tax Services
917 Business Use of a Car

Copies of most of these publications are available at many public libraries. You also may order them by calling 1-800-TAX-FORM (1-800-829-3676) 8 a.m. to 5 p.m. weekdays and 9 a.m. to 3 p.m. Saturdays.

You can also get free help from the IRS in preparing returns. Look under "Telephone Assistance—Federal Tax Information" in the index of your tax form. The IRS listing in your phone book can give you more information about free tax preparation help available in your area.

LAW AND THE WRITER

History offers few greater mismatches than that of publisher vs. writer. On one side, one of the world's largest and most profitable industries with armies of lawyers at its disposal. On the other, one of the world's most competitive, low-paying and unprotected professions. Many writers live in large part by trusting editors and publishers they've never met, without benefit of written contracts or anything else prudent souls would consider security.

As a writer, you probably can't afford to level the playing field by having a lawyer on retainer. But you can learn your way around the legal terrain, and with luck, bypass some of the quagmires and minefields.

CONTRACTS: THE BEST AND WORST OF PROTECTION

Clearly the best security you can have as a writer is a written contract. For books, contracts are the norm. But understanding the contract's implications can be difficult. For articles, contracts are less common. Though many national consumer magazines and some trade journals offer them, many more don't.

While better than nothing, a contract sometimes isn't *much* better. A contract is only as good as your ability to enforce it. If the language is vague, or the cost of a lawsuit would far outweigh any return, the contract becomes fairly useless. If drafted the wrong way, a contract can become more like a chain than a bond. Clauses that give publishers dibs on unwritten, unconceived and quite unintended work have been inserted in book and periodical contracts.

Here are some pointers that could keep you from selling yourself into slavery or poverty.

BOOK CONTRACTS

Book contracts fall within a fairly standard format. But writers have every right to negotiate the terms. The following are some of the major contract issues that may come up between author and publisher.

- Does the author have the right to review the copyedited manuscript? If so, how long is the review period?

- If arbitration of contract disputes is called for, the arbitration should be in accordance with the rules of the American Arbitration Association. Also, does the contract state the place for the arbitration? If so, it should be a locale equally convenient to both parties.

- Does the contract have a non-compete clause prohibiting the author from writing, editing or publishing another competing book without written permission of the publisher? Some clauses are so vaguely worded that they seemingly would give the publisher control over virtually anything else the author produces. The Authors Guild in its model trade book contract recommends against any non-compete clause whatsoever. If you must have such a clause, make sure it's narrowly worded.

- Does the contract provide a time frame in which the manuscript is considered to be accepted even if the publisher does not expressly do so? A period of 60 days is reasonable for the publisher to accept or reject a manuscript or revision.

- Does the contract specify a time frame in which the author must complete any revisions? If so, is it enough time?

- Is there a provision for an audit of the publisher's records in accounting for royalties due the author?

- When is the advance to be paid? If payable in three stages, as is the norm, what are they? If some stages are beyond the author's control, is there a time limit to prevent foot dragging by the publisher?

- If the book is to be indexed, who is responsible for hiring and paying the indexer? Who is responsible for the cost of providing photographs and illustrations? If the author is responsible for such costs, are they to be withheld from the advance or royalties? The latter is in the writer's best interest.

- If an accepted manuscript is never published, does the contract become void, allowing the author to sell it elsewhere? If so, does the author retain the advance?

- Does the contract provide for free copies to be furnished to the author and a discount for the author to purchase additional copies?

- Does the contract specify a dollar commitment for publisher's promotional expense? Does it obligate the author to make promotional appearances without provisions for payment or expenses?
- Does the contract give the publisher any options on future works by the author? The Authors Guild in its contract guide finds all such clauses unacceptable. Unless the publisher wants to pay you for this option, you should probably reject it.
- Does the author have veto power over the title of the book and the design of the book jacket?
- Do publication rights revert to the author when the book goes out of print?
- Does the author have the right of consent to any sales of subsidiary rights, such as motion picture, book club or anthology? Is there a provision for full subsidiary rights to revert to the author should the publisher fail to exercise such rights in a specified time?
- Does the publisher promise to pay for legal expenses arising from any libel action in connection with the book? If so, does the author have the right to choose his or her own lawyer?
- Is the author responsible for any of the publisher's legal costs?
- Does the publisher agree not to settle any claim without the author's consent?
- Can the publisher freeze royalty payments after a suit is filed? If so, what are provisions for resumption of payment following a settlement and assignment of claim among the publisher and author?

There are no "right" ways to handle these issues. But you should hold out for the best deal you can. Regardless of your excitement about getting a contract offer, take a cold hard look at how you're treated under the contract or get a lawyer who can. It's the mark of a professional.

Some of the most common book contract problems involve subsidiary rights, says David Weinstein, a Denver attorney affiliated with the National Writers Club. In some cases, writers hand over potentially lucrative rights to negotiate motion picture deals, book club contracts, microfiche reproduction and more to publishers who have little interest in or ability to market those rights.

"Find out what the publisher's track record is in negotiating those deals," Weinstein says. Publishers may recognize they have limited ability to negotiate subsidiary deals and be willing to license such rights for a nominal fee.

DEALING WITH AGENTS

Similar situations arise with agents, Weinstein says. "Authors should try to find out about the agent's ability and track record," Weinstein says, "before they sign a contract."

Some writers organizations, such as the National Writers Union, maintain database lists of agents that could be of help in making your selection.

Agents customarily make at least nominal contact with all the appropriate publishers once a writer has contracted with them, Weinstein says. How vigorously and competently they handle those contacts is another issue. If the writer entirely through his or her own efforts later lands a deal with one of those publishers, the agent could still be entitled to a cut based on a perfunctory contact.

Contracts with agents should spell out the agent's responsibilities clearly, Weinstein says, and prevent agents from claiming a share from contracts they didn't procure. That's one reason Weinstein prefers short-term agent contracts, such as 60 days, rather than long-term relationships.

Another issue to look out for is reading fees. Some agents charge less experienced writers fees of several hundred dollars merely to review their manuscripts. The fees don't obligate the agent to make any other effort on your behalf.

MAGAZINE CONTRACTS

Compared to book negotiations, contracts and negotiations for periodicals seem simple. Yet the perils of taking insufficient precautions can be as great.

Getting written contracts for articles can be tough. Many publications operate on informal, verbal assignments without so much as a letter of confirmation, much less a contract. Listings in *Writer's Market* and other directories may be a useful guide to publications' practices, but they don't constitute a binding legal obligation. And many publications ask unproven writers to submit work entirely on speculation.

"I've worked a lot of times with editors who just told me to go ahead and do it, and it hasn't been a problem," says Steven Meyerowitz, a freelance writer and lawyer in East Norwich, N.Y. "Writers get paid poorly enough, and if you're going to start refusing work because you can't get anything in writing, you might as well give it up all together."

Still, some kind of written agreement is preferable, if only an informal assignment letter from the editor. You can also try sending your own confirming letter to the editor. If nothing else, such a letter may clear up misunderstandings before it's too late to do anything about them. The

American Society of Journalists and Authors offers members a suggested letter of agreement to be used when the publication doesn't offer written confirmation of an assignment.

"But if the letter isn't signed by the editor, the editor changes jobs or they decide they just don't like your work, that doesn't really offer you much protection," Meyerowitz says.

Among points to confirm on an article assignment are:

- The deadline
- The fee
- Whether any of the fee will be paid in advance
- What kill fee the publisher will pay if the finished article is rejected
- Under what circumstances will a kill fee be paid? In other words, will the author get a kill fee if the editor rejects the manuscript or only if the assignment is terminated for some other reason?
- What rights are conferred? First North American Serial Rights are a good starting point.
- Will you be paid on acceptance? If so, how long does the editor have to accept or reject the manuscript? And how soon after that will the publisher pay?
- What expenses will the publisher pay—and when?
- Will you have the right to approve a final edited version of the article?

The National Writers Union negotiated the following points in its contract with the *Columbia Journalism Review* that may serve as guidelines in your negotiations with publishers.

- A kill fee of 33% of the article fee.
- A 66% kill fee on rejected assignments that involve rewrites.
- Full payment for accepted articles even if not published.
- Payment for exploratory research or updating assigned articles.
- Automatic protection from libel suits.
- Right to approve edited versions.
- Acceptance or rejection within four weeks of submission.
- Payment within six weeks of acceptance.
- Exclusive rights that revert to the author after first publication.

You'll find few takers for all of these terms. But you can use them as a point of departure and try to keep the journey as short as possible.

PROTECTING YOUR RIGHTS

Understanding what rights you're selling a magazine is also important. The word "selling," in fact, is something of a misconception. Ideally, you should only lease your work to a magazine.

First North American Serial Rights, a standard deal for a magazine article, only gives a publication the right to use your work first in North America. After that, rights revert to you. That means if the publisher wishes to reprint the article in another publication or another form, it must negotiate additional payment with you.

Many publications say they buy all rights, which essentially gives them ownership of the piece. That means they can reuse it in any form without paying you anything more. It also means you can't sell secondary rights to anyone else.

Even if a publication says it buys all rights, that is a negotiable issue. If you don't expect to sell the piece again, and you feel the payment you received is fair if the publisher wants to reuse the piece in another form, then selling all rights probably makes no difference. Otherwise, you may want to do some bargaining.

Keep in mind that a publisher has to get your signature on a contract in order to buy all rights. In absence of a written agreement otherwise, with some minor exceptions, the Copyright Law of 1978 states an author gives a publisher only one-time rights. These are much like first rights, only they don't guarantee the publisher first use.

Some writers feel so strongly about the issue that they refuse to sell all rights to any piece. In practical terms, many articles are so closely tailored to a magazine's format that no one else would want them anyway. In that case, you lose little by selling all rights.

Similar to selling all rights to a piece is a work-for-hire arrangement. A work for hire becomes property of the publisher. Generally, something is considered a work for hire if produced by an employee for an employer, such as a staff writer for a publication. Freelancers, however, have also been subjected to work-for-hire arrangements.

In 1989, the U.S. Supreme Court ruled that independent contractors own the rights to creative works unless they transfer those rights in written agreements.

Even if you do sign away all your rights, all is not lost. "You're just selling the rights to those 2,500 words in that particular order," Meyerowitz says. "The writer can still take the information, twist it, put another slant on it, and write it for another publication."

In some cases, you can sell your work to two or more publications at the same time if they don't have overlapping circulations. You should always inform the editor of simultaneous submissions out of professional courtesy, if not legal obligation.

COPYRIGHT

Technically, the only thing you must do to copyright work is put it down on paper. Since the United States accepted the Berne Convention in 1989, no formality such as a copyright notice is required. Some additional steps, however, can protect your copyright better.

- By adding a copyright notice to your work, you can defeat any claim by a publisher of "innocent infringement."
- By registering your copyright, you can bring suit against someone for infringing your copyright. Works created in foreign countries need not register their copyrights to have the right to sue. But you must register works created in the U.S. before you can file suit. You may still register your copyright after an infringement and then sue. But this means you can't recover attorney fees and some damages from the defendant. See listings at the end of this chapter for the address to write to register a copyright.

Even a registered copyright can't protect something writers often feel are most vulnerable — their ideas. Most articles are written on the basis of an idea proposal. That protects you from finishing a piece without having a market for it. But since you can't copyright an idea, you're left with little choice but trusting the editor who fields your query not to rip it off. Fortunately, the vast majority of editors are trustworthy. Sometimes editors may seemingly take your idea. But what appears to be piracy could be the result of a project that was already in the works before your query. An editor should, however, inform you of this when rejecting your query.

The American Society of Journalists and Authors Code of Ethics and Fair Practices defines a story idea as a "subject combined with an approach." It says a writer shall have a proprietary right to an idea suggested to an editor and have priority in developing it. Though not a legal right, this is an ethical standard that any editor with integrity should respect.

GETTING PAID

Even if you've protected your rights throughout the process and turned in a manuscript that was accepted, you still have one big hurdle to pass — getting paid. Even having your rights spelled out doesn't put a check in your pocket.

During a recession, you may have to be a little more patient. It's likely your publisher is also getting paid slowly by advertisers and may not have any choice but to string its creditors along some. But don't be too patient. No matter how bad the publisher's cash flow, it's probably better than yours. In hard times, companies tend to put bills from freelancers and other independent professionals at the bottom of the stack. After all, you can't evict them, turn the lights off or repossess inventory like other creditors.

Even in good times, checks seem to travel through accounting departments and post offices at speeds that are in inverse proportion to their size. But even more aggravating is getting stiffed for a relatively paltry sum.

Whatever the size of the check, waiting for it is one of the most nerve-racking parts of being a freelancer. Even if you don't need the money right away, a doubtful proposition for the average shallow-pocket writer, you're still stuck with simmering resentment and the embarrassment of feeling like a sucker.

The resentment is called for but useless. The embarrassment is uncalled for and potentially debilitating. After all, several bank executives in Manhattan have been sitting in their corner offices waiting for a check from Mexico for years. So stop feeling bad and get to work. You may have to earn your money all over again, but at least you'll get it.

Here are some steps.

1. After payment is 30 days past due, call and/or write immediately. You need not be confrontational. Simply send a late notice or call to check on the status of payment or make sure your invoice wasn't lost. But do get a commitment from the editor or accounting office on when the payment will be sent.

2. Hold them to the promise. If payment isn't in your mailbox by the time promised, call to ask why. Be a little more persistent this time. If you have a long-term relationship with the publication, this is a good time to let them know you won't be able to send any more work until payment is received. Your leverage is increased markedly if you're working on an assignment that's needed soon.

3. If payment isn't forthcoming the second time you call or write, the time for further action is nearing. Send a final notice informing the publisher that you will have to turn the account over for collection or legal action if payment isn't received by a specified date.

4. Take that "further action" promptly if the deadline passes. It could be a letter from a lawyer. Or you may want to hire a collection agency.

Some clubs, such as the National Writers Club, will write on behalf of members to publications that have not paid for published work. Several other organizations will note non-payments in their newsletters as a warning to other members, and a few associations may even pursue legal action for members who have not been paid. If you learned about the publication in a directory, inform the directory's staff of your problem.

They may also write on your behalf and consider deleting the publication from the next edition of the directory.

A letter from a third party is an attention-getter that will disgorge a check from many slow payers. But if you have reason to believe the publisher is failing and could be headed for bankruptcy, skip this rather time-consuming step, or at least start the next one immediately.

5. If all else has failed, it's time to consider serious legal options such as small claims court. In most cases, this is your only realistic option. Any higher court will require a lawyer, whose fees will likely outweigh anything you might be owed for an article. If it's a book, more expensive options probably are warranted.

SMALL CLAIMS COURT

When worse has come to worst, small claims court can be a writer's best friend. Filing fees are nominal. Lawyers aren't required. And novices are tolerated.

Expect to invest some time, though. You must wait in line to get papers to file, then wait in line to file them. In front of you will be lots of people who are as familiar with the process as you are. So expect to take at least an hour. Later, you may have to press your case in a sort of cattle-call hearing that can take much of the day before your case comes up.

Unfortunately, small claims court won't handle every situation. Depending on the state, the court will have a claim limit of $1,000 to $5,000. Also, you may not be able to sue an out-of-state publisher in your local court.

"You can't sue anybody in your state if they don't do business in your state," Meyerowitz says. If the publisher has an office in your state or a significant percentage of its circulation there, you can probably sue locally. If not, you'll have to file suit out of state, which could increase your costs beyond the value of your claim.

With luck, your suit will convince the publisher to pay you. If not, be prepared to make your case in court. This is one situation in which a written agreement is a definite plus. You should also bring copies of any invoices you sent, a copy of your manuscript and, if the piece has been published, a copy of the publication with your article in it.

If you had an oral agreement, you may need to subpoena the editor to prove your case. This step will cost you more money, since you must pay a subpoena fee and the travel costs of any witnesses you call. If the editor is out of town, it may not be an affordable step. And the strategy will only work if you expect the editor to tell the truth. But in the right situation, a subpoena can be quite effective. Faced with the prospect of a day in court, the editor may become your staunchest advocate before the accounting department.

Even if you don't have a written contract and it seems unwise to subpoena anyone, you should still consider a suit. Possibly, the publisher won't send anyone and you'll win by default.

Sadly, winning your suit doesn't guarantee you'll be paid. You may need to follow up by filing for an attachment of the publisher's bank account. And if the bank is out of state, you may not succeed.

One reason to sue quickly if you suspect a publisher is failing is that bankruptcy could thwart you. A bankruptcy filing automatically stays all legal proceedings against the debtor. And, as you'll soon see, your chance of getting paid after a bankruptcy filing is razor thin.

DEALING WITH BANKRUPTCY

If you're ever a creditor in a bankruptcy case, you'll wonder why debtors prisons were abolished. That's because bankruptcy puts creditors, particularly small fry like you, at a distinct disadvantage.

Bankruptcy lawyers, banks with loans backed by collateral and employees all have priority over you in getting paid. As an "unsecured creditor" you might get paid cents on the dollar if anything's left. If it eases your pain any, you do rank ahead of the owners, so they shouldn't get anything unless you do.

To protect your rights in a bankruptcy, you'll need to file a proof of claim. You can get the appropriate form by calling the U.S. Bankruptcy Court clerk where the debtor filed for bankruptcy or from the federal courthouse nearest you. The clerk can also tell you the deadline for filing the proof of claim. You'll need to attach any supporting documents, such as your contract or invoice. If you don't have a written agreement, you can still file a proof of claim and hope the debtor accepts it anyway.

"You might as well file the proof of claim, because it doesn't cost you much," says Meyerowitz, who has had one magazine that owed him money go bankrupt. "But in most cases, you might as well write it off."

LIBEL ISSUES FOR FREELANCERS

Besides deadbeat publishers, the next most likely thing to land you in court is a libel suit. A wide-ranging discussion of libel issues for writers is beyond our scope here. An AP Stylebook and Libel Guide should give you the basic background you need. And regular reading of a journalism trade magazine, *The Wall Street Journal* or *The New York Times* should keep you up-to-date on new developments.

Freelance writers do have some special issues of concern with libel.

First, keep in mind that you aren't necessarily going to be defended by the publisher if your article or book prompts a libel suit. Conceivably, you could be sued and the publisher not, though it's hard to imagine a plaintiff not going after the deeper pockets of a publisher, too. Even if the publisher alone is sued, it could come after you for some of the damages if it loses.

You may have an agreement from a publisher indemnifying you in case of any libel suit. But make sure you don't sign an agreement indemnifying the publisher in case of a suit.

To protect yourself, it's good to have tapes to back up your notes of interviews. Keep in mind that taping phone conversations may be illegal in your state unless you tell the other party that the conversation is being taped. And an illegally obtained tape would never be admissible in court.

Not all libel suits may stem from anything you did. An overly aggressive headline writer or ham-handed editor could also provoke one. The best protection against this is getting to review a proof of the edited version, including headlines and photo captions. Since that's not always possible, keep a hard copy of manuscripts you send, particularly ones that seem like candidates for a libel action.

A manuscript need not be published in a magazine to be libelous. If you circulate it to editors, you've published it for the purpose of libel. Though rare, it could spark a suit without being published, if say, a fact-checker or editor calls to verify points of the article and alerts a subject to libelous content. In that case, the publication is completely off the hook, while you're wiggling on it for all your life.

RESOURCES

Several groups offer legal advice and help for writers, ranging from research reports to consultations with attorneys. For a listing of writers associations and clubs along with the services they offer, see Chapter 2. In some cases, members can consult with an affiliated attorney for no charge and arrange fees if further work is needed.

Volunteer Lawyers for the Arts has chapters in 27 states, plus the District of Columbia, Puerto Rico and Canada. VLA also sells a variety of handbooks on such legal issues as small claims court, book contracts and taxes. VLA members can consult volunteer lawyers for free and then arrange further work if needed. Most VLA chapters have an income ceiling of $15,000 a year or less. But even if you don't meet the guidelines, a VLA chapter may be an excellent source for referral to a lawyer experienced with problems like yours.

For more information, contact:

Volunteer Lawyers for the Arts
1285 Avenue of the Americas
Third Floor
New York NY 10019
(212)977-9270

Your local bar association can also refer you to an attorney in your area experienced in copyright law, collections, etc. You may be able to arrange a consultation with a lawyer for a relatively small fee before committing yourself to further work.

To register a copyright, request the proper form from the Register of Copyrights, Library of Congress, Washington DC 20559. You'll need to send the completed form and a $20 registration fee.

EMPLOYMENT AGENCIES, JOB BANKS AND CONTACTS FOR WRITERS

Writing can seem like a lonely profession when the mailbox brings a stream of rejection notices and nary a trickle of checks. Fortunately, you're not really alone. In many places, writers have banded together for mutual aid in getting work. National, regional and local groups offer help for writers seeking anything from freelance assignments to full-time jobs.

How the job programs work, however, varies significantly from group to group. The National Writers Club and its affiliated group, Associated Business Writers of America, offer information about freelance market opportunities through their monthly newsletter, *Flash Market News*.

The American Society of Journalists and Authors offers members listings in an annual directory that may be used by editors in search of writers. It also offers its Dial-A-Writer referral service, which allows editors to call with specific needs for freelance writers and be referred to writers who meet those needs.

The Society of Professional Journalists offers members a national job bank called Jobs for Journalists for an annual fee of $25. Journalists are entered in a pool of employment applicants nationwide. But jobs handled by the bank are mostly full-time positions.

Women in Communications Inc. has a toll-free hotline listing national job opportunities for members. After listening to a recorded message about jobs, members can call for details about applying for them, says Membership Director Margaret Jenkins. Local chapters of WICI also have groups that list job seekers for potential employers and jobs submitted by employers. Most of WICI's job listings are for full-time employment, Jenkins says, because local networks and agencies seem to get most of the traffic from freelancers and clients.

Local organizations or local chapters of national groups also offer job banks. The Editorial Freelancers Association offers a database of its members for potential clients in the New York City area through its Job Phone line. The National Writers Union has job banks with listings of opportunities for writers in New York, Boston and San Francisco. And Dana K. Cassell, executive director of freelance writer organizations in Florida and Texas, says her groups also put members on a database available to potential clients.

See Chapter 2 for individual group listings.

WRITING-RELATED AGENCIES

Many areas also have for-profit agencies that provide work for freelance writers and editors. The agencies generally screen freelance writers to determine their interests, credentials and fee schedules. Then they put freelancers on databases available to their clients. The agencies mark up the fees charged by freelancers to cover their costs and profit.

Such agencies can provide a sort of business support system to you as a freelancer. They become your marketing department and your collection bureau. For a talented, experienced writer who's new in town, such an agency can plug them into instant work. The disadvantage is that you might make more by marketing your work directly to the end user, since you might be able to charge both your fee and at least part of the markup the agency gets.

Different agencies have different specialties, such as technical writing, advertising copywriting or book editing.

For instance, The Write People, a Dayton, Ohio, agency, mostly handles technical writing because of the city's heavy concentration of defense contractors and other high-tech industries, says President Roger Summers. But the agency has also provided writers for advertising copy, direct-mail pieces, and speeches for corporate executives. Jobs range from a few hours to full-time placements lasting a year or more.

"There are two classes of people we've found we can't help," Summers says. "They are people just out of school and people thinking of changing careers who have no writing experience."

Writers handled by The Write People are classified as employees of the agency, Summers says, though they have the leeway to set their own fees. "We tell them what the market bears," he says, "but we don't tell them what to charge us."

A slightly different twist is provided by Creative Consortium Inc., a full-service marketing communications agency based in Cincinnati, with associated professionals in cities around the U.S. Creative Consortium handles writers, graphic artists and marketing specialists, says President Judith Hoyt Pettigrew.

"We're a brokerage firm for marketing communications talent," Pettigrew says. "We're really a marketing department for hire, though we provide talent for end users and advertising agencies as well."

Writing jobs handled by Creative Consortium include copywriting, employee and operations manuals, newsletters, scriptwriting for audio-visuals and press releases, to name a few.

"We've found a lot of people go through freelancing as a revolving door in and out of corporate jobs," Pettigrew says. "We look for professional independent writers who are prepared to stay out there living as freelancers."

Writers for Creative Consortium are independent contractors, which helps the company keep its rates competitive, Pettigrew says. Freelancers bid their fee for the job at the outset and are free to accept or reject any project, she says.

STANDARD EMPLOYMENT AGENCIES

More traditional employment agencies and temporary services firms can also provide work for freelancers in some instances. Employment agencies may handle some full- or part-time jobs, with placement fees paid by you or the employer. Temporary agencies may also have call for copyeditors, proofreaders or copywriters from time to time. You will be an employee of these agencies, which offer full- and part-time temporary assignments that sometimes lead to permanent positions.

But most traditional agencies report they seldom handle jobs for freelance writers. "We've had few writing positions in recent years," says Donald Frieman, spokesman for Snelling & Snelling in New York. Mimi Desmond, spokeswoman for Adia Personnel Services, says specialized agencies and networks of freelancers tend to dominate the editorial services end of the employment agency market in most cities.

OTHER FAST ROADS TO WORK

Besides agencies and writer's groups, most cities also have other opportunities for writers to find work relatively easily. These opportunities can also lodge your foot firmly in the door of better opportunities. Here are a few of your options.

NEWSPAPER STRINGING

Community newspapers and metropolitan dailies never seem to have enough staff reporters to handle all the stories they need. They use stringers extensively to fill the gaps. Stringers cover everything from school board meetings to lower-interest sporting events to breaking spot news if they get there first. Catching on as a stringer is a lot easier than catching on as staffer. Even high school and college students are sometimes used.

Community newspapers are the easiest to break in with, whether they're the chains of suburban weeklies that ring most major cities or independent weeklies and small dailies. Pay for community newspaper stringers, however, is poor even by freelance writing standards. They may pay as low as $15 to $25 per article. But they do provide a means of getting clips that can lead to better and higher-paying work.

While somewhat harder to break in with, metropolitan daily newspapers are by no means insurmountable markets for college graduates with some clips from college or community newspapers.

Community news coverage is by far the greatest need metropolitan dailies have for stringers. The explosion of suburban newspapers in the 1970s and 1980s sparked an equally explosive reaction by metropolitan dailies, which launched zoned suburban editions in hopes of recouping their advertising losses. The zoned editions now get more inches of editorial space than the run-of-press (ROP) metro section in some newspapers. This creates a gaping news hole that most dailies can't afford to fill entirely with the work of staff writers. If you live in the territory covered by zoned editions, contact the editor for the edition. Chances are he or she is eager to add capable stringers to the pool.

Even if you don't live near or in a suburban area, or your daily doesn't have zoned editions, you may still find work covering community news for them. Metro dailies often need stringers in peripheral circulation areas that their reporters rarely visit. Contact the metro editor or managing editor to see if he or she needs a stringer in your area. It could result in a few bylines a year.

Metro dailies may also use stringers to cover high school sports, less-attended college sports like swimming and hockey, or even minor league professional sports. There's also a chance of selling your work to food and lifestyle sections or special sections on such issues as health care, home and garden and automobiles.

Stringing for metropolitan dailies won't exactly make you rich, but it will pay better and generate better clips than community newspapers. Expect to make $35 to $250 per article, with most zoned news articles being in the $35 to $100 range and most articles that make the ROP sections in the $75 to $150 range. The paper may also pay an hourly rate for coverage of local government meetings or a lower rate for news briefs culled from a local government beat. Alternative weekly papers, free-circulation urban entertainment publications and local business newspapers can also be good markets for freelancers in many cities.

WRITING A COLUMN

Columns are another way to get your byline, and possibly your face, into newspapers regularly.

Locally based humor columns are one avenue, though it can be a tough market to crack. Editors see a lot of such column proposals and have their pick of nationally syndicated humor columns, too. But a good column can still win editors over and lead to big returns, including national syndication. Erma Bombeck started writing her column for the *Kettering-Oakwood Times*, a suburban newspaper outside Dayton, Ohio.

If you have expertise in a subject area and writing ability, you could also develop a specialized column. Examples of locally produced columns that have run in community or daily papers include auto and home repair, real estate, education, tax preparation, antiques, nature, and stamp collecting. Community newspapers and zoned editions of metros also frequently use chatty columns that cover local events and personalities.

Of course, the best idea for a column is one that hasn't been done before. That way, the editor can't just rip something else like it off the wire service he or she is already paying for anyway. A copy of *Editor & Publisher's* annual syndicate issue, which may be available in a college or city library, is a good place to check what material is already abundantly available. A superior local column on a subject that's already got several syndicated columns can still sell. But you'll have the added responsibility of proving why yours is better than what's already out there.

The key to selling such columns is convincing the appropriate editor:
- You're an expert in the area;
- You can write;
- Readers will actually be interested.

The first is relatively straightforward. Your academic credentials, business experience or organizational accreditation should be sufficient to prove you're an expert, if you in fact are. If you're not, you may be able to collaborate with someone who is but who can't write.

You'll prove you can write the same way you would with any other market — by showing examples of your work. But with a column, have several installments ready. That will show you can produce it consistently.

The last area may be a little tougher. But if you can show statistics on club membership in your area or point to the universal appeal of your topic, you might succeed.

Pay for columnists is similar to pay for stories in community and metro newspapers listed earlier. No windfall, but it is steady work. And once you get the hang of putting the column out, it may be easy and fast. Bigger payoffs come if you establish a track record for your column and can start selling it to other publications or for national syndication. And even if you don't, a column could make a nice credit to list when sending queries for freelance assignments.

FREELANCE EDITING AND PROOFREADING

Most cities and even small towns offer a wealth of opportunities for freelance copyeditors, content editors and proofreaders. But finding such work means sending out resumes, making calls and knocking on doors.

Even if you don't live in New York, many other cities have smaller book publishers that need freelance content and copyeditors and proofreaders for some of their projects. Book publishers also advertise needs for freelance editors in trade publications such as *Publishers Weekly*.

Printers, typesetters and graphic designers may need proofreaders and copyeditors. Even if they have such people on staff, they may need freelancers to fill in when work gets especially heavy. These same sources can also be good contacts for clients who need copywriting help for anything from brochures to annual reports. See Chapter 5 for more information on selling your writing services in a variety of specialty areas.

EMPLOYMENT AND OTHER AGENCIES THAT USE WRITERS

Communicators Connection Inc.
7638 Holmes Run Dr.
Falls Church VA 22042
(703)849-9191

Creative Consortium Inc.
Suites 331-335
10999 Reed Hartman Hwy.
Cincinnati OH 45242
(513)771-2120

Specializes in marketing communications, with occasional needs for writers nationwide.

CRS Associates Inc.
Suite 1400
509 Madison Ave.
New York NY 10022
(212)688-7255

Specializes in magazine and book publishing personnel.

Mae Daly Agency Inc.
6 E. 45th St.
New York NY 10017
(212)687-3911

Editorial Experts Inc.
Suite 200
66 Canal Center Plaza
Alexandria VA 22314-1578
(703)683-0683

Editorial Service of New England Inc.
126 Prospect St.
Cambridge MA 02139
(617)354-2828

Specializes in technical and general subject areas.

Marilyn Howard Agency
62 W. 45th St.
New York NY 10036
(212)398-9545

Specializes in copywriting.

Phone-A-Writer Inc.
1 Fresenius Road
Westport CT 06880
(203)222-1425

Specializes in providing writers for books, copywriters, technical writers.

Professional Assignments
Suite 1200
31 E. 32nd St.

New York NY 10016
(212)481-8100

Specializes in book and magazine publishing.

Remer-Ribolow & Associates
Suite 1605
275 Madison Ave.
New York NY 10016
(212)808-0580

Specializes in book and magazine publishing.

The Write People
1401 Westbrook Road
Dayton OH 45415
(513)854-0643

Specializes in mostly technical writing, but some copywriting.

Writers Connection
Suite 180
1601 Saratoga-Sunnyvale Road
Cupertino CA 95014
(408)973-0227

Specializes in technical writing.

GRANTS, FELLOWSHIPS, AWARDS AND CONTESTS

As hard as it is to make a living as a writer, it's good to know some kind folks out there want to give you money. For many writers, grants are the only way to stay even marginally solvent through lengthy projects. Fellowships offer opportunities for career-enhancing education that freelance writers may not otherwise get, since they have no chance at paid leaves of absence and financial aid is become scarcer all the time. Contests and awards can offer not only recognition for a job well done, but also money to do the next job well, too.

But as applicants know, these programs are anything but a free ride. It takes hard work and skill to get. Much like selling an article or a book idea, getting a grant, fellowship or award means having a good idea, doing superior work and then searching for the appropriate market. You'll need to find catalogs and directories, then study the listings to find ones whose funding interests match your creative interests.

Many grants have strict eligibility requirements. Grants from state and local arts councils, for instance, require recipients to live in the state or locality. Some organizations allow you simply to apply. Others require nomination from a member of the organization.

The more money in question, the tougher the competition for it. Some of the biggest have rather high hurdles to face even before you apply, such as a number of years of professional experience, having a book previously published or having a set number of articles published in literary magazines.

Every organization approaches the application process differently. So one of your best sources of ways to work with that particular organization may be talking to someone who has received one of its grants in the past.

Generally, the process of applying for a grant or fellowship involves these steps.

1. Call or write to get details or any changes concerning the deadline, eligibility and application process. Be sure to follow exactly any details as far as manuscript preparation or display of published works. And find out if the deadline is when the application must be postmarked or when it must be in the door. You may need to send your application by overnight delivery to ensure on-time arrival.

2. Send in your application, which usually will include samples of your published work and may include an essay or letter of explanation about your plans for future work.

3. Wait for your application to be screened by a committee that chooses finalists.

4. If you've passed that stage, wait for the same committee, or possibly another one in some cases, to decide on winning entries.

5. In some cases, especially for higher-paying fellowships, finalists will be interviewed before the final decision.

Grant application is often framed as a mysterious art best left to experienced practitioners. But in many cases, all the bells and whistles you can muster in a grant application won't make much difference. The quality of your work as viewed by the judges is the primary criterion.

"Our panelists know absolutely nothing about who the writers are," says Bob Fox, literary program coordinator of the Ohio Arts Council. "They read the manuscripts anonymously. So their decision is based entirely on their subjective view of the writer's work."

His only suggestions are to follow the guidelines for submitting manuscripts and submit finished works instead of works in progress, because finished works tend to fare better with judges.

"The single most important thing we're looking for is commitment to the popularization of science and technology," says Victor K. McElheny, director of the Knight Science Journalism Fellowships. "We're looking for people who have tried this, proven themselves to be very competent at it, and intend to go on."

In many cases, selection committees must wade through hundreds or thousands of applications for a handful of awards. Other, more specialized programs, may only have a handful of applicants. For instance, the Knight Science Journalism Fellowships, a prestigious program that offers a stipend of $23,000 and relocation assistance of $2,000, only has about 20 applications for eight fellowships each year, McElheny says.

Like submitting your work for publication, applying for foundation grants and fellowships means getting your share of rejections. Program administrators advise writers not to be discouraged by an initial rejection. Many writers go on from a rejection to find acceptance elsewhere or even from the same program in later years. Things change from year to year. The competition may not be as fierce next time. And you, with an extra year of experience, will have more accomplishments to show judges and more experience with the program.

To find your best prospects among the hundreds of grants, fellowships and awards available, the most comprehensive directory is *Grants and Awards Available to American Writers*, PEN American Center, 568 Broadway, New York NY 10012. Writing and journalism publications discussed later in this chapter are also good sources for notices of grants and the like, and many directories noted later in this chapter have listings of contests.

The following are some other listings that may help. When sending for information from these organizations, include a SASE.

Joan Shorenstein Barone Center on the Press, Politics and Public Policy Harvard University
79 John F. Kennedy St.
Cambridge MA 02138
(617)495-8269

A five-month fellowship for the study of the intersection of the press and politics.

Congressional Fellowship Program
American Political Science Association
1527 New Hampshire Ave., NW
Washington DC 20036
(202)483-2512

A 10-month fellowship for journalists with two to 10 years of experience, preferably outside of Washington, to improve research and reporting on American politics.

Fellowship in Law for Journalists
Yale University
401A Yale Station
New Haven CT 06520
(203)432-1681

A nine-month program leading to a master's degree in legal studies for journalists, preferably with five years of experience.

Gannett Center for Media Studies
Columbia University
2950 Broadway
New York NY 10027
(212)854-8392

A three- to nine-month fellowship to foster exchange between journalists and scholars and develop projects into books.

Gannett Foundation Fellowships
University of Hawaii
School of Hawaiian, Asian and Pacific Studies
1890 East-West Rd., Moore 216
Honolulu HI 96822
(808)948-6083

A one-year fellowship to broaden understanding of Asian studies for working journalists who meet university standards for graduate study.

Kiplinger Midcareer Program in Public Affairs Reporting
Ohio State University School of Journalism
242 W. 18th Ave.
Columbus OH 43210
(614)292-2607, 292-6291

A one-year program to develop enterprise reporting and complete a master's degree in journalism for journalists with B.A. degrees and three years of public affairs reporting experience.

Knight-Bagehot Fellowship in Economics and Business Journalism
Columbia University Graduate School of Journalism
New York NY 10027
(212)854-2711

A nine-month fellowship to improve economic and business reporting through formal study for journalists with four years of experience in business or general reporting.

John S. Knight Fellowships for Professional Journalists
Department of Communication
Stanford University
Stanford CA 94305
(415)723-4937

A nine-month program of non-degree study for journalists with seven years or more experience.

Knight Science Journalism Fellowships
MIT
Room E40-373
Cambridge MA 02139
(617)253-3442

A nine-month fellowship for science, technical and medical writers with three years of professional experience, aimed at bringing them up-to-date on current developments in their fields.

Michigan Journalism Fellows
2072 Frieze Building
Ann Arbor MI 48109
(313)763-2400

An eight-month fellowship for journalists with five or more years experience, aimed at helping mid-career journalists reach peak performance.

Nieman Fellowships for Journalists
Harvard University
1 Francis Ave.
Cambridge MA 02138
(617)495-2237

A nine-month fellowship for full-time editorial employees or journalists with a minimum of three years experience.

The Alicia Patterson Foundation
Suite 120
1001 Pennsylvania Ave., NW
Washington DC 20004
(301)951-8512

Offers journalists a grant to spend one year researching and reporting on a subject of his or her choice.

Quarterly Review of Literature
Colladay Awards
26 Haslett Ave.
(602)921-6976

Award and publication for book-length manuscripts of poetry, a poetic play, a long poem or poetry in translation.

Wallace E. Stenger Fellowships
Creative Writing Program
Stanford University
Stanford CA 94305

WRITERS' PUBLICATIONS

From poetry to public relations, a variety of publications are available to writers who want to know more about everything from the craft of writing to the business of publishing.

Many local and national writers' organizations have their own newsletters and publications available to members. (More information about these is contained in individual Associations and Organizations listings in Chapter 2.) These publications are especially helpful in obtaining information about specialized types of writing and for getting tips on local writing opportunities.

We've included a few of the most widely known publications in each area, along with the major directories for writers in a variety of specialty areas. Many can be found in larger libraries, but you may want to consider a subscription or book purchase if you use the periodical or directory often and need more immediate access than library use can provide.

PERIODICALS

GENERAL WRITING

The Writer
The Writer, Inc.
120 Boylston St.
Boston MA 02116
(617)423-3157

Writer's Digest
F&W Publications
1507 Dana Ave.
Cincinnati OH 45207
(513)531-2222

Poets & Writers
Poets & Writers Inc.
72 Spring St.
New York NY 10012
(212)226-3586

BOOK PUBLISHING

Publishers Weekly
R.R. Bowker
245 W. 17th St.
New York NY 10011

MAGAZINE PUBLISHING

Folio:
The Hanson Publishing Group, Inc.
6 River Bend
P.O. Box 4949
Stamford CT 06907

Magazine Week
Lighthouse Communications Inc.
233 W. Central St.
Natick MA 01760

NEWSPAPER PUBLISHING

Editor & Publisher
Editor & Publisher Co.
11 W. 19th St.
New York NY 10011

BROADCAST JOURNALISM

Broadcasting
Times Mirror
1705 DeSales St. NW
Washington DC 20036

Television Radio Age
Television Editorial Corp.
1270 Avenue of the Americas
New York NY 10020

PUBLIC RELATIONS

Public Relations Journal
Public Relations Society of America
33 Irving Place
Third Floor
New York NY 10003

ADVERTISING

Advertising Age
Crain Communications Inc.
220 E. 42nd St.
New York NY 10017

SCRIPTWRITING

Hollywood Reporter
Billboard Publications Inc.
6715 Sunset Blvd.
Hollywood CA 90028

Hollywood Scriptwriter
#385
1626 N. Wilcox
Hollywood CA 90028

DIRECTORIES

Literary Market Place, R.R. Bowker, 121 Chanlon Road, New Providence NJ 07974. Annual directory covering the book trade. Also publishes an *International Literary Market Place*.

Writer's Market, Writer's Digest Books, 1507 Dana Ave., Cincinnati OH 45207. Annual directory covering book, magazine and greeting card publishers, contests and scriptwriting opportunities. Also publishes these specialized directories: *Novel & Short Story Writer's Market, Poet's Market, Children's Writer's and Illustrator's Market, Humor and Cartoon Markets*, and *Writer's Guide to Literary Agents and Art/Photo Reps.*

The Writer's Handbook, The Writer, Inc., 120 Boylston St., Boston MA 02116. Annual with variety of listings covering writing outlets, organizations and opportunities; also features several articles by professional writers on both craft and business aspects of writing and publishing.

Gale Directory of Publications, Gale Research Co., 835 Penobscot Bldg., Detroit MI 48226. Annual with magazine and newspaper entries; helpful geographic index. Also publishes the *Publishers Directory* and several other directories of interest to writers.

International Writers' and Artists' Yearbook, A&C Black, 35 Bedford Row, London WC1R 4JH. Covers the publishing scene in the U.K.

International Directory of Little Magazines and Small Presses, Dustbooks, P.O. Box 100, Paradise CA 95969. Also publishes *Directory of Poetry Publishers* and *Directory of Small Magazine-Press Editors and Publishers*.

Oxbridge National Directory of Magazines, Oxbridge Communications, Inc., Suite 301, 150 Fifth Ave., New York NY 10011. Also publishes the *Oxbridge Directory of Newsletters*.

The Association of American University Presses Directory, University of Chicago Press, Fourth Floor, 5801 Ellis Ave., Chicago IL 60637.

California Publishing Marketplace, Writers Connection, Suite 180, 1601 Saratoga-Sunnyvale Rd., Cupertino CA 95014. Also publishes *Southwest Publishing Market Place*.

Directory of Florida Markets for Writers and PR Professionals, Cassell Communications, P.O. Box 9844, Fort Lauderdale FL 33310.

Literary Agents of North America, Author Aid Associates, 340 E. 52nd St., New York NY 10022.

Cassell & The Publishers Association Directory of Publishing, Cassell Ltd., Greycoat House, 10 Greycoat Pl., London SW1P 1SB. Covers Great Britain, The Commonwealth, Ireland, Pakistan and South Africa.

Dramatist's Sourcebook, Theatre Communications Group, 355 Lexington Ave., New York NY 10017.

The Writer's Yellow Pages, Steve Davis Publishing, P.O. Box 190831, Dallas TX 75219. Has addresses and phone numbers of everything from agents to word processing equipment.

1991-92 Directory of Publications Resources, Editorial Experts, Inc., Suite 200, 66 Canal Center Plaza, Alexandria VA 22314. Information about reference books, software and desktop publishing, as well as training programs, professional organizations and grammar hotlines.

Another publisher of directories of interest to writers is Running Press, 125 S. 22nd St., Philadelphia PA 19103. (215)567-5080.

Chapter 2

A COMMUNITY
OF WRITERS

Writing can be a solitary occupation, but it doesn't have to be. From writers' groups to conferences to continuing education programs, there are an endless number of ways for writers to learn from others, perfect their craft, and share information about the writing life with other writers.

This section can help you connect with those opportunities. It won't provide you with all the organizations available, but it will let you know where they can be found, how to evaluate the best program for your development, and how to get the best value for your money. If you'd like to start a workshop or be an instructor, we also include tips for entering this side of the writing business.

PROFESSIONAL ASSOCIATIONS
AND ORGANIZATIONS

Writers' groups and organizations are available across the U.S. covering a wide range of interests and offering a variety of services. Some are small groups of writers who meet weekly over coffee around a member's kitchen table to exchange war stories, read each other's work, and offer support. Others are massive nationwide organizations with 5,000 members and services that include medical and health benefits. Your involvement with a professional organization depends a great deal on your needs as a writer.

Professional associations and organizations typically have members nationwide. They frequently concentrate on a single area or target a specific group of people, such as American Medical Writers Association or Women in Communications, Inc. Some have very stringent guidelines for membership, including publishing credits or amount of time spent writing. Because many have a national membership base, they can offer national networking and job bank possibilities along with workshops and professional discounts. The largest associations usually have chapters in large cities to accommodate members.

Many professional associations are formed with an emphasis on helping members tackle the business side of writing. The Authors Guild, for instance, includes members who write everything from textbooks to mysteries. The majority, says Assistant Director Peggy Randall, are not full-time writers. "They're not famous, but they do get published," she says. "We work to get them a bigger piece of the pie." As with many associations, members are classified on more than one level. Authors with a book published in the past seven years or three articles published in the past 18 months are regular members. Authors can join as associate members if a contract offer has been made for a book. The member-at-large category includes agents and other industry people.

According to Randall, most guild members don't have agents and consider the services offered by the guild an alternative. Although she says The Authors Guild has a "tiny, overworked staff," they have computer records, a full-time lawyer on staff, and a quarterly bulletin. They also pride themselves on offering individual advice to members on "all the business aspects of writing." One of the most prized possessions of membership is the guild's contract guide, a document that explains in detail the contract language used by most publishers and the meaning it has for authors. Because most members don't have agents, they feel this information helps them negotiate better contracts, Randall says.

One of the guild's latest and most popular programs is a random audit of a publisher's royalty statements. Although audits are routinely granted in contracts, few authors are likely to pay for an audit, Randall says. The guild will audit only three statements this year, but Randall says the action "puts publishers on notice" concerning royalty statements, which "are bewildering even to authors who know how to read them."

While organizations such as The Authors Guild work on the business side of writing, other associations concentrate on services for specialty writers. The Education Writers Association, for instance, offers referrals, ways of approaching topics, professional development seminars, a guide for covering the education beat, as well as national and regional meetings. According to Executive Director Lisa J. Walker, the group includes print and broadcast reporters and freelance writers whose concentration is "substantially" education-oriented. This doesn't mean "just covering schools," Walker says, but overlaps youth and business interests, covering everything from early childhood education to adult education and training in the workplace for its 600 members.

Sometimes the specialty is not a particular beat as much as a particular constituency. Women in Communications, Inc., includes members in areas ranging from corporate communications to media to education.

About 6% of its members are freelance writers, and 5% of the membership is men. With a membership of 12,200, however, Director of Communications Linda Russman says: "The orientation is toward women. We think women have a great deal of opportunity through us." In addition to monitoring legislation and providing a job hotline and a national network of 189 chapters, the organization offers several services Russman says are "especially helpful for those in business for themselves," including group medical plans, loans and car rental discounts.

While a professional organization may offer many attractive options and services, these programs are not likely to be cheap. The cost of most memberships is $50 or more, with some ranging as high as $500.

WRITERS' GROUPS

Writers' groups are more likely organized around a local or regional, rather than a national, base. Although they may have a specialized focus, they are much less likely to restrict themselves; most, however, concentrate on fiction and poetry. Local and regional groups usually are more open in membership requirements, and less expensive to join. They usually emphasize more feedback and interaction among members than professional associations. A medium-sized city may support three or four writers' groups with a variety of meeting styles and focuses. Writers' groups can range in size from fewer than 10 members to a few thousand members, and their offerings also vary considerably, so it's up to you to determine which one suits you best.

If level of service is your desire with a writers' group, an organization such as the National Writers Club may be your choice. The club, with 5,000 members in 50 states and 17 countries, has both aspiring and professional writers ranging from three to 30 years of writing experience. Executive Director James Young believes writers have several reasons for joining the group. "Initially, I think it's an avenue to get the information they need to get published. The professionals stay with us for our service."

The National Writers Club staff includes two full-time and three part-time members, as well as 12 people under contract to provide information and services. In addition to receiving 200 to 300 letters per week, the staff coordinates newsletter production, writing courses, medical plans, and even a new literary agency service for members.

Service on a more regional basis is the aim of other large groups, such as the Florida Freelance Writers Association and the Austin Writers'

League. Executive Director Dana Cassell says the Florida group, with 1,200 members, emphasizes a newsletter "with the very latest market information," medical plans, a critique service, a writer referral service and a state writers' conference. "The established writer wants in the group for information, writers' referral and more business information," Cassell says. "The part-time writer wants it for networking, conferences and a chance to be part of a group."

Although its name denotes a city-wide group, Executive Director Angela Smith says the Austin Writers' League has about 800 members in the Austin area and 600 outside. An active job bank, professional business information, networking, and several workshops attract members. "The reputation the organization has built up enables us to attract good people" for workshops and, in turn, increases growth, she says.

Whether it's a large group or a smaller, local group without additional services, a writers' group often will be free or fairly inexpensive to join. The highest rate is usually about $100 for a yearly membership to a large group, and local groups are frequently free.

EVALUATING A GROUP

Before you join an association or writers' group, you should evaluate both your needs and goals as well as the group's services.

While joining a group may *help* your career, don't think of it as a magic potion. James Young of the National Writers Club says a high turnover among aspiring writers is not unusual. "A lot of people *think* they want to be in this business. They think because they've joined a writers' group they will be successful."

Consider this information about each association or group before you join:

- Are your goals compatible with the group's? If your aim is to get critical feedback on your latest short story, you may be dissatisfied with a large association that emphasizes business services. If you are a specialty writer, you may not appreciate the far-flung interests of a local group. At least one group in California completely eschews writing technique; members gather to exchange business and marketing information only. You must look at the group as an extension of your business interests in writing; it must provide some payback to justify your time away from the keyboard.
- What programs and other benefits does the group offer? If you are a full-time freelance writer and need medical benefits, you'll want to look for an organization large enough to offer them. If you're a part-time writer and your main interest is in programs, look for a group strong

in that area. If you are a specialty writer, you'll certainly want to check out any related specialty groups as well as the more general ones.

- What's the cost of joining? Annual fees vary widely—from free membership to several hundred dollars—so you want to be sure you'll get the most benefit for your membership fee. If you're paying for a high-service organization but are not using the services, perhaps you should look into a local, less expensive group. If, on the other hand, your local or regional group isn't able to offer everything you'd like to have, perhaps you should weigh the benefits of a more expensive group.
- What's the size of the group? For some people, the most beneficial group is one that's small and allows them to participate in each session. Others value the resources of a large group. Some feel the best of both worlds is available through a local chapter of a large organization. You must determine which best fits your style.
- What kind of programs are offered? Try to visit a meeting before you join to determine whether or not you'll benefit from the group's programs. Some organizations offer small critique groups; others have large, formal meetings. In some, leaders of the group are there merely to facilitate discussion or introduce a speaker; in others they play a stronger role. If possible, talk to a few writers in the organization to determine what they like best about the group and its programs, workshops and other services.
- What's the experience level of writers in the group? Most writers' groups and organizations have a variety of members, ranging from aspiring or beginning writers to those with many years of experience. Beware getting in a group with too many members at one or the other end of the spectrum. If you're experienced and the majority of members are not, most of the programs will be geared to beginners. You eventually may feel your time is being wasted. If, on the other hand, members are very experienced, they may be unwilling to help you develop in a specific area, or you may feel too intimidated to ask questions. Many organizations, especially large ones, have membership surveys that can let you know what the membership experience level is.

FORMING A WRITERS' GROUP

Occasionally you'll find that a national organization doesn't suit your needs but a local group isn't available or doesn't have the programs you want. If you have the time and energy, you may want to form a writers' group of your own.

Remember, even the largest groups started small. Angela Smith says the Austin Writers' League started with three people in 1981 and now has 1,400. She advises organizers to gather as many aspiring writers together as possible. "When you get creative minds together, it's amazing what can happen," she says.

Dana Cassell of the Florida Freelance Writers Association says it's important to check out current groups that meet in the area through local newspapers, libraries and the Chamber of Commerce. To get the word out about a new group, she advises sending press releases to community newspapers and putting notices in adult education bulletins.

If your aim is to form a local chapter of a national organization, James Young of the National Writers Club says it's best to contact the parent group and find out what their requirements are. The National Writers Club, for instance, has a Chapter Development Guide it sends to interested writers with everything from an outline of services to tips on running meetings.

Before you begin meeting, take time to consider these questions about the group you plan to form:

- What are your criteria for membership? Whether you plan to restrict membership to published writers or to a particular genre—or open membership to anyone interested—is something you should decide *before* you start meeting. Sometimes a genre focus can be helpful if there is no other similar group in the area. Mystery and romance writers, as well as poets, frequently benefit more from a group tailored to their needs. Most newly formed groups do not have stringent membership requirements, however.
- What membership fees and services will the group have? When you start small, you usually must make membership free or low-cost because prospective members have nothing on which to judge the value of a membership. Until you know what type of membership base you have, you also can't determine what services you'll be able to support. It's usually best to start slowly in this area and expand as your membership, and its needs, expands.
- What type of programs will you sponsor? Most groups try to set up a fixed time each month, so members can fit that time into their schedules. The format of meetings is less established. Some groups like to have members read from their work and obtain feedback. Others like structured meetings with outside speakers. Many groups try to provide a mixture to attract a variety of participants.

Many more questions will come up as you meet, form plans for a group, and select leaders. With the formation of any group for creative people, keep in mind that flexibility and cooperation will allow you to provide the best service for writers.

SOURCES FOR WRITERS' ORGANIZATIONS

Several sources of information about writers' groups and organizations are available, but there isn't one that's comprehensive. It's simply impossible to gather information about all the organizations, associations and individual groups.

The closest to a comprehensive directory was the *International Directory of Writers' Groups & Associations* printed in 1984-85 by Inkling Publications, Inc. (824 Winnetka Ave. S., Minneapolis MN 55426. (612)546-0422). It contained 2,000 entries of clubs and organizations in the U.S. and internationally. The book is no longer in print and publishers have no plans to reprint it. But at least one club director still uses it and finds a surprising number of references still good. You may be able to find this directory in your library.

Literary Market Place and *International Literary Market Place* (both R.R. Bowker titles) have listings for writers' organizations, mostly the larger associations. *The Writer's Yellow Pages* (Steve Davis Publishing, P.O. Box 190831, Dallas TX 75219) also lists writers' groups and organizations under Associations. National Writers Club, with more specific information in the following listings, also keeps lists of writers' organizations.

Although they probably won't have comprehensive lists, state arts councils sometimes have lists of writers' groups that have received grants. *Grants and Awards Available to American Writers* (PEN American Center, 568 Broadway, New York NY 10012) has listings for state arts councils.

ASSOCIATION AND ORGANIZATION LISTINGS

American Medical Writers Association
9650 Rockville Pike
Bethesda MD 20816
(301)493-0003

Members: 3,400
Individual and institutional memberships
Publications: quarterly journal, annual membership directory

American Society of Journalists and Authors
Suite 302
1501 Broadway
New York NY 10036
(212)997-0947

Associated Business Writers of America
Suite 620
1450 S. Havana
Aurora CO 80012
(303)751-7844

Members: 200
Executive Director: James L. Young
Professional memberships only
Services: electronic mail service, research reports, complaint service, medical plans
Publications: *Flash Market News* (monthly); *Authorship* (bimonthly)

The Authors & Artists Resource Center
P.O. Box 64785
Tucson AZ 85740-1785
(602)325-4733

Members: 300
Director and Literary Agent: Martha R. Gore
Services: medical plan, reference library, answers to reference questions, critiques and editing for fee, workshops
Publications: *TARC Report* (bimonthly)

The Authors Guild Inc.
330 W. 42nd St.
New York NY 10036
(212)563-5904

Members: 6,500
Assistant Director: Peggy Randall
Full voting membership; associate/member-at-large
Services: contract guide, health and life insurance, surveys
Publications: *Authors Guild Bulletin* (quarterly)

Aviation/Space Writers Association
Suite 1200
17 S. High St.
Columbus OH 43215
(614)221-1900

Members: 900
Executive Director: Madeline Field
Regular and student memberships
Sponsors annual news conference and Awards of Excellence program
Publications: *AWA Yearbook* (annual) and *Air Accidents and the News Media*

Christian Writers Guild
260 Fern Lane
Hume Lake CA 93628
(209)335-2333
Members: 1,100
Contact: Norman B. Rohrer
Student (enrolled in 48-lesson home study course) and full members
Services: consultation on manuscripts submitted
Sponsors "Write to be Read" workshops
Publications: *Quill o' the Wisp* (quarterly)

Council of Authors and Journalists, Inc.
1214 Laurel Hill Dr.
Decatur GA 30033
(404)320-1076
Members: 110
Co-chairs: Anthony Grooms, Ann Ritter
Sponsors contests, conference
Publications: quarterly newsletter

Council of Writers Organizations
1 Auto Club Dr.
Dearborn MI 48126
(313)336-1211
Members: 34,000
Contact: Board chairman Len Barnes at address above. President Isolde
Chapin is executive director of Washington Independent Writers, 220
Woodward Building, 733 15th St. NW, Washington DC 20005.
Umbrella organization for 20 writing groups. Sponsors health insurance, no
cost or low cost legal and IRS advice.
Publications: *Word Wrap* (quarterly); newsletters by individual groups

Disabled Journalists of America
484 Hammond Dr.
Griffin GA 30223
(404)228-6491
Members: 150
Contact: David Shapiro
Disabled student and professional journalists
Sponsors quarterly newsletter and phone contacts

Dog Writers' Association of America
9800 Flint Rock Rd.
Manassas VA 22111
(703)369-2384

Members: 350
President: Harold Sundstrom
Professional and associate memberships
Sponsors workshops, awards
Publications: bulletin (10 times/year)

Education Writers Association
1001 Connecticut Ave. NW
Washington DC 20008
(202)429-9680

Members: 600
Executive Director: Lisa J. Walker
Active and associate memberships
Sponsors annual writing awards, publications, seminars, regional
workshops
Publications: bimonthly newsletter, guide to covering education beat,
members directory (annual), occasional literacy newsletter, occasional issue
briefings, urban education newsletter (5 times/year)

Feminist Writers Guild (Chicago)
P.O. Box 25477
Chicago Il 60625
(312)918-2020

Members: 250
Contacts: Amoke Omoleye, Loraine Edwards
Regular and special membership for those retired or unemployed
Services: performances at area bookstores, information about area writing
classes
Sponsors monthly workshops, monthly writing exercise workshop, quarterly
discussion group
Publications: newsletter (monthly) and literary magazine (annual)

Freelance Editorial Association
P.O. Box 835
Cambridge MA 02238
(617)729-9253

Members: 500
One level of membership
Services: Members' Network, member-to-member phone connection, advice
of Fair Practices Committee, free advertising in *Freelance Editorial
Association Yellow Pages*, group insurance
Sponsors discussion groups, meetings and workshops
Publications: quarterly newsletter, *Code of Fair Practice*

International Association of Crime Writers (North American branch)
JAF Box 1500
New York NY 10116
(212)757-3915

Members: 225
President: Roger L. Simon
Executive Director: Mary A. Frisque
Professional membership for authors, editors, booksellers, agents and translators
Sponsors reception for foreign authors and publishers; crime writing conferences abroad
Publications: *Border Patrol* (quarterly)

International Society of Dramatists
P.O. Box 1310
Miami FL 33153
(305)531-1530

Members: 5,000
Contact: A. Delaphaine
Sponsors playwriting contests
Publications: *The Globe* (monthly); *The Dramatist's Bible* (annual)

The International Women's Writing Guild
P.O. Box 810
Gracie Station, New York NY 10028
(212)737-7536

Members: 2,000
Executive Director: Hannelore Hahn
Various levels of membership
Services: medical insurance, literary agents list, workshops, regional meetings
Sponsors 12 conferences per year; annual summer conference

Mystery Writers of America
17 E. 47th St., 6th Flr.
New York NY 10017
(212)888-8171

National Association for Young Writers
215 Valle del Sol Dr.
Santa Fe NM 87501
(505)982-8596

Members: 1,000

Contact: Sheila Cowing
Sponsors contests in fiction, nonfiction and poetry for writers, ages 6 to 14
Publications: *Shoetree* for writers 6 to 14 (3 times/year); *NAYW News* for
teachers and adult writers (4 times/year)

National Conference of Editorial Writers
6223 Executive Blvd.
Rockville MD 20852
(301)984-3015

Members: 566
Executive Secretary: Cora B. Everett
Professional membership
Services: outreach committee (critiques)
Sponsors 2 professional seminars, annual convention, foreign tours,
workshops, awards
Publications: *The Masthead* (quarterly)

National League of American Pen Women, Inc.
1300 17th St. NW
Washington DC 20036-1973
(202)785-1997

Members: 6,000
Contact: National President
Professional memberships in three classifications: letters, art, music
composers
Services: 200 branches in U.S., biennial meetings (April 1992, Washington,
DC)
Publications: *The Pen Woman* (9 issues/year); membership roster printing
planned for December 1992

Outdoor Writers Association of America, Inc.
Suite 101
2017 Cato Ave.
State College PA 16801
(814)234-1011

Members: 1,950
Executive Director: Sylvia G. Bashline
Individual professional, student and supporting (corporate) memberships
Services: insurance, discounted legal services, job file
Sponsors annual conference, member contests, annual international film/
video awards, annual youth writing contest
Publications: *Outdoors Unlimited* (monthly); *OWAA Directory* (annual)

Poetry Society of America
15 Gramercy Park S.
New York NY 10003
(212)254-9628

Members: 2,500
Assistant Director: Cynthia Atkins
Five levels of membership
Services: discounts on readings and lectures
Sponsors contests, workshops, readings and awards
Publications: newsletter (3 issues/year)

Romance Writers of America
13700 Veterans Memorial Dr. #315
Houston TX 77014
(713)440-6885

Science Fiction and Fantasy Writers of America, Inc.
5 Winding Brook Dr. #1B
Guilderland NY 12084
(518)869-5361

Members: 1,100
Executive Secretary: Peter Dennis Pautz
Active, affiliate, graphic illustrator, institutional, estate memberships
Services: grievance committee, circulating book plan, insurance program
through Council of Writers Organizations
Sponsors SFWA Nebula Awards
Publications: *SFWA Bulletin* (quarterly); *SFWA Forum* (bimonthly); annual
membership directory; handbook; Nebula Awards Report (bimonthly)

Society for Technical Communication
901 N. Stuart St.
Arlington VA 22203
(703)522-4114

Members: 13,000
Services: employment information, group insurance, scholarships, research
grants
Sponsors annual conference, regional and local conferences, competitions,
fellowships, electronic bulletin board
Publications: *Technical Communication* (quarterly); *Intercom* (10 times/
year); *Internchange* (quarterly for students); chapter newsletters; STC library
of publications

Society of American Travel Writers
Suite 500
1155 Connecticut Ave. NW

Washington DC 20036
(202)429-6639

Society of Children's Book Writers and Illustrators
22736 Vanowen St.
Suite 106
West Hills CA 91307
(818)888-8760

Members: 6,500
Contact: Sue Alexander
Associate and full membership
Services: grants, insurance, regional meetings, members' manuscript
exchange
Sponsors annual conference, merit awards
Publications: *Bulletin* (bimonthly)

Society of Professional Journalists
P.O. Box 77
Greencastle IN 46135
(317)653-3333

Members: 17,000 (300 chapters)
Membership contact: Penny Williamson
Professional and student memberships
Services: CareerNet job search
Sponsors annual convention and regional conferences, awards
Publications: *Quill* (monthly)

Women in Communications, Inc.
Suite 417
2101 Wilson Blvd.
Arlington VA 22201
(703)528-4200

Members: 12,000
Professional and student memberships
Services: insurance programs, member loan program, Member Card, job
hotline, national directory, car rental discounts
Sponsors annual national professional conference
Publications: *The Professional Communicator* (bimonthly); *Leading
Change* (3 times/year)

Writer's Forum
6115 Gilbert Dr.
Pello Cedra CA 96073

Contact: Karen Todd

Writers Guild of America
(West) 8955 Beverly Blvd.
West Hollywood CA 90048
(213)550-1000

(East) 555 W. 57th St.
New York NY 10019
(212)245-6180

Members: 7,500
Professional members only
Services for members only
Publications: *Journal* (11 times/year)

Writers Information Network (W.I.N.)
P.O. Box 11337
Bainbridge Island WA 98110
(206)842-9103.

Members: 600
Director: Elaine Wright Colvin
Professional association for Christian writers
Services: 2 annual writers conferences and monthly workshops
Publications: bimonthly newsletter

UNION

National Writers Union
13 Astor Place
New York NY 10003
(212)254-0279

Members: 3,000
President: Jonathan Tasini
Associate Director: Anne Wyville
Services: contract advising, agent database, grievance handling, health care plans, New York and San Francisco job banks
Publications: *American Writer* (quarterly); local newsletters

WRITERS' GROUPS

Arizona Authors' Association
Suite 117
3509 E. Shea Blvd.
Phoenix AZ 85028
(602)996-9706

Members: 200

President: Velma Cooper
Services: information and referral service
Sponsors monthly meetings, workshops and seminars, contests
Publications: newsletter (bimonthly)

Austin Writers' League
1501 W. 5th St., E-2
Austin TX 78703
(512)499-8914

Members: 1,400
Executive Director: Angela Smith
Individual, student and senior citizen, and corporate memberships
Services: discounts on books and audiotapes, job bank, study groups
Sponsors fall and spring series of workshops, informal classes, weekend
seminars, awards program
Publications: *Austin Writer* (monthly)

The Byliners
P.O. Box 6015
Corpus Christi TX 78466-6015

Members: 180

California Writers' Club
2214 Derby St.
Berkeley CA 94705
(415)841-1217

Members: 900
Contact: Dorothy V. Benson
Sponsors biennial writers' conference, workshops and smaller conferences
by branches, monthly meetings, contest for nonmembers (with prize of
tuition to conference)
Publications: *California Writers' Club Bulletin* (monthly except July/August);
also branch newsletters

Florida Freelance Writers Association
P.O. Box 9844
Fort Lauderdale FL 33310
(305)485-0795

Members: 1,200
Executive Director: Dana K. Cassell
Services: medical plans, critique service, legal hotline, toll-free help hotline,
writer referral service
Sponsors seminars, contest, state conference. Also has similar regional

associations for Georgia and Texas. Both are based in Florida but have regional directories of writers and markets.
Publications: *Freelance Writer's Report* (monthly); annual guide to Florida writers; annual directory of Florida markets

Georgia Freelance Writers Association
(see Florida Freelance Writers Association)

Members: 150

Golden Triangle Writers Guild
4245 Calder
Beaumont TX 77706
(409)898-4894

Members: 900
President: Ben Lee, Kay or D.J. Resnick
Regular and associate memberships
Services: writer support group
Sponsors monthly meetings, annual conference (October)
Publications: *Scene & Sequel* (monthly)

National Writers Club
Suite 620
1450 S. Havana
Aurora CO 80012
(303)751-7844

Members: 5,000
Executive Director: James L. Young
Associate and professional memberships
Services: research reports, critiques, marketing information, medical plans, complaint service, small press, literary agent, agent referral, writing courses
Sponsors periodic workshops
Publications: *Authorship* (bimonthly); *NWC Newsletter* (monthly); *Flash Market News* (monthly for professional members)

The Nebraska Writers Guild, Inc.
P.O. Box 30341
Lincoln NE 68503-0341
(402)435-4607

Members: 140
President: David Kubicek
Treasurer: Rosalie Shimerda
Secretary: Diane Kirkle
Active and associate memberships
Services: manuscript critiques, audiotape library, editorial information pool

Sponsors 2 conferences each year (April and October)
Publications: *Bulletin* (February and September), *The Broadside* (June and December)

New England Poetry Club
137 West Newton St.
Boston MA 02118

Members: 250
President: Diana Hovanessian; Membership chair: Victor Howes
Student, honorary, friend, associate and full memberships
Sponsors regular meeting, prizes, annual workshop
Publications: *Writ* (semi-annual)

Ozark Writers League
P.O. Box 1433
Branson MO 61656
(417)334-6016

Members: 235
President: Dr. Robert K. Gilmore
Sponsors quarterly seminars
Publications: newsletter (quarterly)

Philadelphia Writers Organization
P.O. Box 42497
Philadelphia PA 19101
(215)387-4950

Members: 300
President: William Wartman
Student, associate and full memberships(requires proof of publication)
Services: disability insurance, medical plan, small group discussions
Sponsors monthly meetings, workshop, writers' meeting and editors' marketplace
Publications: newsletter (11 issues/year)

San Diego Writers/Editors Guild
3235 Homer St.
San Diego CA 92106
(619)223-3634

Members: 110
Contact: Betty Smith
Professional and associate memberships
Services: monthly meetings, discounts on conference
Sponsors yearly conference
Publications: newsletter (monthly)

Texas Freelance Writers Association
(see Florida Freelance Writers Association)

Members: 200

Washington Christian Writers Fellowship
P.O. Box 11337
Seattle WA 98110
(206)842-9103.

Members: 250
Director: Elaine Wright Colvin
Various levels of membership
Services: critique, marketing, how-to, networking, press card, instruction
Publications: newsletter (bimonthly)

Washington Independent Writers
#220, 733 15th St. NW
Washington DC 20005
(202)347-4973 or 347-4067

Members: 2,200
Executive Director: Isolde Chapin
Full, associate, senior, student and dual memberships
Services: group health insurance, Job Bank, legal services plan
Sponsors monthly workshops, spring writers conference, freelance basics
course
Publications: newsletter (monthly); directory of members (every 2 years)

West Florida Literary Federation (Francis P. Cassidy Literary Center)
P.O. Box 1644
Pensacola FL 32597
(904)434-6070

Members: 275
President/Board of Directors: Fran D. Cassidy
Chairman/Board of Governors: Ron Cannon
Student, individual, family, business memberships
Services: education programs, Student Writers' Network, annual
scholarship, poet laureate of West Florida (every 3 years)
Sponsors monthly meetings, poetry readings, presentation by Readers'
Showcase Group, informal discussion groups, contests
Publications: annual anthology *Emerald Coast Review*, for regional writers;
poet laureate chapbook (every 3 years); *The Legend* newsletter (monthly)

Writers Alliance
12 Skylark Ln.
Stony Brook NY 11790

Members: 125
Contact: Kiel Stuart
Individual and corporate/group memberships
Services: technological help for writers
Sponsors workshops
Publications: *Keystrokes* (quarterly)

The Writer's Center
7815 Old Georgetown Rd.
Bethesda MD 20814
(301)654-8664

Members: 2,000
Executive Director: Jane Fox
Student, regular, family and business associate memberships
Services: workshop and Book Gallery purchases, reference library, laser printing and typesetting services
Sponsors four sessions of workshops each year in all genres; readings series
Publications: *Carousel* (bimonthly); *Poet Lore* (members receive a subscription discount)

Writers Connection
Suite 180
1601 Saratoga-Sunnyvale Rd.
Cupertino CA 95014
(408)973-0227

Members: 2,500
Various levels of membership
Services: seminars, books, reference library, referral service, job shop, grammar hotline
Sponsors "Selling to Hollywood" weekend conference (August)
Publications: Newsletter (monthly)

OTHER

Poets & Writers, Inc.
72 Spring St.
New York NY 10012
(212)226-3586

Non-membership organization
Executive Director: Elliot Figman
Services: information center for the literary community

Co-sponsors readings throughout New York and California
Publications: *Poets & Writers* (bimonthly magazine); *A Directory of American Poets & Fiction Writers*, 1991-92 with names, addresses and telephone numbers of more than 6,600 poets and fiction writers. Organized alphabetically by state [use]. The cost is $21.95 and $2.50 for postage and handling.

Poets & Writers also offers these publications of interest to writers' groups: *California Resources List* with writing information on magazines looking for work from California writers; services for writers; and literary landmarks. Updated annually and available for $2 plus a self-addressed, stamped envelope. Also available is "Living Rooms for Literature: Literary Centers in the U.S.," a reprint of a magazine article with 18 gathering places for writers. Cost is $2 and a self-addressed, stamped envelope.

COLONIES, RESIDENCIES AND RETREATS

Some writers are happiest working in their own homes or offices and find they are very productive there. Others have a desire to get away from the regular routine at a colony or retreat. Among the colonies available, some are just for writers, while others are open to artists and performing artists. Few of the colonies could be considered tourist meccas, and some, such as Dorland, are extremely Spartan.

The advantage of a colony is not in the accommodations, but the opportunities it provides. Colonies are not for every writer, but time at one can be extremely useful as a change of pace to get the most out of your creative powers in a short amount of time. A colony "is for people who don't have enough concentrated time," says Jill Charles of The Dorset Colony.

Writers have a variety of reasons for attending colonies. Elizabeth Goheen, of Ucross Foundation in Wyoming, says writers want "the time—and for a lot of people, this is a region of the country they aren't familiar with. This is a really beautiful area, authentic West, with a lack of glitz." At Yaddo, President Myra Sklarew says colonists "are completely protected. We provide absolutely guaranteed time and a community of writers. They never have to step away from the work if they don't want to." Other writers like the informal atmosphere of a place such as The Dorset Colony. "If they had the money to buy their own home in the country, this is what they'd have," Jill Charles says.

Characteristics of colonies vary widely. Some put a premium on unrestricted time and freedom from interaction with anyone. Others seek a balance of colonists so they can learn from each other. Very few have a regimented schedule, but a few require a plan from writers about what they will work on while they stay at the colony. You'll find that some are very competitive and others have a more open policy. Nearly all require that you bring any equipment you plan to use (typewriter, personal computer) while you're there.

Some colonies operate year-round, but others are open only in the fall and spring. Especially when applying for a highly competitive colony, consider going in the off-season to take advantage of fewer applicants. Many writers want to attend in the fall or spring, so you may want to consider applying for a summer or winter position if the colony will be open then.

At the Ucross Foundation, for instance, about 250 to 300 applications are received per year for 17 positions. A panel meets to choose "a good mix" of residents who will live in a home and eat dinner together, but have separate studio space. Jill Charles says most residents have other employment but are on sabbatical or vacation and "find a way to make it work with their creative lives." The colony is expanding to accommodate eight residents at a time for an average stay of about six weeks.

Yaddo, one of the oldest and most well-known colonies, has about 780 applicants in writing and art, of which 220 are accepted. The focus is on poetry, fiction and playwriting, but Myra Sklarew says "we never ask what they're working on." The colony, open year-round, has a recommended payment of $20 per day. Sklarew says the average stay is one month.

Flexibility is the key at The Dorset Colony. About 60 to 75 writers and performing artists make use of the space during the year, with some who have been there before calling ahead and getting approval for a weekend stay. In addition, writers cook their own food when they want. The average stay is about two weeks in a large house in a rural village.

Before applying at a colony, consider these points about each:

● What are the requirements for application? Colonies almost always require an application, some with accompanying writing samples, recommendations or references, and a deposit. At Yaddo, for instance, applicants are judged as if it's the first time they have applied even if they have been there before. The Dorset Colony, on the other hand, requires no formal application after the first time. After you've selected a colony for application, begin getting your material together about eight months or more before you would like to attend. This is necessary because applications are frequently considered about six months before attendance. Most colonies will let you know their requirements by phone; several have brochures or flyers they can send for a self-addressed, stamped envelope.

- What's the cost? Some colonies offer free accommodations to chosen applicants; many have a recommended daily fee of $10 to $40. A few charge weekly fees. The majority of colonies stress that payment is voluntary and no qualified applicant will be turned away simply because he cannot pay.
- How many other residents are there? Writers attending colonies frequently want the kind of freedom away from other people they can't get at home. If you're that type of person, consider a colony with few residents and perhaps one in which the individual cooks his own meals. After concentrating on your work for several hours each day, you may enjoy some social time with other colonists, however.
- Does the colony fit your lifestyle? Some colonists think they'd like nothing better than a rural atmosphere, but later find they don't. Writers sometimes like to cook their own meals at their convenience, but others would rather have their meals prepared and ready at a regular time. These are all considerations you need to make before applying. Myra Sklarew says it's a self-evaluation process: Decide how you work best and which colony can help you accomplish that. "Isolation is a gift. Or it can be overwhelming to have 18 hours per day for work," she says.
- How much time do you need? A few colonies offer residencies as short as a weekend, but the majority of colonies want you to stay two to eight weeks. Because most writers find they work more quickly and efficiently at a colony, you need to have a plan for what you'd like to accomplish while you're there—even if the colony doesn't require it for application. If possible, talk to other writers who've been to colonies to find out how they used the experience. Most use it to finish up a project, start a new one or revise or reassess a "stalled" piece of writing.

RESOURCES

Several reference books have information and listings of writers' colonies. Check *The Guide to Writers Conferences* (Shaw Associates). As a service to its members, The Authors Guild compiles a list of several colonies, and *Poets & Writers* frequently carries advertisements and notices of colonies. You may also want to check with your state arts council to see if officials there know of any colonies in the state.

LISTINGS

Atlantic Center for the Arts
1414 Art Center Ave.
New Smyrna Beach FL 32168

Program Director: James J. Murphy
(904)427-6975
Estab. 1978

Offers 3-week interdisciplinary sessions 5 to 6 times/year. Cost is $200 for non-resident; $600 resident fee. Provisions include private room/bath, work space, meeting space, copy machine, limited access to typewriters. (Computers and word processors planned for future). Accommodates 10 to 15 per residency. Submission procedure varies with each Master Artist, but examples of writing are sent directly to that person, who then selects "associates." College credit may be available.

Blue Mountain Center
Blue Mountain Lake NY 12812
Director: Harriet Barlow
(518)352-7391
Estab. 1982

Offers 4-week sessions during summer and fall at no cost other than transportation to center. Provisions include private room (bedroom and study), breakfast and dinner in dining room, serve-yourself lunch, laundry, Xerox machine, tennis court, lakes, boats, trails, recreation room. Accommodates 15 residents at one time. Submissions required by Feb. 1; decisions made by March 31. No college credit.

Cummington Community of the Arts
RR #1, Box 145
Cummington MA 01026
Executive Director: Lucius Parshall
(413)634-2172
Estab. 1923 as "Music Box"

Offers 1 to 3-month residencies from April through November; family facilities are available. Cost is $500/month in June, July, August and September; $400/month in April, May, October and November; and $400/month for children. Deadlines are Jan. 1, March 1, and June 1. Under the community work program, each family prepares meals once a week. Isolated cabins and studios are available. Accommodates 20 residents at one time. No college credit.

Dorland Mountain Arts Colony
P.O. Box 6
Temecula CA 92390
President: Mary Morton
(714)676-5039
Estab. 1979

Offers 1 to 3-month residencies year-round. Cost is $140 per month.

Provisions include cabin with kitchen, bedroom, private working area. Meals are responsibility of resident. Accommodates 6 residents at a time. Request application with SASE; deadlines are Sept. 1 and March 1. No college credit.

The Dorset Colony
Church Street, Box 519
Dorset VT 05251
Director: Dr. John Nassivera
(802)867-2223
Estab. 1982

Offers sessions from one week to one month Sept. 1 to Dec. 1 and March 15 to May 15. Cost is $75/week voluntary fee. Provisions include private room in 3-story house, kitchen, dining room, library/sitting room, phone room, porch area. Accommodates 8 residents at a time. Submit letter, résumé, brief statement of material/project to work on during stay. No college credit.

Fine Arts Work Center in Provincetown
24 Pearl St./Box 565
Provincetown MA 02657
Contact: writing coordinator
(508)487-9960
Estab. 1968

Offers 7-month residencies from Oct. 1 to May 1. Fellows are provided with live-in studio and a monthly stipend of $375. Accommodates 8 first-year fellows and 2 returning fellows at a time. Application and information available ($20 application fee). Feb. 1 deadline. No college credit.

William Flanagan Memorial Creative Persons Center
("The Barn")
Edward F. Albee Foundation
14 Harrison St.
New York NY 10013
Foundation Secretary: David Briggs
(212)226-2020

Offers 1-month residencies, June 1 to Oct. 1. Provisions include room for writers and composers; room and studio space for visual artists. Accommodates 4 artists per month. Application forms available. Résumé, 2 letters of recommendation, letter outlining proposed project, 2 mailing labels and SASE for return of material required. Applications accepted between Jan. 1 and April 1. No college credit.

Green River Writers' Retreat
11906 Locust Rd.
Middletown KY 40243

President: Mary E. O'dell
(502)245-4902
Estab. 1986

Offers 2-week residency in July. Cost is $10 membership, $20 regular fee. Provisions include private and semi-private rooms (available in dorm housing at additional fee of $18 per night). Accommodates 40 residents at a time. Contact for application information. No college credit.

The Tyrone Guthrie Centre
Annaghmakerrig, Newblish
County Monaghon, Ireland
Director: Bernard Loughlin
047-54003
Estab. 1981

Offers 3-week to 3-month residencies year-round. Cost is Ir 1,200/month. Provisions include private apartment, all meals. Accommodates up to 12 residents at a time. Requires samples of work for writers, slides of photographs for visual artists, and tape recordings of work from musicians. No college credit.

The Hambidge Center for Creative Arts & Sciences
P.O. Box 339
Rabun Gap GA 30568
Executive Director: Judy Barber
(404)746-5718
Estab. 1975

Offers 2-week to 2-month residencies from May to October. Cost is $100/week. Provisions include private housing, studios, dinner, laundry. Accommodates 7 residents at a time. Applications ($10 fee) are reviewed by committee. No college credit.

Kalani Honua Conference Center and Retreat
RR 2, Box 4500
Pahoa HI 96778
Director: Richard Koob
(808)965-7828
Estab. 1980

Offers full-payment residencies year-round; stipended residencies as space is available, usually May to June and September to December. Cost is $40 to $100 per day including meals; with stipend $30 to $60 per day including meals. Provisions include option of private room with shared or private bath, work space/studio and meals. Accommodates 80 residents at a time. Write or call for application ($10 fee); documentation of work required. College credit must be applied for separately through University of Hawaii-Hilo.

MacDowell Colony
100 High St.
Peterborough NH 03458
Admissions Coordinator: Shirley Bewley
(603)924-3886
Estab. 1907

Offers up to 2-month residencies year-round. Cost is "pay what you can." Provisions include studio space, room and board. Accommodates about 10 residents at a time. Deadlines are Jan. 15 for May through August; April 15 for September through December; and Sept. 15 for January through April. No college credit.

Millay Colony for the Arts
Steepletop, P.O. Box 3
Austerlitz NY 12017-0003
Assistant Director: Gail Giles
(518)392-3103
Estab. 1976

Offers 1-month residencies year-round. Provisions include private room, studio space, all meals. Accommodates 5 residents/month. Application deadlines are Feb. 1 for June to September; May 1 for October to January; Sept. 1 for February to May. No college credit.

O'Neill Theater Center
Suite 901
234 W. 44th St.
New York NY 10036
Artistic Director: Paulette Haupt
(212)382-2790
Estab. 1978

Offers 3 to 4-week residency in August. No cost. Provisions include stipend, transportation from New York to Waterford, Connecticut, housing and meals. Minimally staged and unstaged readings. Accommodates 8 to 10 residents at a time. Send SASE for application form and guidelines, accepted between Nov. 1 and Feb. 1.

Palenville Interarts Colony
P.O. Box 59
Palenville NY 12463
Artistic Director: Joanna Sherman
(518)678-3332
Estab. 1982

Offers 1-week to 2-month residencies between June 1 and Sept. 30. Suggested fee of $175 is requested. Open to writers, composers, performing artists and visual artists. Provisions include private or semi-private rooms or cabins, studio space, shop, darkroom and video equipment, all meals, swimming and hiking. Send SASE for application and information; must be returned by April 1. Two copies of up to 40 pages of a completed manuscript or playscript or a selection of short stories and/or poetry required with résumé/biography. Charges $10 handling fee.

Ragdale Foundation
1260 N. Green Bay Rd.
Lake Forest IL 60045
Director: Mike Wilkerson
(708)234-1063.
Estab. 1976

Offers 2 to 8-week residencies in June and the last two weeks of December. Suggested cost is $10 per day; financial aid and full or partial waivers are available. Accommodates 12 residents at a time. Provisions include separate studios; prepared evening meals. Deadlines are Jan. 15 for May through August; April 15 for September through December; and Sept. 15 for January through April. No college credit.

Mildred I. Reid Writers Colony
Penacook Rd.
Contoocook NH 03229
Director: Mildred I. Reid
(603)746-3625
Estab. 1942

Offers 1 to 6-week residencies in July and August. Cost is $125 and up. Provisions include private room, breakfast, classes and conferences. Accommodates 8 to 12 residents at a time. Send SASE for information. No college credit.

Ucross Foundation
2836 U.S. Highway 14-16 East
Clearmont WY 82835
Program Director: Elizabeth Goheen
(307)737-2291
Estab. 1981

Offers 2 to 8-week sessions in January through May and August through November. No cost. Provisions include a private studio and room, meals. Accommodates 4 residents at a time—a mix of writers, visual artists and composers. Send SASE for brochure and application. Deadlines are March 1 and Oct. 1. No college credit.

Villa Montalvo Center for the Arts
P.O. Box 158
Saratoga CA 95071
Director of Programming: Sam Nuccio
(408)741-3421
Estab. 1952

Offers 1 to 3-month residencies. Accommodates 5 residents at a time. No cost except food. Applications are reviewed in October and April each year.

Virginia Center for the Creative Arts
Mt. San Angelo
Sweet Briar VA 24595
Director: William Smart
(804)946-7236
Estab. 1971

Offers 1 to 3-month residencies available year-round. Cost is $20/day suggested fee. Provisions include a private room, studio and meals. Accommodates 11 residents at a time. Send SASE for application. Deadlines are Jan. 25, May 25 and Sept. 25. No college credit.

Helene Wurlitzer Foundation
P.O. Box 545
Taos NM 87571
President, executive director: Henry A. Sauerwein Jr.
(505)758-2413
Estab. 1954

Offers varying residencies from April 1 to Sept. 30. No cost. Provisions include a furnished house including free rent and paid utilities. Accommodates varying number of residents. Send SASE for application.

CONFERENCES AND WORKSHOPS

With thousands of conferences and workshops available, writers can choose from a variety of subjects, lengths and locations to suit their writing needs and schedules.

Writers have many goals when they attend conferences and workshops. Some want to explore a new writing area or learn from a particular instructor. Others are interested in making publishing contacts with writers, editors and agents attending the conference. Still others like the inspiration and concentrated time with fellow writers.

Whatever your motivation for exploring conferences, you'll probably find that several sound interesting from written descriptions. Explore these further, obtaining any literature the conference has available and talking to previous attendees.

At a primarily statewide and regional conference such as the New Orleans Writers' Conference, Beverly Gianna says the aim "is to bring the national marketplace to New Orleans." The emphasis is on meetings with agents and editors at the four-day conference. Now in its third year, the conference is limited to 300 participants and has a 28% return rate. "We try to keep it small enough so you can benefit from others," Gianna says. The cost to writers of $175 is kept fairly low because faculty members volunteer their time.

Registration at the Santa Barbara Writers' Conference also is limited to 300 people and attracts participants from as far away as Australia. The conference features a number of bestselling writers and has classes for both beginners and advanced writers, including several genre classes. "The caliber of the workshops attracts people," says Mary Conrad.

A slightly smaller week-long conference is the Cape Cod Writers' Conference with about 150 participants. Nonfiction, fiction and poetry are always covered, along with a fourth rotating writing specialty. The conference attracts a large number of returning participants who credit it with providing them with ideas and industry contacts.

Consider these aspects of the conference, too:

- Who is on the faculty? For some writers, this is the most important of all criteria. They want a well-respected, published writer from whom they can learn for a day, a weekend or a week. Look for writers who have credits in the particular area they will teach *and* can communicate with other writers without simply lecturing. Marion Vuilleumier of the Cape Cod Writers Conference says she looks for "teachers who are teachers *and* published. We don't want a college class." The New Orleans Writers' Conference is one of a few that offers one-on-one consultation and free manuscript evaluation. Director Beverly Gianna says, "We try to select faculty that are good and have a sharing, approachable attitude."

- How many people attend the conference? There is very little one-on-one instruction in large conferences, but some offer individual conferences with editors, agents and other instructors—usually for an additional fee. Obviously, your chances of individual meetings or instruction are greater if the conference is smaller, but smaller conferences frequently attract less prominent speakers, too. Instead of focusing on the total number attending the conference, ask about the number in each session. If you find this number is 30 or less, you'll probably have more of a chance to ask questions or discuss your work with the instructor.

- What type of sessions does the conference offer? Is the format set up in a lecture style or does it involve some give-and-take with instructors and speakers? Are there panels with writers, editors and agents who may offer their opinions on subjects of interest to the group? Are the programs geared to beginners, intermediate or professional writers? These are questions you will want to evaluate against your own preferences.

- What kind of personal feedback can you expect? As stated before, most individual conferences, manuscript evaluations and other personal feedback must be arranged ahead of time and paid for separately. That doesn't mean you can't make contact with people in the business, but you usually can't count on it. If you are paying or making an appointment, however, you have every right to know what to expect from the meeting. Don't go in expecting to find an editor who will want to publish your work or an agent who will want to represent it. Certainly, this kind of serendipitous meeting has happened before. Just don't be disappointed if it doesn't.

- What's the average level of other writers at the conference? Most conferences attract a variety of writers, ranging from beginners to professionals. A quick look at the program offerings can give you a clue to whether most sessions are geared to beginners or professionals, and you may want to avoid a conference, or at least those sessions, that seems too far below or above your level of experience.

- How much does the conference cost? Last, but certainly not least for any writer, is the value for the dollar. Many writers save money by attending regional conferences where they can stay at home and commute each day. Others combine vacation and work and attend a conference in Cape Cod or Santa Barbara, California, for instance. The average cost for a one- or two-day workshop ranges from $15 to $50, although some run as high as $200. Conferences that last from four days to a week usually will cost from $100 to $800 and most often include lodging and meals.

STARTING A CONFERENCE

A great deal of work has to go on behind the scenes to pull off a conference for 300 people, so it's typical for organizers to wonder, after the conference ends, how they accomplished it.

Mary Conrad's husband, Barnaby, taught at a prep school and set up the first writers' conference for 35 students from the school. It's no longer affiliated with the school or restricted to students and has become one of the largest and most well-respected conferences in the U.S. "It just steadily increased," she says. "We never dreamed it would be this big."

Likewise, Marion Vuilleumier says a group of writers on Cape Cod wanted to start its own conference "because we couldn't go away in the summer because we were taking care of guests." She consulted with editors at *The Writer* magazine who advised her on ways to attract participants and teachers. The programs offered now include a young writers' section, a literacy program, a TV book show, and a workshop arts program.

If you'd like to start your own conference, follow these tips from current conference directors:

● Start small, perhaps with a weekend workshop, to work out scheduling.
● Offer a mixture of programs to appeal to beginners and advanced writers.
● Look for ways the conference can provide individual feedback and personal attention to participants.
● Take advantage of contacts you may have made in the publishing business through magazines, book publishers or writers you've met at other workshops.
● Most important to the success of the venture: Organize the type of conference you'd like to attend.

SOURCES

The best source for writers' conferences is probably *The Guide to Writers Conferences*. The third edition is currently available from Shaw Associates, Publishers, Suite 1406, 625 Biltmore Way, Coral Gables FL 33134. (305)446-8888. Doreen Kaplan says they do a "massive mailing" to obtain listings from 313 sponsors of writers conference, workshops, seminars, residencies, retreats and organizations. The guide has an index by month, a geographic index, subspecialty index, as well as information on conferences that provide continuing education or college credit, award scholarships, and sponsor contests. *The AWP Official Guide to Writing Programs* (Dustbooks, P.O. Box 100, Paradise CA 95967) also has information on writers conferences, colonies and centers. The May issue of *Writer's Digest* also has conference listings and many directories mentioned in Chapter 1 also will have details on workshops.

Other sources include *Writers Conferences*, with dates, addresses, fees, deadlines and workshop leaders for 200 conferences, available March 1 each year from Poets & Writers, Inc., 72 Spring St., New York

NY 10012. (212)226-3586; fax: (212)226-3963. Cost is $6 with $1.50 for postage and handling. The group also offers a New York City Workshops List of free and fee-charging poetry and fiction workshops in the New York metropolitan area. It's issued in January, May and September. Cost is $2 plus a self-addressed, stamped envelope for each copy. Also available is *Author & Audience: A Readings and Workshops Guide* which covers 400 organizations that present readings or workshops, arranged alphabetically by state. It also has information on running successful programs. Cost is $7.95 and $2.50 for postage and handling.

Another source is *How to Conduct a Successful Writing Workshop*, by Melinda Wiley and Mary J. Davis, JLC Future Publications.

LISTINGS

Alabama Writers' Conclave
University of Montevallo
Montevallo AL
Contact: Ann Moon Rabb
(205)822-3086
Estab. 1923
1991 dates: August 7, 8, 9

3-day workshop covering fiction and poetry, scriptwriting when possible. Send SASE after Feb. 1 for details about workshop and cost.

Arkansas Writers' Conference
1115 Gillette Dr.
Little Rock AR 72207
Director: Clovita Rice
(501)225-0166
Estab. 1944
1991 dates: June 7, 8
1992 dates: first weekend in June

2-day conference on various types of writing and marketing. Cost: $10 both days; $5 for one day. Program includes $2,000 in contest awards. Information available by Feb. 1.

American Society of Journalists and Authors
Grand Hyatt Hotel, 42nd and Lexington
New York NY
Executive Director: Alexandra Cantor
(212)997-0947
Estab. 1971
1991 dates: May 4

1-day workshop with various panels concentrating on topics of interest to journalists. Cost: $125.

Antioch Writer's Workshop
P.O. Box 494
Yellow Springs OH 45387
Director: Susan Carpenter
(513)767-9112
Estab. 1985
1991 dates: July 7-13
1992 dates: July 5-11

1-week workshop covering novels, poetry, short stories, screenwriting and nonfiction. Includes daily classes, mini-workshops. Cost: $425 tuition plus room and board.

Appalachian Writers Workshop
P.O. Box 844
Hindman KY 41822
Director: Mike Mullins
(606)785-5475
Estab. 1977
1991 dates: Aug. 5-9
1992 dates: Aug. 3-7

5-day workshop covering fiction, nonfiction, poetry, children's writing and playwriting. Cost: $200.

Arizona Christian Writers Conference
P.O. Box 5168
Phoenix AZ 85010
Director: Reg A. Forder
(602)838-4919
Estab. 1981
1991 dates: Nov. 1, 2

2-day conference with 15 workshops covering writing (including music) for the religious market. Cost is $850.

Bay Area Writers Workshop at Mills College
P.O. Box 620327
Woodside CA 94062
Director: Laura Jason
(415)430-3127
Estab. 1988
1991 dates: 5 summer weekends

3-day workshops on poetry and fiction. Cost: $200 per weekend.

Biola University Writers Institute
13800 Biola Ave.
La Mirada CA 90639
Associate Director: Susan Titus
(213)903-4805
Estab. 1984
1991 dates: July 28-31

4-day conference on nonfiction and fiction books, article writing, writing for children, marketing and curriculum. Includes 43 classes, 30 publishing houses, article writing contest and manuscript critique service. Cost: $275 plus room.

California University Writers' Conference
8465 Jane St.
San Diego CA 92129
Director: Diane Dunaway
(619)484-8575
Estab. 1988
1991 dates: May 18, 19

2-day conference covering fiction, nonfiction, screenwriting, consultations with editors and agents, and critiques. Cost: $188.

California Writers' Conference
2214 Derby St.
Berkeley CA
Contact: Secretary
(415)841-1217
1991 dates: July 12-14

3-day conference covering all genres; includes agents and editors panels. Cost: $295 resident; $195 commuter.

Cape Cod Writers' Conference
% Cape Cod Conservatory, Rt. 132
W. Barnstable MA 02668
Executive Director: Marion Vuilleumier
(508)775-4811
Estab. 1963
1991 dates: Aug. 18-23

1-week conference covering fiction, nonfiction, poetry, juvenile writing, and a fifth course that rotates. Cost: $60 registration, $50 per course, $60 for manuscript critique, $30 for personal interview with staff (plus housing and meals). Average cost is $200 to $300. Group also sponsors Cape Literary Arts Workshops on a variety of topics.

Carter Caves Writer's Workshop
Carter Caves State Resort Park
Olive Hill KY 41164
Director: Lee Pennington
(502)245-0643
Estab. 1980
1991 dates: June 2-8
1992 dates: June 7-12

1-week workshop covering fiction and poetry. Cost: $65 plus food and lodging.

Chisolm Trail Writer's Workshop
P.O. Box 32927
Fort Worth TX 76129
Director of TCU Press: Judy Alter
(817)921-7822
1991 date: June 8

1-day conference, generally on fiction with a Western flair. Cost: $500 to $575.

Christian Writers Institute Conference
388 E. Gundersen Dr.
Carol Stream IL 60188
Office Manager: Jean Kasmerski
(708)653-4200
Estab. 1948
1991 dates: June 4-7

4-day workshop on fiction, nonfiction, poetry, children's writing, tract writing, humor, writing for women, public relations, inspirational romance, marketing—all Christian inspirational. Cost: $300 for workshop, room and board.

Christopher Newport College Annual Writers Conference
50 Shoe Lane
Newport News VA 23606
Coordinator: Doris Gwaltney
(804)594-7158
Estab. 1981
1991 dates: April 6

1-day workshop covering nonfiction, poetry, fiction and juvenile fiction. Includes writing contest. Cost: $65.

Colorado Mountain Writers' Workshop
Spring Valley, 3000 County Rd. 114
Glenwood Springs CO 81601
Associate Professor: Doug Evans
(303)945-7481 (ext. 261)
1991 dates: July 22-26

1-week conference covering novels, poetry, short fiction, nonfiction and scriptwriting. Cost: $350 out of state, $150 in state, $100 in district.

Desert Writers Workshop — Canyonlands Field Institute
P.O. Box 68
Moab UT 84532
Program Coordinator: David Williams
(801)259-7750
Estab. 1985
1991 dates: Oct. 17-20

4-day conference covering creative nonfiction, fiction, poetry (all with emphasis on landscape). Cost: $195.

Fiction from the Heartland
P.O. Box 32186
Kansas City MO 64111
Conference Chair: Judy Johnson
(816)254-4901
Estab. 1988
1991 dates: Feb. 8, 9
1992 dates (tentative): Feb. 7, 8

2-day conference covering commercial fiction — romance, mystery/suspense, fantasy/science fiction, horror. Cost: $50.

The Flight of the Mind
622 SE 29th Ave.
Portland OR 97214
Director: Judith Barrington
(503)236-9862
Estab. 1984
1991 dates: July 24-Aug. 4
1992 dates: July 26-Aug. 2

1-week, all women's conference covering fiction, poetry and nonfiction. Other offerings vary. Cost: about $450, including room and board. Offers scholarships for low-income participants. Brochure for 1 first-class stamp, no SASE.

Florida Space Coast Writers Conference, Inc.
P.O. Box 804
Melbourne FL 32902
President: Dr. Edwin J. Kirschner
(407)727-0051
Estab. 1981
1991 dates: Nov. 2, 3

2-day conference covering a variety of media and concentrations. Cost: $54 for members, including lunch.

Great Lakes Writers' Workshop
3401 S. 29th St.
Milwaukee WI 53215
Director, Telesis Institute: Debra Pass
(414)382-6177
Estab. 1986

1-week conference covering a variety of subjects. Cost: less than $100.

Green Lake Christian Writers Conference
American Baptist Assembly
Green Lake WI 54941-9599
Director of program: Dr. Arlo R. Reichter
1-800-558-8898
Estab. 1948
1991 dates: July 13-20
1992 dates: July 11-18

1-week conference covering nonfiction, devotional, poetry and fiction. Cost: $80 tuition; room and meals additional.

Hofstra University Children's Literature Conference
Hofstra University
Memorial Hall 232
Hempstead NY 11550
Director, Liberal Arts: Lewis Shena
(516)463-5016
Estab. 1983
1991 date: April 13

1-day conference covering children's writing: fiction, nonfiction, picture books, submission procedures. Cost: approximately $47.

Hofstra University Summer Writers' Conference
Hofstra University
Memorial Hall 232
Hempstead NY 11550

Director, Liberal Arts: Lewis Shena
(516)560-5016; (516)463-5016
Estab. 1971
1991 dates: July 8-19

12-day conference covering fiction, nonfiction, poetry, children's books and stage/screenwriting. Cost: $495.

Iowa Summer Writing Festival
116 International Center
The University of Iowa
Iowa City IA 52242
Director: Peggy Houston
(319)335-2534
Estab. 1987
1991 dates: June 9, 16 and 22; July 7, 14 and 21

1-week conferences offering 60 different classes. Cost: $245 per week.

Maple Woods Community College Writers Conference
2601 NE Barry Rd.
Kansas City MO 64156
Coordinator: Barbara Cakarnis
(816)436-6500
Estab. 1983
1991 date (tentative): Oct. 19

1-day workshop covering a variety of writing and publishing topics. Cost: $30.

Midland Writers Conference
Grace A. Dow Memorial Library
1710 W. St. Andrews
Midland MI 48640
Reference Librarians: Eileen Finzel or Margaret Allen
(517)835-7151
Estab. 1979
1991 date: June 15

1-day conference covering poetry, writing for children, and fiction. Cost: $45 until June 1; $55 after June 1. Senior citizens and student discounts.

Midwest Writers Workshop
Department of Journalism
Ball State University
Muncie IN 47306
Co-Director: Earl L. Conn
(317)285-8200

Estab. 1972
1991 dates: July 31-Aug. 3

4-day conference covering fiction, nonfiction, poetry, plus one or more specialized areas. Cost: $150.

Moody Write-to-Publish Conference
820 N. LaSalle
Chicago IL 60610
Director: Leslie R. Keylock
(312)329-4030
Estab. 1971
1991 dates: June 17-21
1992 dates: June 15-19

5-day conference with a variety of levels and classes. Conference includes visit to publishing house. Cost: $225 by April 15; $250 by May 15.

Mount Holyoke Writers' Conference
P.O. Box 3213 W.
Mount Holyoke College, South Hadley MA 01075
Director: Michael Pettit
(413)538-2308
Estab. 1988
1991 dates: June 8-16
1992 dates: same

8-day conference covering fiction and poetry, including agents' and editors' panels. Cost: $625 tuition, room and board. Scholarships are available.

Napa Valley Writers' Conference
Community Education Office
Napa Valley College
Napa CA 94558
Program Director: Sherri Hallgren
(707)253-3073
Estab. 1981
1991 dates: July 28-Aug. 2 (tentative)

1-week conference covering fiction and poetry. Cost: $350.

The New Orleans Writers' Conference
1520 Sugar Bowl Dr.
New Orleans LA 70112
Conference Director: Beverly Gianna
(504)566-5090
Estab. 1989
1991 dates: Sept. 25-28

3-day conference covering fiction, nonfiction, poetry, play/screenwriting, juvenile writing, romance, mystery. Free manuscript evaluation, agent/author consultation and awards to promising unpublished writers included. Cost: $175 before Aug. 28.

Ozark Creative Writers Inc.
6817 Gingerbread Lane
Little Rock AR 72204
Director: Peggy Vining
(501)569-8771
Estab. 1973
1991 and 1992 dates: second weekend of October

2-day conference covering fiction, nonfiction, writing for children, and poetry. Cost: $30 registration, approximately $59 for lodging and food, approximately $25 for 2 banquets. Held at Ozarks Convention Center.

Port Townsend Writers' Conference
Centrum/Box 1158
Port Townsend WA 98368
Director: Carol Jane Bangs
(206)385-3102
Estab. 1974
1991 dates: July 12-22
1992 dates: July 9-19

10-day conference covering mainstream and experimental fiction, poetry, nature writing, essay writing, and writing for children. Cost: $295 for tuition; approximately $250 for room and board.

Professionalism in Writing School
4308 S. Peoria, Ste 701
Tulsa OK 71405
Coordinator: Norma Jean Lutz
(918)PIW-5588
Estab. 1980
1991 dates: March 15, 16
1992 dates: second weekend in March

2-day conference for Christians who write broad spectrum (includes all genres, Christian and secular). Cost: $125.

St. Davids Christian Writers Conference
Eastern College
St. Davids PA 19087
Mail should be addressed to:
1775 Eden Rd.

Lancaster PA 17601
Registrar: Shirley Eaby
(717)394-6758
Estab. 1958
1991 dates: June 23-28

5-day conference with rotating workshops, including adult and children's fiction, journalism, articles, feature and devotional writing, poetry, serious and humorous writing and scriptwriting. Cost: $180 to $245 for housing, $100 to $275 for tuition.

San Diego State University Writers Conference
5630 Hardy Ave.
San Diego CA 92182
Extension Director: Jan Wahl
(619)594-2514
Estab. 1984
1992 dates: Jan. 18, 19

2-day conference covering fiction, nonfiction and screenwriting. Cost: approximately $185.

Sandhills Writers' Conference
Augusta College Continuing Education
2500 Walton Way
Augusta GA 30910-0299
Director, Continuing Education: Theresa Bryant
(404)737-1636
Estab. 1974
1991 dates: May 9-11. Conference always held the second Thursday, Friday
and Saturday in May.

3-day conference covering fiction, nonfiction, poetry, screen and playwriting, children's literature, novel/novella writing. Cost: $40 to $110, depending on number of events attended, manuscripts reviewed.

Santa Barbara Writers' Conference
P.O. Box 304
Carpinteria CA 93014
Directors: Mary and Barnaby Conrad
(805)684-2250
Estab. 1973
1991 dates: June 21-28
1992 dates: June 19-26

1-week conferences covering all genres of writing. Cost: $325 for 1991 conference and $350 for 1992 conference. Single hotel and conference (without meals) is $800; double (shared occupancy) hotel room is $600.

Society of Children's Book Writers & Illustrators Summer Retreat
1712 Morning Dr.
Loveland CO 80538
Rocky Mountain Chapter SCBWI
President: Ellen Javerniak
(303)667-2793
Estab: 1981
1991 dates: July 19-21

3-day conference with workshops on writing for children. Cost: $165 for SCBW members and $185 for non-members (tentative).

Steamboat Springs Writers Conference
P.O. Box 774284
Steamboat Springs CO 80477
Director: Harriet Freiberger
(303)879-8079
Estab. 1981
1991 dates: Aug. 2, 3

2-day conference covering fiction, nonfiction, general creativity and/or poetry. Cost: $50 by June 15; $60 after June 18.

Stonecoast
University of Southern Maine
Portland ME 04103
Director: Barbara Hope McGrath
(207)780-4291
Estab. 1981
1991 dates: late July-early August

12-day conference covering fiction, poetry, scriptwriting, and nonfiction. Cost: $375 plus room and board.

Trenton State College Writers' Conferences
Department of English
Hillwood Lakes CN 4700
Trenton NJ 08650
Director: Jean Hollander
(609)771-3254
Estab. 1981
1991 date: April 2

1-day conference covering fiction, poetry, newspaper and magazine journalism, playwriting, scriptwriting, literature for young people, and nonfiction. Cost varies.

UCLA Extension Screenwriting Workshops
The Writers' Program
10995 Le Conte Ave., #313
Los Angeles CA 90024-2883
(800)825-9064

1-, 2- and 4-day formats for beginners and advanced writers. Classes in various locations in the U.S.

University of Wisconsin School of the Arts at Rhinelander
727D Lowell Hall
610 Langdon St.
Madison WI 53703
Administrative Coordinator: Kathy Berigan
(608)263-3494
Estab. 1964
1991 dates: July 22-26

1-week conference covering fiction, nonfiction, poetry, creativity; also classes in visual arts, folk arts, dance, photography, drama. Cost: $150, not including food and lodging.

Vassar College Institute of Publishing and Writing: Children's Books in the Marketplace
P.O. Box 300
Poughkeepsie NY 12601
Associate Director of College Relations: Maryann Breeno
(914)437-5903
Estab. 1984
1991 dates: June 16-23

1-week conference covering children's books (fiction and nonfiction), illustrating, and understanding the market. Cost: $600; includes room and board.

Wesleyan Writers Conference
Wesleyan University
Middletown CT 06457
Director: Anne Greene
(203)347-9411 (ext. 2448)
Estab. 1956
1991 dates: June 23-28. Held last week of June.

1-week conference covering fiction, poetry, literary journalism and nonfiction. Scholarships available. Cost: $410 (tuition), $160 (meals), $75 (room).

Western Reserve Writers and Freelance Conference
Lakeland Community College
Route 306 and I-90
Mentor OH 44060
Coordinator: Lea Leever Oldham
(216)943-3047
Estab. 1984
1991 date: Sept. 14

1-day conference covering fiction (romance, science fiction, short stories); nonfiction (books, articles and humor); poetry, photography, cartooning. Cost: $39, including lunch.

(Also sponsors Western Reserve Writers Weekend at Cedar Hills Conference Center, July 19-21, 1991. Covers fiction, nonfiction and general writing, editing and marketing information. Cost: $175, including sessions, room and board.)

Wildacres Writers Workshop
233 South Elm St.
Greensboro NC 27401
Director: Judith Hill
(919)273-4044
Estab. 1984
1991 dates: June 23-30

1-week conference covers fiction, poetry and playwriting. Cost: less than $300.

Woodstock Guild's Byrdcliffe Arts Colony
34 Tinker St.
Woodstock NY 12498
Program Director: Michael Perkins
(914)679-2079
Estab. 1902
1991 dates: first weekend in June

Weekend conference covering writing and publishing. Cost: varies.

World-Wide Writers Conference
186 N. Coleman Rd.
Centereach NY 11720-3072
Director: Dr. David Axelrod
(516)736-6439
1991 dates: Nov. 5, 6

2-day conference covering all genres. Cost varies.

Write On The Sound
700 Main St.
Edmonds WA 98020
Arts Coordinator: Linda McCrystal
(206)775-2525 (ext. 269)
Estab. 1986
1991 dates: Oct. 4, 5

2-day conference covering various fiction and nonfiction writing. Cost: $25 for pre-registration; $30 on day of registration.

Writers Studio Spring Conference
1115 Brown
Davenport IA 52804
President: Jean Heritage
(319)324-4815
Estab. 1970
1991 date: April 7

1-day conference of general interest, with 18 1-hour workshops in poetry, fiction, nonfiction, romance, illustration. Cost: free

Writers in the Rockies: Television and Movie Screenwriting Conference
1980 Glenwood Dr.
Boulder CO 80304
Director: Carolyn Hodges
(303)443-4636
Estab. 1984
1991 dates: Aug. 17, 18

2-day conference covering screenwriting topics. Cost: $200, includes materials and 2 catered meals.

Writing for Money
34200 Ridge Rd., #110
Willoughby OH 44094
Contact: Lea Leever Oldham
(216)943-3047

1-day workshops held in educational institutions in northeastern Ohio, covering business and submission topics as well as general writing tips.

Yellow Bay Writers' Workshop
Center for Continuing Education
University of Montana
Missoula MT 59812
Program Manager: Judy Jones

(406)243-6486
Estab. 1988
1991 dates: Aug. 25-31
1992 dates: Aug. 16-22

1-week conference covering poetry, nonfiction or personal essay, and fiction. Cost: $325 registration; $195 for lodging and meals (tentative).

WRITING INSTRUCTION

If you're looking for writing instruction, or you'd like to supplement your income as an instructor, you have choices ranging from university degree programs to correspondence schools. In addition, several professional writers' groups offer regular classes and workshops for members. See the listings under Professional Associations and Organizations and Writers' Groups for more information, and check out individual offerings from other groups in your area.

Choosing a writing program or course means evaluating what benefits you want, how much you can spend, how much time you have to write, and what type of instruction you find best suits you.

UNIVERSITY PROGRAMS

Writing programs offered through universities typically demand at least part-time attendance at group classes and workshops. Some universities offer independent study; inquire about this if it is your only option and you'd like to work on a degree. There are a few drawbacks to degree-granting programs. The application process can be confusing; and you may be unsure what degree you want to pursue. In addition, university writing programs are fairly expensive and time-consuming. If you are writing part-time and have a full-time job, or you're earning a fairly good living writing full time, the pursuit of a degree may cost more than you can comfortably afford to spend.

On the other hand, writing programs have proliferated on college campuses for good reason. Michael Bugeja, in a *Writer's Digest* article, says the programs are considered "the minor league for writers." Writers enroll for many reasons, most having little to do with the actual degree. More often they look for the opportunity to study with a particular writer, concentrate more fully on techniques of the craft, hone their writing skills and establish industry contacts.

A good writing program may provide you with an entrance to the world of publishing. Not only do agents scout the major programs for talent, some students have their work recommended to editors and agents by writing program faculty members. Universities also support more experimental writing and have literary magazines that will publish noncommercial writing.

Tips on choosing programs:

● Have a few choices available. Don't bank on acceptance from one program and only apply there. The competition is quite daunting in some programs. The Iowa Writers Workshop, for instance, receives about 560 applications in fiction and 300 in poetry and it only accepts 25 students in each category.

● Weigh the benefits of a local program versus an out-of-state one, both in terms of what's offered and what you can afford.

● Make sure your writing samples are ready to go. Now's the time to polish them and select the best ones for the program to which you're applying. A sample poetry submission will have 10 to 20 poems, and a fiction or nonfiction sample includes three stories.

● Register to take any tests required for entrance or be sure your test scores are available.

● Decide what approach you want in a program. Some writers prefer a small program where they'll receive individual attention; others want a large program with a prestigious faculty. If you can, talk to other graduates of the program. A master's degree usually requires more reading while a master of fine arts program requires more writing but fewer literature classes. (At least one program, Stanford, doesn't even confer a degree.) Some programs are conducted in a straight classroom setup, but a typical workshop approach has about 12 students and a teacher. During a class session, one student will bring in work to be critiqued by the teacher and students.

● Evaluate the "extras." The community of writers around the program may be very helpful in your development as a writer. Look for the caliber of visiting writers in addition to faculty and the literary magazines, readings and festivals that also may be offered.

● Cost of programs is nearly always a consideration for writers, so find out what kind of financial aid is available and what teaching assistantships are available. In addition, you'll want to look at the cost of living in the area.

Here are some other tips offered by graduates of writing programs:

"Look for track records—where writers are going who are coming out of the program."

"You're going to be there two years or more, so choose a place you'll like to be."

"Financial aid is fairly available, but you should look into this early."

"Know who's teaching. Read their work. It will help you select the best submissions to make from your own work."

"Line up your references early. Start a reference file, so professors won't have to write several times."

"Know the little things about the programs. If you choose someplace like Columbia, it'll be easier to make connections with other writers and editors since you'll be in New York. At Iowa, you know there'll be editors and agents scouting, so you can be in touch with the publishing industry. If you just want to write, though, you may not want some place that's so competitive and distracting."

LISTINGS

The best source of information on writing programs is *The AWP Official Guide to Writing Programs*, edited by D.W. Fenza and Beth Jarock. The fifth edition covers 1990-91. The book includes information about 328 writing programs in the U.S. and Canada, both at the undergraduate and graduate level, and has indexes by state and degree offered. Write to Associated Writing Programs, Old Dominion University, Norfolk VA 23529-0079 or order through Dustbooks, P.O. Box 100, Paradise CA 95967. Following are some of the more well-known writing programs.

Boston University
236 Bay State Rd.
Boston MA 02215
(617)353-2510

Offers bachelor's degree in English; master's in creative writing. Contact: Leslie Epstein, Creative Writing Program.

Brown University
P.O. Box 1852
Providence RI 02912
(401)863-3260

Offers a 2-year master's degree in writing. Contact: Graduate Writing Program.

Columbia University
School of the Arts
Writing Division
404 Dodge Hall

New York NY 10027
(212)854-4391

Offers a 2-year MFA in creative writing; also offers undergraduate writing classes through School of General Studies. Contact: Writing Division, School of the Arts.

Cornell University
Goldwin Smith Hall
Ithaca NY 14853
(607)255-6802

Offers bachelor's degree in English with creative writing component; MFA in creative writing, and MFA/PhD program. Contact: Director of the Creative Writing Program, English Department.

Indiana University
Bloomington IN 47405
(812)855-8224

Offers a bachelor's degree in English, an MFA in creative writing, a master's in English with a concentration in creative writing, and a PhD. Contact: Director, Creative Writing Program, Department of English.

Johns Hopkins University
Baltimore MD 21218
(301)338-7544

Offers bachelor's degree in the writing seminars; master's in the writing seminars: fiction, poetry, nonfiction prose, or writing about science. Contact: Jane Wenk, admissions secretary, the Writing Seminars.

Louisiana State University
Baton Rouge LA 70803
(504)388-2236

Offers bachelor's and MFA degrees. Contact: Kate Daniels, Director of Creative Writing, % the English Department.

Ohio University
Athens OH 45701
(614)593-1000

Offers bachelor's in English with concentration in creative writing; master's in English and PhD in English. Contact: Paul Nelson, Director, Creative Writing, Department of English.

San Francisco State University
1600 Holloway Ave.
San Francisco CA 94132
(415)338-1891

Offers bachelor's and master's degrees in English with concentration in creative writing. Contact: Secretary, Creative Writing Department, School of Humanities.

Stanford University
Stanford CA 94305
(415)723-2637

Stanford Writing Program confers no degree; fellows in creative writing attend a weekly workshop. Contact: Secretary, Creative Writing Program.

Syracuse University
Syracuse NY 13244-1170
(315)443-2173

Offers a master's in English with creative thesis. Contact: Sally Bennett Segall, coordinator, Creative Writing Program, Department of English.

The University of Alabama
Tuscaloosa AL 35487
(205)348-5065

Offers bachelor's degree in English with minor in creative writing; MFA in creative writing. Contact: Director, Program in Creative Writing, Department of English, P.O. Box 870244.

University of Arizona
Tucson AZ 85721
(602)621-3880

Offers bachelor's degree and MFA with major in creative writing. Contact: Steve Orlen, Director of Creative Writing, Department of English.

University of California, Irvine
Irvine CA 92717
(714)856-6712

Offers bachelor's degree in English with creative writing emphasis; MFA in writing. Contact: Administrator, The Program in Writing, Department of English and Comparative Literature.

University of Houston
Houston TX 77204-3012
(713)749-3640

Offers master's in English and creative writing; PhD in English and creative writing. Contact: Associate Director, Creative Writing Program, Department of English.

University of Iowa
Iowa City IA 52242
(319)335-0416

Offers a bachelor's degree in English and an MFA in creative writing. Known informally as the Iowa Writers' Workshop. Contact: The Writers' Workshop.

University of Massachusetts
Amherst MA 01003
(413)545-0643

Offers an MFA in English. Contact: Director, MFA Program in English, 452 Bartlett Hall.

University of Michigan
Ann Arbor MI 48109-1045
(313)764-6330

Offers a bachelor's degree, an MFA in creative writing, a master's, PhD, and DA degrees. Contact: Nicholas Delbanco, Director, MFA Program in Creative Writing, Department of English.

University of Montana
Missoula MT 59812
(406)243-5231

Offers bachelor's in English with creative writing emphasis; MFA in creative writing. Contact: Lois M. Welch, Director of the Creative Writing Program, Department of English.

University of North Carolina at Greensboro
Greensboro NC 27412
(919)334-5459

Offers bachelor's in English with concentration in creative writing; MFA in creative writing; and PhD in English with creative writing dissertation. Contact: Denise Baker, Director of Graduate Studies in English, Department of English.

University of Oregon
Eugene OR 97403
(503)686-3911

Offers bachelor's, master's and MFA in creative writing. Contact: Director of the Writing Program, Department of English.

University of Southern Mississippi
P.O. Box 5144
Hattiesburg MS 39406
(601)266-4321

Offers bachelor's in English; master's and doctorate in English with creative writing emphasis. Contact: Rie Fortenberry, Southern Station.

University of Utah
Salt Lake City UT 84112
(801)750-2733

Offers bachelor's with creative writing emphasis, master's degree, MFA and PhD. Contact: Director of Creative Writing, Department of English.

University of Virginia
143 Wilson Hall
Charlottesville VA 22903
(804)924-7105

Offers bachelor's in English and MFA in creative writing. Contact: Creative Writing Program, English Department.

Washington University
Campus Box 1122
St. Louis MO 63130
(314)889-5190

Offers a 2-year MFA in writing. Contact: Eric Pankey, Department of English.

CORRESPONDENCE SCHOOLS

Correspondence schools have some advantages over traditional university programs. If you live in a rural area without easy access to a university writing program, or if your schedule prevents you from meeting at a regular classroom time, you may want to explore a correspondence course. In addition to the advantage of scheduling and access, most courses offer you one-on-one instruction with the same teacher throughout the course. You also have the advantage of being able to work at your own pace.

Correspondence work has its disadvantages, too. Usually the course is set up with the average student in mind, and you may be unable to adapt the course to your needs. If you are the type of person who finds it difficult to meet deadlines, a correspondence course is not for you. Correspondence allows you to set your own pace up to a point, but most courses have a deadline and getting an extension may cost you. Many writers also enjoy the "community" feeling and feedback that comes with interaction among students and teachers.

When you see advertisements or brochures for correspondence schools, don't let that information be your only guide. Evaluate courses with these things in mind:

- Does the course suit your needs? Some courses offer a smorgasbord of topics, and you'll study everything from news writing to fiction in a single course. Others concentrate on a single subject such as the romance novel or the short story. You need to decide what you want to study and whether or not the course fits that need. It's also nice to be able to inspect the course for a week to 10 days and be able to return it if it's not suitable. Look for this feature and/or ask if it's available.
- What's the length of the course? Most correspondence or home study courses can be finished in a year or less. That may be more time than you want to invest, or perhaps you'll see the course and think it's not *enough* time to learn everything you need to know about the particular type of writing.
- What's the cost? Costs of correspondence courses vary widely, from as low as $200 to as high as $1,500. Not only should you compare the course against other comparable courses but compare it against other writing instruction available in your area. Also ask what kinds of payment plans are available and if refunds are offered within a certain amount of time if you decide to withdraw from the course.
- What's the experience level of the instructor? A correspondence school should be willing to give you information about the caliber of its instructors, and it also should be willing to reassign you to another instructor if things don't work out. In a correspondence course, feedback from the instructor can make or break your learning experience, so it's important to get a good match. Look for instructors who not only know the subject but have recent sales in the area.
- What amount of feedback can you expect? Will your instructor provide you with a detailed critique of your work, pencil in grammar and style corrections, or just give you an overall evaluation? How often—and how soon after you return an assignment—can you expect feedback? This is an important part of correspondence school learning, so you need to be sure you'll get the type of feedback you can use to improve your writing.

Finally, be wary about amazing claims, or business practices that seem out of the ordinary. As the saying goes, if it sounds too good to be true, it probably is.

TEACHING IN CORRESPONDENCE SCHOOLS

If you think you'd like to be on the other side of the mailbox, you can do several things to enhance your chances.

Some correspondence schools ask professional organizations for references or place notices in association newsletters. A scan of these will usually tell you whom to call and what credentials are required. Most school directors will ask for a résumé and writing samples, along with your credentials to teach. (If you haven't seen an advertisement or notice but are interested, write to the director of the school and ask if instructors are being sought.)

You should ask for information about the course, including your role in shaping the course, the feedback expected, and the general level of students enrolled. You'll also want to know the pay rate, of course, and the number of students typically assigned to an individual instructor.

LISTINGS

Two books contain listings of correspondence instruction: *Guide to Independent Study Through Correspondence Instruction* (Peterson's Guides) and *The Correspondence Educational Directory* (Racz Publishing). Check with your local university to see if it offers correspondence or independent study courses. Some clubs, such as the National Writers Club, also offer correspondence instruction.

Selected writing correspondence programs:

Creative Writing: Poetry, an Independent Study Course, University of Wisconsin at Madison
631 Lowell Hall
610 Langdon St.
Madison WI 53703

Hollywood Scriptwriting Institute
Suite 216
1605 North Cahuenga Blvd.
Hollywood CA 90028
1-800-SCRIPTS

Offers courses in professional screenwriting, playwriting. Optional resident training available.

International Romance Writers' Institute
P.O. Box 7916
Aspen CO 81612
1-800-882-8148

In Connecticut or outside the U.S., call collect (203)438-1599.

Offers 10 lessons, including technique and business aspects of writing romances. Other editorial services also available for fee.

Long Ridge Writers Group
Long Ridge Road
West Redding CT 06896-0802.

Covers articles and short stories.

National Writers School
(see National Writers Club in Writers' Groups section)

NRI School of Writing
McGraw-Hill Continuing Education Center
4401 Connecticut Ave. NW
Washington DC 20008

Nonfiction and fiction writing courses

Writer's Digest School
1507 Dana Ave.
Cincinnati OH 45207
1-800-759-0963. Outside U.S., (513)531-2222.

Variety of writing courses in fiction and nonfiction.

Writers Institute
112 West Boston Post Rd.
Mamaroneck NY 10543

CONTINUING EDUCATION PROGRAMS

Continuing education programs are offered by a variety of groups ranging from professional associations to local high schools. Check professional magazines such as *Publishers Weekly* for notices of professional classes and workshops too. Local classes are usually publicized through writers' groups, library bulletin board notices and free distribution catalogs. Call your local university's continuing education department to ask about offerings. Classes often are available through community-based programs at high schools or "free university" workshops too.

Although few continuing education programs offer credit, they can provide you with a fairly inexpensive way to explore new types of writing. Most courses of this type cost $50 to $100, and the average length is six to nine weeks. It may not be long enough for you to learn everything you want to know, but it should give you an indication of whether or not you want to pursue the subject more seriously. With the exception of professional continuing education programs, which usually focus on a narrow topic such as indexing, most continuing education programs offer information for the beginner.

The caliber of instruction is an important consideration here. Although you won't be investing a considerable amount of time and money, you certainly don't want to waste it. Tom Clark, *Writer's Digest* senior editor and a frequent workshop instructor, counsels writers to look for an instructor with experience as an editor, publisher or writer. "It's important to look for relevant credits too," he says. "Don't go to someone who's only written nonfiction for a fiction class or to a novelist for newspaper writing."

Because continuing education programs usually have open enrollment, you may or may not find fellow students helpful in your development as a writer, and your instruction will rarely involve any individual attention from the teacher. On the other hand, a local program can help you determine what direction you want to go with your writing without a major investment of time and money. It can also provide you with local contacts, a valuable source for any writer.

TEACHING IN CONTINUING EDUCATION PROGRAMS

If you have the credits and interest in sharing with other writers, you may want to explore continuing education programs as a supplemental source of income.

First, find out what's offered in your area. It's always helpful to sit in on an existing class to find out more about the students and what works and doesn't work for you. Sometimes it also can give you ideas about a new class you'd like to propose.

Contact the director of the continuing education program about your idea for a class; most are very flexible and eager to offer new courses of potential interest. Follow up that contact with a formal outline proposal for the course and include a statement of your qualifications to teach the class.

From there, be prepared to back up your proposal with a solid class that will continue to interest students. The majority of continuing education programs have minimum student enrollments necessary to justify holding a class.

Chapter 3

RESEARCHING IT

Research. The very word brings sweaty palms to most writers, no doubt a throwback to the days of slogging through a dusty card catalog only to find that, with your first real deadline looming, all the available books on Beowulf had been checked out by your fellow student/writers.

But we've grown up, and research has grown up, and new technologies have streamlined the process and made it far less sweaty.

Volumes have been written about how to conduct research, whether it be for a short nonfiction article, a historical novel, a family genealogy or any other purpose for which you have to look something up. This chapter is by no means a short course in library science, just a primer to some of the most used (and some relatively unused, but nevertheless valuable) resources available to writers.

One of the best guides anywhere to finding information is *Knowing Where to Look: The Ultimate Guide to Research*, written by Lois Horowitz (Writer's Digest Books). Horowitz is a reference librarian and newspaper columnist who takes your hand and leads you gently through the maze of reference sources. A condensed version, but still information packed, is *A Writer's Guide to Research* (Writer's Digest Books).

Overall, the advice offered time and again by professionals interviewed for this chapter was "Put yourself in the hands of a good research librarian." Some writers, perhaps not wanting to appear as rank amateurs, eschew the services of a librarian—rather like the traveler who, preferring to make all his or her own reservations, avoids the services of a travel agent.

Both are missing a good bet.

A good travel agent can save you money, time and headaches, lead you to some exotic, sometimes unexpected, locales, and generally ensure a pleasurable, sometimes profitable, trip.

An illustration: John Graham, currently in the History and Government Department of the Public Library of Cincinnati and Hamilton County, tells of helping a writer in Tulsa, Oklahoma, research a book on the development of Route 66. A search of conventional sources and databases turned up little, but Graham and the writer had a sudden brainstorm.

The writer sang the lyrics to the "Route 66" theme song—which lists many of the cities along the route—and Graham compiled a list of other agencies—newspaper libraries, state highway departments and tourism boards—in those cities. The writer, who probably would have hit a dead end in his research otherwise, now had a whole new road map to follow, one that provided a lot of useful information.

A postscript: A busy public library may not be the best source if you'll need to spend a significant amount of time with a reference librarian. A university library reference staff might be less rushed, and they are generally very willing to help if you clearly explain the type of project that you're working on. It's best to call in advance to see if the reference librarian is available and let her know what you're interested in researching so perhaps she can get a head start on pulling out the sources you need.

LIBRARIES

The first word that writers generally speak in the same breath as "research" is "library" but, thanks to interlibrary loan and new technology, the modern library's scope extends far beyond the walls of your neighborhood branch. Interlibrary loan allows writers far removed from large metropolitan libraries access to a staggering number of sources in far-flung locales.

Lonnie Wheeler, a freelance sportswriter and author, for example, enlisted the services of a research librarian at the University of Cincinnati to help him prepare a biography of Hank Aaron. The librarian was able to send for microfilm copies of the *Indianapolis Recorder*, a Black newspaper, old photographs and other resources that added richness to Wheeler's account of Aaron's career.

For those unacquainted with interlibrary loan (ILL), it's the cooperative lending of materials between libraries. Generally governed by lending rules established by the American Library Association (ALA), it takes only a valid card from the library system that will be making the ILL request for you, and the title of the work or works you're looking for.

Suppose, for example, you're researching a major piece on global warming, and a book that is the definitive work on the subject is not available anywhere in your library's system. The librarian checks the request against the Online Computer Library Center (OCLC), a catalog network of more than 10,000 libraries in the U.S., Canada and around the world. The OCLC database contains information on and locations for books, serials, records, audiovisual material, maps, manuscripts and computer files. The search will turn up which library or libraries hold the particular book or other material for which you're searching.

A note here for computerphiles: OCLC introduced EPIC service, an on-line reference system available to members and nonmembers of OCLC, in January, 1990. Though it plans to add a variety of databases to the service, the Online Union Catalog is the first service available. It's expensive for the individual—$110 per connect hour at this writing—but it allows, for the first time, search of OCLC by subject, meaning a researcher can determine where books on his particular subject are available anywhere in the OCLC system. For further information, call or write OCLC, 6565 Frantz Road, Dublin OH 43017-0702. (800)848-8286 or (614)764-6000.

Armed with this information, the librarian can process the request. The library from which you are requesting materials sets the rules on whether they will loan particular materials or not. Reference materials, rare books, audiovisual materials and recordings, microfilms and fiches are frequently not circulated through ILL, but most libraries will comply with requests for photocopies of these materials. They also set the rules on how long you can keep things—generally three or four weeks. Overdue charges usually are based on those of your home library.

The cost of ILL to you will primarily be postage, copying charges and sometimes a processing charge. (Check with the library originating the ILL request for you to find out the approximate charge and the form of payment they require for these materials. Some library systems require a check or money order made out to the library system sending you the materials, *not* your home library.)

Other tips for using interlibrary loan:

- Allow enough time for processing requests and for requesting renewals on materials. Receipt of materials through ILL can take two to four weeks—or longer—depending on the availability of the material you're requesting and the work load of the libraries on each end of the request. To renew the materials in your possession, give your local library at least a week's notice to process a renewal.
- Give the librarian all the available information you have—author, title, publisher and year published, if available—and be sure it's accurate. If you request the wrong issue of a magazine, for instance, you'll more than likely have to pay for the mistake nonetheless.
- If processing a large number of ILL requests (for example, for book

research) through a large public library, it might be wise to file your requests a few at a time. That way, all your research materials won't arrive at the same time.

• ILL materials must be picked up and dropped off at the library branch initiating the request.

PHONE AND FAX

For library research that needs a quick answer, most libraries will answer questions by phone. Some larger libraries have also instituted fax service—i.e., transmittal of information by telefacsimile (fax machine). If you don't have a fax machine, some libraries will fax the information to a branch library near your home. This can be costly, though. The Cincinnati library, which instituted fax service this year, charges 25¢ per page, plus a $1 service charge per article or citation within the county; 30¢ per page, plus a $2 charge outside the county; and 40¢ per page, plus a $3 service charge outside the state. (They'll even fax you an invoice for the service.)

LIBRARY CO-OPS

Most writers, unless they have very specialized research needs and/ or unlimited travel budgets, will patronize libraries within a comfortable driving distance from home, and then network through these to obtain the necessary materials through interlibrary loan. It pays, then, to know the locations and policies of these institutions, some of which may be off the beaten path. If your local library belongs to a regional consortium or cooperative, you may discover local libraries you had not been aware of, and be entitled to borrow materials directly from any of its member institutions, return materials to a more convenient location, and benefit from other perks such as free parking, reduced photocopying charges and the like. The Greater Cincinnati Library Consortium, for example, represents 37 academic, public, school and special libraries that will honor a valid college, university, public library or company ID card to grant lending privileges.

The *American Library Directory*, published by R.R. Bowker, lists public, academic, government and special libraries throughout the U.S. and Canada. Arranged geographically, the notations include subject interests and whether the library is open to the general public. The *Library and Book Trade Almanac* (also known as the "Bowker Annual") is available in most libraries and lists these networks, consortia and other cooperative arrangements by state. Phone numbers are included. The *Encyclopedia of Information Systems and Services*, published by Gale Research, also carries a section listing these cooperative library groups.

SPECIAL LIBRARIES

If your research runs to the exotic, or if you're seeking materials outside the ken of public or academic libraries, you might investigate special libraries. More than 10,000 special libraries exist across the U.S., representing information sources vital to any number of entities, from banks to businesses, museums to media relations experts, nonprofit groups to news organizations. The Special Library Association, 1700 18th St. NW, Washington D.C. 20009, maintains a list of 12,500 members, but does not generally provide information about locations and subject matter of member libraries, according to Kathryn Dorko, manager of information resources for SLA.

When a writer calls the SLA seeking a special library, whether it deals with the art of tattooing or the collected works of Mark Twain, the association refers the caller to the *Directory of Special Libraries and Information Centers*, Gale Research Co. The book describes more than 19,000 libraries and information centers in the U.S., Canada and 80 other countries. A *Subject Directory of Special Libraries*, also by Gale, reorganizes the subject into three volumes: business, government and law libraries; computer, engineering and science libraries, and health science libraries. Both resources are available at larger libraries.

About six regional Special Library Association chapters, in addition, publish directories that describe the special libraries within their geographical area. These include the New Jersey chapter, Philadelphia chapter, Rhode Island chapter, New Mexico chapter, Rocky Mountain chapter, San Andreas chapter, southern California chapter and Toronto chapter. Directories range in price from $5 to $75 and must be ordered through the individual chapter. Contact the SLA for information, (202)234-4700.

NEWSPAPER LIBRARIES

For background on a prominent citizen, a natural disaster, a crime in the headlines, or other localized topic, don't overlook the library (or "morgue") of the local newspaper office. Two caveats here, however: Due to staff shortages and the disinclination to handle a lot of requests, many larger newspapers have closed their libraries to the general public. A letter outlining your legitimate research request may get you around that problem. The second warning: Also due to lack of staff, the quality of newspaper libraries is spotty. Some "libraries," especially at small town papers, are nothing more than two or three file cabinets stuffed full of poorly filed clippings.

Also, many of these facilities can't — or don't — correct errors that may have appeared in the file materials, perpetuating the errors through the researchers who use them.

Despite all this, newspaper libraries can provide exciting "on the scene" looks at events and people who have shaped that region. The SLA publishes a directory of *Newspaper Libraries in the U.S. and Canada*, arranged by geographical location and also by newspaper chain. It's available for $18.50.

Also on the subject of specialized libraries, The Medical Library Association, (Suite 300, 6 North Michigan Ave., Chicago IL 60602, (312)419-9094), publishes two useful finding tools if your specialty is medical writing: *The MLA Directory* ($46 for nonmembers) and *MEDLINE: A Basic Guide to Searching* the database, covering some 3,000 medical journals ($32 for nonmembers).

Other special-interest library associations:

Music Library Association, P.O. Box 487, Canton MA 02021. (617)828-8450.

Art Libraries Society of North America, 3900 E. Timrod St., Tucson AZ 85711. (602)881-8479.

LIBRARY OF CONGRESS

The "nation's library" holds more than 98 million items, including books, music, pamphlets, disks, tapes, maps, microforms, photographs, prints, drawings and personal papers from some of America's most distinguished citizens. It publishes the *National Union Catalog*, a record of publications held by more than 2,500 libraries in the U.S. and Canada, and also serves as headquarters of the federal Copyright Office.

Housed in three buildings within walking distance of the Capitol (it maintains its original purpose as a research facility for members of Congress to the present day) it's a fascinating place to browse and, obviously, a first-rate reference site for researchers in the Washington, D.C., area. Those writers working on projects needing extensive use of the general collections may want to contact the Research Facilities Office (Library of Congress, Washington D.C. 20540) to inquire about assigned desk space or study shelves.

For researchers outside the Washington area, the Library of Congress does participate in interlibrary loan service to academic, public or special libraries making requests on behalf of persons doing serious research, provided the materials can't be procured elsewhere. This is an important proviso—the Library of Congress staff reports, in all seriousness, that it is the "library of last resort."

Photoreproductions of many materials in the collections are available from the library's Photoduplication Service. A price list is available on request.

The Library of Congress doesn't ordinarily provide large numbers of items for a single project, nor will it lend out certain materials—those frequently used by Congress, for example, or certain rare books and other items. ILL requests should be made through your librarian. For single reference questions, a note or phone call may suffice. Direct written inquiries to the General Reference Division or, in the case of photoreproductions, to Photoduplication Service, Library of Congress, Washington D.C. 20540. The phone number for reference questions is (202)707-5522; for general information, (202)707-6400.

NATIONAL ARCHIVES

Anyone who's visited Washington is usually acquainted with the National Archives, 7th Street and Pennsylvania Avenue NW, where researchers with a valid ID card can browse. But a lesser known fact is that the archives also maintains 11 field branches throughout the U.S. where copies of many of the same documents (usually chosen on the basis of regional interest) are housed. For a list of field branches, a description of archives policies, or to pose a specific question in a research area, call or write National Archives and Records Administration, Washington D.C. 20408, (202)501-5402. The office is open weekdays from 8:45 a.m. to 5:15 p.m. EST.

OTHER NATIONAL LIBRARIES

Information on almost any facet of medicine and the health sciences is available at The National Library of Medicine, 8600 Rockville Pike, Bethesda MD 20894.

Materials are available on the premises, and the library participates in interlibrary loan. The National Library of Medicine maintains MEDLARS, a group of databases indexing more than 3,000 medical journals from around the world. MEDLARS is adding databases regularly—an AIDSLINE was added in 1988, and is considered *the* database for serious medical research.

Out-of-town researchers who contact NLM by phone will generally be referred to one or two medical libraries in their area, or else to relevant organizations and/or associations. The reference number is (301)496-6095.

The National Agricultural Library, United States Department of Agriculture, NAL Building, Beltsville MD 20705, contains 2 million volumes and 27,000 periodical titles received annually from throughout the world.

NAL, too, participates in interlibrary loan. Brief questions can be answered by phone through the reference branch, (301)344-4479, or by mail (address queries to USDA, National Agricultural Library, Public Services Division, Reference Branch, Room 111, Beltsville MD 20705).

Its collections can be searched on-line through the AGRICOLA database by a number of the commercial vendors (see Databases section).

FINDING SPECIAL COLLECTIONS

Libraries have strengths in specialized areas much as writers do. If you're seeking in-depth information on a particular topic, you might want to determine what library or libraries have specialized collections that may lend an added fillip to your research. (This is particularly helpful in researching fiction.)

Subject Collections: A Guide to Special Book Collections and Subject Emphases, by R.R. Bowker, catalogs 20,000 special collections housed in more than 9,000 university and college libraries, public libraries and special libraries and museums in the U.S. and Canada.

If you were writing the definitive guide on the paranormal, for example, *Subject Collections* would point you to the American Society for Psychical Research, a 7,000-volume library in New York, the Parapsychology Foundation, also in New York, with more than 9,300 volumes, plus about a dozen other public and other libraries throughout the U.S. with significant holdings in that subject.

Special Collections in College and University Libraries, published by MODOC Press Inc. (Macmillan Publishing Co.), catalogs these collections in academic libraries. The general index here is helpful for subject browsing. Entries are arranged geographically, which gives you a clue to the treasure troves that might be available in your own backyard.

USING THE TECHNOLOGY

Rather than drudgery, library research can be intriguing, challenging and sometimes even serendipitous. The key things to remember are to be flexible, to use the technology and to keep an eye out for other avenues to explore through cross-references and other clues.

Suppose you've been assigned a story for a general interest women's magazine on television violence and its effect on adolescent behavior. The old method might have been to head first for the *Reader's Guide to Periodical Literature*. But the General Periodicals Index, and several other helpful indexes, are available in CD-ROM (Compact Disc-Read Only Memory) format which means you can not only type in a general description of your topic and see what turns up, but also possibly have a printer make a copy of the relevant citations, rather than, as in past, laboriously copying them by hand.

The General Periodicals Index, for example, has you type in "Television" followed by "Psychological Aspects." Out of two dozen citations, you turn up seven that are most promising.

Susan Hettinger, of the Education Department of the Public Library of Cincinnati and Hamilton County, would head for the Wilson Indexes, the set of indexes covering journals in the social sciences, education, art and a wide range of topics, to find out what type of research has been done in the subject.

In the Social Sciences Index, for example, a check of "Television – Psychological Aspects," turns up an article on "Adolescents and death on television: a follow-up study" in *Death Studies* journal. If you scan further, under "Violence in Motion Pictures," an article titled "Does a single exposure to filmed violence affect aggressive tendencies?" in *Psychological Reports* might be of interest.

Education Index also turns up a listing under "Television broadcasting and children" of "Why Children's Television Should Be Regulated," an article in *Education Digest* that might provide an insight for your article, or maybe even the name of an expert to interview.

Speaking of experts – and we'll treat that at greater length later – if you scan *Subject Guide to Books in Print* or *Forthcoming Books in Print*, you'll no doubt find one or more authors of books on the subject as live interview subjects. And the writer's old stand-by, the *Encyclopedia of Associations*, lists dozens of associations dealing with television and/or violence. The National Coalition on TV Violence might provide you with other interview possibilities.

You get the idea. There are, of course, even more avenues to pursue – database searches to find additional information on the topic, searches of statistical sources, probably even government studies dealing with television and its sociological effects. All of these possibilities will be touched on in the sections that follow.

ADDITIONAL RESOURCES

Map Collections in the United States and Canada: A Directory, 4th Edition, David K. Carrington, ed. and Richard W. Stephenson (Special Libraries Association).

Archives, Libraries, Museums and Information Centers with Index Archivum, Michael Duchein, ed. (K.G. Saur).

Guide to the Use of Libraries and Information Sources, 6th ed., by Jean Key Gates (McGraw-Hill Book Co.).

World Guide to Special Libraries, by Helga Lengenfelder (K.G. Saur).
Archives: A Guide to the National Archives Field Branches, by Loretto Szucs and Sandra Luebking (EIG Publishing).
Finding Facts Fast, by Alden Todd (Ten Speed Press).

DATABASES

If you use a computer for writing and don't at least look into the research opportunities that it and a modem can afford you, it's a little like investing in a fine racehorse and tethering it in the backyard to give the neighborhood kids pony rides. Of course it will do the job, but it could be doing so much more for you on the track at Santa Anita!

By computer, a writer can, with racehorse speed, access any number of library indexes, statistical resources, encyclopedias, or any of a number of other fascinating data sources at any time of day or night, all without leaving the comfort of home.

Gathering information from databases need not be expensive—though it certainly *can* be. The trick is to become adept at defining the parameters of your research, learning the best sources for finding that particular information and even finding some free or low-cost databases offering the information.

The Modem Reference by Michael A. Banks (Brady Books) is a good handbook for learning your way around. Banks, a veteran of the freelance wars, treats databases and how to use them most efficiently and effectively, as well as describing, in nontechnical language, the numerous other capabilities of the computer modem. It's user-friendly, thorough and professional.

If you're a novice at telecommunications, the idea of database searching might sound intimidating. It isn't. A database can be any collection of data—from the hours of operation at your local library to the entire contents of *Grolier's Encyclopedia*. Searching it generally entails typing in a key word or two, sometimes a cross-reference. The computer then searches out any and all entries that fall into those parameters, saving you time in searching through the stacks and paging through mountains of books that you would have had to go through in the old days of research.

The speed and ease of database searching can be addictive. So we'll add a piece of advice from professional researchers: Don't become so enamored of the technology that you begin to think database searching is the only way to research. Since many of the services came on line only in the 1970s, database searching is not comprehensive and may not include older materials. Scrolling around on a screen produces a kind of tunnel vision, not allowing for the types of browsing that book research does, along with the serendipitous discoveries that paging through a book can. Database searching, though, is unparalleled for specific current research topics with definite parameters: e.g., what's been written of late on AIDS and its effect on interest in blood donations?

So where do you access these wonderful fonts of information? Some of them are available at a cost, while others can be had for little or no money, if you know where to find them.

COMMERCIAL VENDORS

Think of commercial database vendors as somewhat like department stores. Most of them offer access to a wide range of research materials, some of them duplicated by other vendors and others offered as exclusives. The bases offered by the commercial vendors are truly staggering, from *Books in Print* and *Magazine Index*, familiar to most writers, to more esoteric offerings such as Coffeeline, summarizing articles and data from more than 5,000 publications relating to that industry, to releases from the Xinhua News Agency, the English language news service originating in Beijing.

In addition, commercial vendors also offer other services — on-line shopping, electronic mail (or E-mail), financial information — that can be useful to nonwriting endeavors. Some offer custom clipping services that let you type in a subject of particular interest, monitor the bases for new information on that subject while you're off-line and then deliver the full text next time you sign on. This is a real time-saver if you're looking for up-to-the-minute information on a particular topic as you're writing.

Of course, you pay for the dazzling array and the convenience. Most charge a basic per-hour or per-minute connect time with surcharges for accessing specific bases — and some of these can be expensive. You often can get a break by working at off-hours (i.e., evenings and weekends), which have cheaper rates.

Most of the vendors offer a variety of methods for learning your way around their systems — from extensive training manuals to video instructions to actual training seminars. You'll also find that many offer credits for service when you sign up.

Like department stores, too, commercial vendors advertise heavily and are only too happy to send potential customers descriptions of what they offer and how much they charge. Call them for an information packet and rate sheet, and compare carefully costs, services, etc.

Here are some of the better known of the commercial vendors and a sampling of what they offer:

CompuServe is perhaps the best known of the vendors, certainly the fastest growing (it absorbed The Source in July, 1989). As do all of the other services listed here, CompuServe is continually adding services to tempt you to join — one of the latest is an on-line directory of 800 numbers from AT&T.

At present, a CompuServe membership is $39.95 (which includes a $25 usage credit). CompuServe gives you no price break on evening hours or weekends. For more information, write CompuServe Information Services Inc., Dept. L, Box 477, P.O. Box 18161, Columbus OH 43272-4630, or call (800)848-8199. In Ohio, the number is (614)457-8600.

Dialog, which bills itself as the "world's largest on-line knowledge-bank," was developed by Lockheed originally as a tool for NASA researchers. Accessible are more than 380 databases and 1,100 full-text journals, magazines, newspapers and newsletters. Dialog Business Connection™ and Medical Connection™ add information from directories, journals and the latest reports in those specialized fields. Given most writers' budgets, the cost of subscribing to Dialog would be a tad steep.

For writers with leaner pocketbooks (or to get your feet wet in electronic information retrieval), Dialog also offers Knowledge Index, an after-hours service (between 6 p.m. and 6 a.m.) that offers reduced rates — at this writing, $24 per hour. Knowledge Index provides access to more than 75 of Dialog's most popular databases, including Medline, *Magazine Index*, *Books in Print* and ERIC (Educational Resources Information Center), used primarily by academic libraries and institutions.

Information about Dialog and Knowledge Index is available through Dialog Information Services Inc., 3460 Hillview Ave., Palo Alto CA 94304. (800)-3-DIALOG or (415)858-3785.

GEnie (for General Electric Network for Information Exchange) is, besides Knowledge Index, the vendor probably most used by writers. Among the services it offers are NewsGrid, a news service compiled from many of the world's largest wire services, Quiknews, a custom clipping service, and medicine, law and education roundtables. Sign-up fee at this writing is $29.95 ($10 of free connect time), with connect rates for non-prime time hours (6 p.m.-8 a.m. Monday through Friday, weekends and holidays) between $5 and $10 per hour. Prime-time connect fees are $18 per hour. For more information, contact GEnie, 401 N. Washington St., Rockville MD 20850. (800)638-9636.

NewsNet provides information from more than 360 newsletters and other information services in roughly 45 subject areas. For news junkies,

NewsNet scans 11 major domestic and international newswires. Its NewsFlash service acts as an electric clipping service from 450 business newsletters in 30 different industries.

A one-year subscription to NewsNet is $120 (on-line charges are additional), which includes $60 of free on-line time for a new user. Charge for NewsFlash is 50¢ per headline.

For information, contact NewsNet at 945 Haverford Rd., Bryn Mawr PA 19010. (800)345-1301; in Pennsylvania, (800)537-0808. Outside the U.S., (215)527-8030.

For business and financial reporting, Dow Jones News/Retrieval permits you to scan 55 selected databases of local, regional and national business publications, including *The Wall Street Journal*, as well as stock quotes, industry forecasts, and other information of interest to investors and others. Archival access to 500 publications is available too.

But it's not cheap. A standard membership is $29.95 for a start-up, with an $18 annual service fee waived the first year. Usage charges range from 21¢ to $2.90 per minute. For information, contact Dow Jones & Co. Inc. Information Services Division, P.O. Box 300, Princeton NJ 08543-9963. (800)225-3170 or (609)520-4649.

BRS (for Bibliographic Retrieval Service)/BRS After Dark is the information retrieval service dealing with information in medicine, the life sciences, business, education, the humanities and physical and social sciences, through more than 150 databases. BRS Colleague specifically references medicine and biomedical research and offers reduced rate searching for the medical community. BRS/After Dark allows access to BRS's most popular databases, at reduced rates, from 6 p.m. to 4 a.m. Monday through Friday, 6 a.m. to 2 a.m. Saturday, and 9 a.m. to 4 a.m. Sunday. BRS is part of Maxwell Online, which also includes Orbit and Information on Demand, a document retrieval service. For information, contact BRS Information Technologies, 8000 Westpark Dr., McLean VA 22102. (800)955-0906.

Although most freelancers will find it out of their league price-wise, Lexis/Nexis offers extensive information on legal cases. Cost is $7 per use, with a $50 subscription fee and a $35 per hour fee for the phone use. Contact Mead Data Central, 9393 Springboro Pike, Dayton OH 45401. (513)865-6800.

PAYING FOR A SEARCH

If you'd prefer not to invest in one of these services (though those writers who get involved with them invariably get hooked), or if you have a onetime project and/or a looming deadline, it's possible to contract for database searching by any number of sources. Most major public libraries offer data retrieval services. Check with yours for rate scale and available databases.

One of the largest is the Cleveland Public Library's Research Center (formerly Facts for a Fee). Angela Bowie, who directs the center, has worked with reporters all over the world on searches and other research assistance. Rates for on-line searching vary with the database used. For information, write or call Cleveland Research Center, 325 Superior Ave., Cleveland OH 44114-1271. (216)623-2999.

With the explosion of computer technology, in fact, a growing number of individuals have set up their own database search services as a cottage industry of sorts. The benefit of dealing with one of these services, if you're a neophyte in computing, is that you won't be frustrated by the sometimes confusing, frequently expensive trial and error process of learning your way around on-line services. In addition, many of these individuals and companies have access to a broader range of vendors/databases than the average writer could afford.

For more information on finding search services, these directories are available at most larger libraries:

Directory of Fee-Based Information Services, by Helen P. Burwell (Burwell Enterprises, Inc.). Divided by states, indexed by company name and subject areas.

1990 Encyclopedia of Information Systems and Services by Amy Lucas, ed. (Gale Research Inc.) The Information on Demand section lists firms that conduct customized research, provide bibliographies, and do other legwork for writers willing to pay for someone else to do it.

FREE INFORMATION ON-LINE

As advances in telecommunications knit the world closer together, a great deal of useful information can be accessed by modem at little or no charge. Government, business and educational institutions — historically collectors of massive quantities of data — have established data banks and bulletin board systems. (These systems, called BBSs, are less formal and less powerful than on-line databases but can provide the writer/researcher with valuable information nonetheless.)

Mark Leff, a reporter for CNN in Atlanta and a member of the Society of Professional Journalists' Technology Committee, eschews the services of the commercial vendors, as there is so much valuable information on the BBS. Two of his favorites, for instance, are ALF, the BBS run by the National Agricultural Library in Berwyn, Maryland, (301)344-8510, and the Economic BBS, (202)377-2870, run by the Commerce Department.

(The latter charges a fee for downloading information, but it's interesting just to look around at this BBS, Leff notes.)

Many colleges and universities run BBS on a number of specialized topics. Your best bet for uncovering this information source is through membership in a local BBS.

Unfortunately, there's not a definitive listing of the free and low-cost BBS available, primarily because the boards seem to come into and go out of existence frequently, the numbers change without notice "and most book listings of BBSs are outdated almost as soon as they're published," Leff notes.

He's managed to collect a good variety of numbers, which he publishes monthly on the Rock & Roll Atlanta BBS, (404)982-0960, through networking with other computerphiles, reading the popular computer magazines and newsletters, and even finding lists of other BBSs on BBSs he's accessed. (ALF, for instance, has a list of other agricultural BBSs available.)

Users of BBSs are generous about sharing information—most ask that you leave any corrections about the information listed or new information you have on the board. Once you're plugged into the network, you should have all the information you'll possibly need.

Here are a few book sources on free databases/bulletin boards available at press time:

Information USA by Matthew Lesko (Viking) includes about a half dozen absolutely free databases run by the U.S. government that you can contact yourself, such as the Alternative Fuel Data Bank and the Climate Assessment Data Base. The book is a pricey ($50) but worthwhile addition to your personal bookshelf, as it lists other government giveaways, from free coloring books to start-up money for small businesses.

Lesko's Information U.S.A. Inc. also publishes *The Federal Database Finder: A Directory of Free and Fee-based Databases and Files Available from the Federal Government*, 2nd ed., edited by Sharon Zarozny. This helpful volume identifies more than 400 government-generated databases plus sources for tapes and diskettes sold by agencies and departments. The information runs the gamut from the Acid Rain database compiled by the Fossil Energy Information Center in Oak Ridge, Tennessee, to the World Fertilizer Market Information Service, headquartered in Muscle Shoals, Alabama.

Some of the bases listed in the latter are not directly accessible by outside users, but some will have staff run searches for you. Some are free, while others charge fees to cover the cost of computer and staff time and office services.

REPORTING IN THE ELECTRONIC AGE

Beyond accessing traditional research sources, computers are beginning to be recognized as invaluable tools for processing and analyzing other electronic data as well, and that power is giving rise to a new form of journalism.

Computer-assisted reporting is taking nonfiction writers beyond the shoe leather approach to newsgathering. For example, the *Providence Journal-Bulletin* won a Pulitzer Prize after it analyzed 30,000 mortgage records to uncover evidence of fraud in a state housing agency.

Techniques for using computers in newsgathering and analysis are beginning to be taught through seminars and workshops. Two programs providing information on such training are the National Institute for Advanced Reporting, Indiana University School of Journalism, IUPUI, ES 4106, 902 West New York St., Indianapolis IN 46202, (317)274-5555, and the Missouri Institute for Computer Assisted Reporting, % University of Missouri School of Journalism, 120 Neff Hall, Columbia MO 65211, (314)882-0684.

ADDITIONAL RESOURCES

Directory of Online Databases (Cuadra/Elsevier). Published quarterly, lists 4,200 databases available through one or more of the 622 on-line services. (It also indicates whether CD/ROM versions of the data are available.) An index grouping the services by subject is especially helpful.

Data Bases: A Primer for Retrieving Information by Computer, by Susanne Humphrey (Prentice-Hall).

Computer Readable Databases, Kathleen Young Marcaccio, ed. (Gale Research Inc.).

Answers Online: Your Guide to Informational Databases, by Barbara Newlin (Osborne-McGraw).

Encyclopedia of Business Information Sources, 6th ed., by James Woy (Gale Research). Lists on-line sources as well as other sources for business data. Includes phone numbers and 800 numbers for contact.

GOVERNMENT DOCUMENTS

A word about the amount of information produced by and for the federal government: The volume is so huge, and the means of searching, sorting through, and selecting any of it for use by the average citizen so mystifying, that nearly an entire industry has grown up around how and where to get government information.

TITLES FOR SALE

The Government Printing Office (GPO), while not the largest printer of government materials, is nonetheless a prolific one. GPO publishes about 30,000 new titles a year from a variety of federal agencies, ranging in subject from consumer oriented pamphlets like "Eating Better When Eating Out" to esoteric training manuals for federal employees. If you're seeking information on nearly any subject, from care of the aging to NASA exploration of the planet Neptune, more than likely some publication on the topic has rolled off the GPO presses on it.

More than 14,000 titles are available for direct sale from the Superintendent of Documents, U.S. Government Printing Office, Washington D.C. 20402-9325. For ordering new publications and getting a periodic update of new offerings, you can dial the office directly, (202)783-3238. Note: The lines are frequently busy; you also can fax inquiries and orders to (202)275-0019.

GPO documents can also be ordered on-line by subscribers to Dialog (see Databases) and selected titles may be purchased directly at any of the following two dozen U.S. Government bookstores across the country.

Alabama
O'Neill Bldg.
2021 Third Ave., North
Birmingham AL 35203
(205)731-1056

California
ARCO Plaza, C-Level
505 South Flower St.
Los Angeles CA 90071
(213)894-5841

Room 1023, Federal Bldg.
450 Golden Gate Ave.
San Francisco CA 94102
(415)556-0643

Colorado
Room 117, Federal Bldg.
1961 Stout St.
Denver CO 80294
(303)844-3964

World Savings Bldg.
720 North Main St.

Pueblo CO 81003
(719)544-3142

District of Columbia
U.S. Government Printing Office
710 North Capitol St., NW
Washington DC 20401
(202)275-2091

1510 H St., NW
Washington DC 20005
(202)653-5075

Florida
Room 158, Federal Bldg.
400 W. Bay St.
Jacksonville FL 32202
(904)791-3801

Georgia
Room 100, Federal Bldg.
275 Peachtree St., NE
P.O. Box 56445
Atlanta GA 30343
(404)331-6947

Illinois
Room 1365, Federal Bldg.
219 S. Dearborn St.
Chicago IL 60604
(312)353-5133

Maryland
Warehouse Sales Outlet
8660 Cherry Ln.
Laurel MD 20707
(301)953-7974; (301)792-0262

Massachusetts
Thomas P. O'Neill Bldg.
10 Causeway St.
Room 179
Boston MA 02222
(617)565-6680

Michigan
Suite 160, Federal Bldg.
477 Michigan Ave.
Detroit MI 48226
(313)226-7816

Missouri
120 Bannister Mall
5600 E. Bannister Rd.
Kansas City MO 64137
(816)765-2256

New York
Room 110
26 Federal Plaza
New York NY 10278
(212)264-3825

Ohio
Room 1653, Federal Bldg.
1240 E. 9th St.
Cleveland OH 44199
(216)522-4922

Room 207, Federal Bldg.
200 N. High St.
Columbus OH 43215
(614)469-6956

Oregon
1305 S.W. First Ave.
Portland OR 97201-5801
(503)221-6217

Pennsylvania
Robert Morris Bldg.
100 North 17th St.
Philadelphia PA 19103
(215)597-0677

Room 118, Federal Bldg.
1000 Liberty Ave.
Pittsburgh PA 15222
(412)644-2721

Texas
Room 1C46, Federal Bldg.
1100 Commerce St.
Dallas TX 75242
(214)767-0076

Texas Crude Bldg.
Suite 120
801 Travis St.
Houston TX 77002
(713)653-3100

Washington
Room 194, Federal Bldg.
915 Second Ave.
Seattle WA 98174
(206)442-4270

Wisconsin
Room 190, Federal Bldg.
517 E. Wisconsin Ave.
Milwaukee WI 53202
(414)201-1304

A GPO title you might want to add to your reference shelf is *The United States Government Manual* — $21 at this writing, stock number 069-000-00022-3.

The Consumer Information Center, an arm of the General Services Administration, also processes requests for certain GPO titles, but don't order from this source if you're on a tight deadline. They're painfully slow.

A good, basic, and free reference from CIC, familiar to many freelancers, is the *Consumer's Resource Handbook*. It's available, along with a catalog of other publications, by writing CIC, Pueblo CO 81009. Expect to wait four to six weeks by mail.

TITLES AS REFERENCE

To access government publications as reference materials, you have to understand something of how and where government documents are stored and also something of the myriad indexes used to catalog them.

To serve as a collection point for many of the government's publications — those issued by the GPO but also many other agencies — a depository library system was created. This designated some 1,400 public and academic libraries around the country to receive, free of charge, those publications considered of informational value to the general public. Fifty have been designated as regional depositories, which means they retain a permanent collection of material, plus provide interlibrary loan service for the other depository libraries in the area. A list of the addresses of these depository libraries is available free from the U.S. Government Printing Office, Superintendent of Documents, Stop: SM, Washington D.C. 20402. Ask for publication 570W, "Directory of U.S. Government Depository Libraries."

Especially in researching through government documents, consulting with a reference librarian who specializes in this area is valuable for several reasons:

Most libraries that house government documents shelve them in a manner that parallels their regular collection (using the Superintendent of Documents — SuDocs — numbering system rather than Library of Congress numbering. SuDocs numbering is according to issuing agency, rather than subject matter, which makes for a somewhat illogical arrangement of documents to the uninitiated.)

Few government documents are listed in most libraries' conventional card catalogs. And unless the library has a specific Documents department, the information on a particular agency you're looking for just might turn up in an unexpected location. (The Uniform Crime Reports at our local library, for example, are included in the Education Department, rather than the Government Department you might expect.)

Another reason for seeking out a librarian well versed in this area, which can be especially daunting to the novice, is that all government documents are not created equal. A librarian experienced in dealing with government publications should be able to tell you, for instance, which statistics (for example, those provided by the Census Bureau) are rock solid, and which were compiled by part-timers hired to do a "quick and dirty" government report. A librarian trained in dealing with government documents can help you sort out the best sources of information. Poorly chosen information sources reflect poorly on your writing.

Another tip: If you're after a particular document, be sure you have the complete and official name of the document, not the popular title, or as much information about it (subject matter, issuing agency, year, etc.) as possible. Presidential commission reports, librarians complain, pose particular headaches. If you come in asking for the "Red Book," for example, most librarians will point you to the Standard Directory of Advertising Agencies, but there's a Hotel/Motel Redbook and other references commonly known by that title.

If you expect to do an extensive amount of work with government documents and can't find someone to help, an excellent reference — one recommended by documents librarians—is *Tapping the Government Grapevine: The User-Friendly Guide to U.S. Government Information Sources*, by Judith Schiek Robinson (Oryx Press).

Also by Oryx, the two-volume *Using Government Publications*, by Jean L. Sears and Marilyn K. Moody, breaks the hunt down according to your quarry. Search by subjects and agencies, statistics, or for more esoteric information, patents and trademarks, standards and specifications, etc.

Another nifty little volume is *Easy Access to Information in U.S. Government Documents*, by Julia Schwartz. Published by the American Library Association, Schwartz's guide leads you very gently through two dozen of the major indexes to government documents. This is available at many libraries or by ordering through the American Library Association, Publishing Services, 50 E. Huron St., Chicago IL 60611. It's $12.95.

Armed with the above advice, we can proceed with a short course on some of the most frequently used indexes of government documents:

The prime reference for the latest offerings of the Government Printing Office is the *Monthly Catalog of U.S. Government Publications*, available at most libraries. It is indexed semiannually and many libraries have a computer version that lists publications issued back to 1976. The monthly catalog indicates which publications are available for sale and which are available through depository libraries.

Publications Reference File (PRF) is a microfiche version of the monthly catalog.

A note from some librarians regarding catalog browsing versus screen browsing to find government documents: Though computer technology might seem the quickest way to plow through government-related (or any research), there's still much to be said for old-fashioned browsing through paper copies of listings. Because the *Monthly Catalog* is divided by departments, you might uncover unexpected listings by paging. (Anyone who's scrolled back and forth on a computer knows how screen myopia can set in.) And because most of these computer catalogs didn't come on-line until 1976, they're useless for finding older documents.

Not everything the government prints, though, ends up in the monthly catalog. Reams of reports, documents, findings, etc. are produced annually by the federal bureaucracy, and it would be a perfect world for researchers if the government also had the mechanisms in place for finding them.

Unfortunately, it's not a perfect world, and it's fallen to "civilian" publishers to sort out much of Uncle Sam's paperwork. Below are listed several of the most commonly used indexes of government information.

Keep in mind, though, that even if your local public library has an impressive array of these indexes in its reference section, it may or may not have the actual documents on hand (they're expensive). But the document you're looking for, if not in house, can more than likely be borrowed through interlibrary loan.

Congressional Information Service Inc., based in Bethesda, Maryland, publishes several indexes that are excellent sources regarding legislative matters. *Index to Publications of the U.S. Congress* catalogs the reports, prints (i.e., background data), and important press releases, issued by that body since 1970. It also publishes a *U.S. Congressional Committee Hearings Index*, an index to the *Federal Register*, where rules of the regulatory agencies, Presidential documents and other information are published, and other indexes that can help you wade through the bombast and bureaucratic baggage to find what you need.

Congress in Print, issued weekly by Congressional Quarterly Inc. and available in larger libraries, lists reports of Congressional Committees, subcommittees and how to order them. There is no charge for ordering copies of bills, reports and public laws, but there's a limit on the number of requests that will be filled per day.

For current U.S. legislation, consult *The Digest of Public Bills*, which includes a summary of the text, or *CCH Congressional Index*.

Index to U.S. Government Periodicals is issued quarterly by Infordata International Inc. of Chicago. This indexes 175 major periodicals produced by the government, from *Agricultural Outlook* to *Woman and Work*.

Government Reference Books, A Biennial Guide to U.S. Government Publications, catalogs the most important directories, indexes, handbooks, statistical works and almanacs produced during the previous two years, by subject. Libraries Unlimited, Englewood CO 80155-3988.

PAIS Bulletin, published by Public Affairs Information Service, indexes more than 1,000 periodicals, books, pamphlets and reports of federal, state and city governments and public and private agencies "related to business, economic and social conditions throughout the world."

SCIENTIFIC DOCUMENTS

Another government agency and a higher volume printer by far than GPO (80,000 titles annually) is the National Technical Information Service. NTIS collects, reprints and catalogs the thousands of technical reports produced by government contractors on various subjects. (A story on the Fernald Uranium Processing plant, for example, could be researched through NTIS documents.) NTIS indexes are very specialized and very expensive; therefore, they may not be in your public library, but may be available from a specialized library in your area. Check academic and business libraries in your area; your public librarian may be able to give you leads on locating NTIS documents.

Another commonly used index for scientific data is *Government Report Announcement and Index* (GRA&I), which also indexes technical reports financed or sponsored by the federal government.

THE NUMBERS GAME

If you're looking for statistics, some of the commonly available resources librarians will steer you to are listed below. Note that all three indexes cover not only government-generated statistics, but also those compiled by business, industry, and other sources:

American Statistical Index (ASI) covers federal statistics from 1972 to date. Also available on-line.

Statistical Reference Index (SRI) covers non-federal statistics from state and industrial sources.

Index to International Statistics.

Speaking of statistics, the recent collection of census material brings up that rich resource, available through state and regional offices and data centers, as well as through the Bureau's Customer Services office, Washington D.C. 20233. (301)763-4100.

If you'd rather conduct your statistical search by computer, a good reference is *Federal Statistical DataBases: A Comprehensive Catalog of Current Machine-Readable and Online Files*, edited by William R. Evinger (Oryx Press). The book provides 2,500 abstracts of statistical and related databases managed by various government agencies. The abstracts include the cost and availability to outside users and are indexed by subject and agency, and also alphabetically.

GOING TO THE SOURCE

If it's a specific fact or statistic you're after, of course, it may be quicker—and more fruitful—to try to get it firsthand from the proper governmental office or agency. If, for example, you're looking for information on the surgeon general's latest recommendations on the American diet, you might contact that office directly. Notice we said "may be quicker." Anyone who's ever gotten the runaround from a government bureaucrat may feel differently. But try the Public Affairs or Public Information office of the department you're contacting, identify yourself as a writer and explain the type of project for which you need information.

Most information officers, if they can't help you, can point you in the direction of someone who will. That's their job.

For finding phone numbers of these agencies, and—always a good idea—specific names of key personnel there, there are a number of popularly priced directories available. One is:

FEDFind: Your Key to Finding Federal Government Information, by Richard J. D'Aleo (ICUC Press).

Matthew Lesko's *Information U.S.A.*, described in the Databases section, provides names and phone numbers, too.

The problem with buying such directories, of course, is that the information quickly becomes outdated.

Larger libraries may have copies of the *Federal Yellow Book* (Congressional and State Yellow Books may also be available), published quarterly. See the Resources section later in this chapter for more information on these. And in addition, the *Information Report* published monthly by Washington Researchers, 918 16th St. NW, Washington D.C. 20006, lists information available free from the government. An annual subscription is $39.

If you don't have a clue as to which federal agency is the correct one to address, you might try calling a Federal Information Center (FIC) office, listed in most major city phone books under U.S. Government. FIC offices are designed to direct citizens' questions to the proper agency.

ADDITIONAL RESOURCES

Directory of Federal Libraries describes more than 2,400 libraries serving the U.S. government here and overseas, their collections, whether they are open to the public, etc., William R. Evinger, ed. (Oryx Press).

United States Government Publications Catalogs, 2nd ed., Steven D. Zink, ed. (Special Libraries Association).

Congressional Publications & Proceedings: Research on Legislation, Budgets and Treaties, by Jerrold Zwirn (Libraries Unlimited).

BIBLIOGRAPHERS

The idea of compiling a bibliography *before* starting a writing project might seem like putting the cart before the horse. When writing that college paper on Beowulf, for instance, most of us probably stumbled along collecting books in our research, used some portion of them in the actual writing, and gratefully included the whole lot of them in a bibliography at the end as a means of turning in the required 10 or 25 pages.

A bibliography compiled at the beginning of a project can save time by doing some of the legwork for you, eliminating some of the dead ends and time-wasters.

Don't overlook some of the subject bibliographies already prepared at your local library—many on current topics—e.g., substance abuse, divorce and children, nutrition and health, teen suicide. While not exhaustive treatments of the subjects, and not necessarily geared toward your particular project, they can sometimes provide a starting point—or a clue to what's been covered, or not covered, on the subject.

Subject bibliographies are available from other sources as well. The Government Printing Office publishes a Subject Bibliography Index listing nearly 240 bibliographies on a wide variety of topics. (Some of its historical bibliographies may also be of help to fiction writers.) The Index (SB-599) is free, as are the bibliographies listed in it. These are available through the Superintendent of Documents, U.S. Government Printing Office, Washington D.C. 20402.

The Library of Congress, described elsewhere in this chapter, also provides interesting subject bibliographies, especially on current topics— e.g., the presidential election process. Unfortunately, as these are prepared by individual Library of Congress departments, there's no centralized and printed listing of them. A few are mentioned in the Library of Congress's *Publications in Print*, available from the Library of Congress Central Services Division, Washington D.C. 20540. Otherwise, write or call the LOC department dealing with your subject area to find out what resource list may already have been pulled together.

COMMERCIAL BIBLIOGRAPHIES

Some editorial services, too, help writers in the preparation of bibliographies. Though most often the customers are scholars carrying out in-depth research, some writers, too, call on professional bibliographers for help.

"Researching is like following a tree that may have many branches," observes Karen Pangallo, a freelance bibliographer and indexer based in Salem, Massachusetts. A skilled bibliographer will know which branches bear fruit and which are barren. Because they know the terminology to pursue research topics, have access to more databases and other sources than the average writer might, and may specialize in a field—natural history, for instance, or French literature or American poets—the services of a bibliographer can be worth pursuing.

Most charge an hourly rate from about $12 an hour at the low end of the spectrum to $50 per hour and up at the high end. They ask that, above all, the writer/client knows what he or she wants—i.e., defines the parameters of the writing project as well as the parameters of the sources they wish to use. (Note: Some bibliographers are trained to provide foreign-language sources as well as English.)

LISTINGS

Literary Market Place provides a list of bibliographers under the Editorial Services heading. In addition, the *Directory of Fee-Based Information Services* published by Burwell Enterprises Inc. also lists some of these firms.

Following are some of the firms that provide bibliography services:

Berlow Communications
9 Prairie Ave.
Suffern NY 10901
(914)357-8215

Victoria Holmes
Information Unlimited
3744 Congreve Ave.
Cincinnati OH 45213
(513)396-7970

Barry R. Koffler
Featherside
High Falls NY 12440
(914)687-9851

Karen L. Pangallo
27 Buffum St.
Salem MA 01970
(508)744-8796

Publishers Editorial Services
23 McQueen St.
Katonah NY 10536
(914)232-5246

Wollheim Publishing Services
531 Main St., #516
Roosevelt Island NY 10044

Wordsworth Associates Editorial Services
9 Tappan Rd.
Wellesley MA 02181
(617)237-4761

PERMISSIONS

Sooner or later in doing research, every writer runs across the perfect quote, the succinct and absolutely on-target description, the clear-as-a-bell explanation that will add the right fillip to the project at hand. The problem: the quote, or the passage of description, or the paragraphs of explanation are under another writer's byline.

Gaining permission to use another's material—and knowing when and where such permission is even necessary—is a mysterious and muddied area to many writers, especially in light of recent revisions in the copyright law. This section will go somewhat beyond the scope of research. While offering help on how to avoid infringing on another's work, it will include a basic description of the procedures you'll use to protect your own. Let's start with the second part first.

Revisions to the federal Copyright Law over the years have been refinements to the original Constitutional provision protecting "authors and inventors" from having their "writings and discoveries" ripped off—to use a distinctly 20th century expression.

Under the law, your magazine article, short story, novel or essay, whether published or unpublished, is protected from the moment it exists in "fixed form"—i.e., typewritten, in longhand, shorthand, on a tape recording or however you choose to write. Not eligible for copyright protection are works *not* in fixed form (e.g., a speech delivered but not written or recorded), works made up of information that is "common property" (e.g., tables of weights and measures), ideas, concepts and principles, and titles, slogans and short phrases (although, as we'll see later, these may have their own protection as registered trademarks).

Copyright Law revisions during the last century represent changes in the duration of copyright protection and also in the requirements for formal registration.

The Copyright Act of 1909, for example, differentiated between unpublished works (protected only through state copyright protection) and published ones (which required a system of formal registration with the Copyright Office to protect a work for a renewable period of 28 years).

The Copyright Act of 1976, which took effect Jan. 1, 1978, remedied some of the weaknesses in the 1909 act concerning protection for writers who had failed to formally register their works. It also revised the period of copyright protection to the "life of the author plus 50 years" or, in the case of anonymous or pseudonymous works, to a single term of 75 years.

In 1989, the U.S. joined the Berne Convention which, as John H. Baker wrote in *Publishers Weekly*, helped "weave the U.S. more firmly into the pattern of international copyright agreements."

Joining the Berne, among other things, meant the elimination of the requirement for copyright notice and copyright registration—which many writers had ignored anyway. So is it still important for writers to register their works?

Attorney Ellen M. Kozak, in her excellent book, *Every Writer's Guide to Copyright and Publishing Law* (Henry Holt and Co.) notes that, if your work is infringed upon, and is registered, you may recover statutory damages and have your attorney's fees reimbursed by the infringer. If you've not protected your work ahead of time, you will be entitled only to compensation for your actual losses—and you'll bear your own legal costs.

Though you may still register your work after it's been infringed upon, delays in processing your application through the Copyright Office can delay your action against the infringer—who all the while may be making money at your expense. Better to be safe than sorry, Kozak cautions.

Registering the copyright on a piece of work is a simple procedure. Call the Copyright office and request the proper form. (TX for nondramatic literary works; PA for works of the performing arts, including musical and dramatic works; SE for serial works intended to continue indefinitely—e.g., if you're publishing your own newsletter, magazine, newspaper or journal.) The fee (nonrefundable) for registering a copyright is $20.

A number of helpful circulars are available by calling or writing the Copyright Office, Library of Congress, Washington D.C. 20559. Those you might want to add to your library include R1, "Copyright Basics," R1c, "Registration Procedures," and R22, "How to Investigate the Copyright Status of a Work."

The Copyright Office Forms Hotline number is available 24 hours a day at (202)707-9100. To speak to an information specialist in the Copyright Office, call (202)479-0700.

For a further discussion of copyright and other legal matters of interest to writers, another useful book is the *Writer's Friendly Legal Guide*, edited by Kirk Polking and published by Writer's Digest Books. The guide covers copyright, libel, contracts, taxes and other matters dealing with the business side of writing.

USING OTHERS' MATERIAL

The Copyright Law that protects your creative works, of course, extends similar protection to the works of countless other creative individuals. This section deals with the procedures for securing permission to use portions of others' copyrighted works, and those instances when no permission is required.

To take the latter case first, works that fall into what is referred to as the "public domain" require no permission to reprint. These include works created before the institution of the Copyright Laws, works on which copyright permission has expired, works which by their nature cannot by copyrighted—e.g., the exemptions discussed at the beginning of this section, and publications of the U.S. government.

The Copyright Law also contains a "fair use" provision that covers those situations in which you can quote from another's work without first seeking permission. But fair use is a gray area, and perhaps the best advice to follow is "If you want to use a portion of someone else's material, no matter how small, it's safest if you ask."

The fair use provision holds that the work to be quoted must be used in a "reasonable manner." But what is "fair" and what is "reasonable" are open to discussion. Some writers and publishers use a rough rule of thumb to determine what constitutes fair use (say, for example, 5% of the total of a novel, or up to 100 words of a short story or article).

But copyright experts such as Kozak will tell you in no uncertain terms that nowhere is a numerical formula for fair use written down and, in an increasingly litigious society, this yardstick may afford you no protection.

The courts consider these four criteria in copyright infringement cases:

● The purpose and character of the use, including whether such use is of a commercial nature or is for nonprofit educational purposes;

● The nature of the copyrighted work—i.e., is it largely factual, with information that is readily obtainable, or interpretative;

● The amount and substantiality of the portion used in relation to the whole (that is, how much of the work are you borrowing?) and

● The effect of the use upon the potential market for or value of the copyrighted work.

Another mistaken notion is that simply paraphrasing a passage or section can absolve you from needing permission. Detailed summaries of books, articles, studies, etc. would probably put you on thin ice with the courts; better get permission before undertaking anything of this nature.

How to begin? If you're preparing a book manuscript and have contracted with a publisher, the publisher may have its own permissions department that handles the necessary requests or can advise you how to proceed. It's best early on to make clear in your contract who will pay the fees that some permissions grantors require. Some publishers will agree to bear all or some of these costs; some may grant a special advance just for this purpose; some will stipulate that these fees will be paid out of the author's royalties; and some will place all of the responsibility for securing/paying for permissions on the writer himself.

If you're working on your own to secure permissions for a book, article or other project, the process, while time-consuming and sometimes frustrating, need not be a mystery. It simply takes common sense, thoroughness and a bit of advance planning.

Barbara Bartolotta, manager of the Copyrights and Permissions Department of Scott, Foresman, Inc., a textbook publisher, says many writers simply "do not understand what information a [permissions] grantor needs," which is as complete a description as you can provide of the material to help the grantor identify the passage and know what use you plan to make of it.

To know who to contact, look for the copyright notice on the title page of the book or magazine from which you're quoting (or the page following it) to see who holds copyright on the work. It's wise, too, to check the acknowledgments page of a book to make sure that the passage you're interested in quoting hasn't been reprinted from another work. (You must contact the original copyright holder then.)

Write to the Permissions Department of the book or article's publisher. If no address is supplied, check *Literary Market Place* or the *Gale Directory of Publications* and give the following information: Title of the work, name of author or editor, and edition (if relevant), year of publication (for a magazine article, complete date and year), page the passage appeared on, and a copy of the original selection. If you plan to alter the original (e.g., use ellipsis, use the material as the basis of a parody, etc.) you should mention that as well. The copyright holder may not agree to the proposed alterations.

The writer should be very explicit in detailing how the material will be used, Bartolotta notes, as that will be used by the grantor to determine if permission will be forthcoming and whether—and how much of—a fee will be charged. The information should include the number of copies to be made—or how large a press run is planned—what form the copied material will appear in (a softcover or hardcover book, photocopied newsletter, magazine article, etc.) and how and when it is to be distributed. In the case of a book, you can obtain this information from your publisher.

A sample letter used by authors for Writer's Digest Books appears below, and will give you an idea of how to frame your request:

Dear _____

I am writing a book, tentatively titled _____,
which Writer's Digest Books plans to publish in the _____
of _____ . The book, which will be a _____ edi-
tion of approximately _____ pages, will retail for about $_____ . An
initial printing of _____ for the trade market is planned.
I would like your permission to include the following excerpt(s) (photocopies attached):

I'm seeking nonexclusive world publishing rights in all languages, including subsequent editions and special nonprofit editions for use by the
handicapped.

I am looking forward to receiving your permission. Please indicate the acknowledgment you wish to have printed in the book.

Thank you very much for your help.

Sincerely,

William Righter

Bartolotta, who has "two shelves full" of books on the subject of copyright law, says the simplest and most helpful resource for writers to understand the basics of the permissions process is the annual *A Writer's Guide
to Copyrights* published by Poets & Writers Inc. The guide includes sample forms and glossary for $6.95 plus $1.50 postage and handling (New
York State residents must add appropriate sales tax). Ordering address is
72 Spring St., New York NY 10012.

If a publisher charges you a fee for the privilege of using copyrighted material, how much can you (or your publisher) expect to pay? *Publish-ers Weekly* reports the going rate for permissions can be anywhere from

$15 to $100 per page of prose, and $5 to $25 per line of poetry. Music lyrics (whose copyrights are jealously guarded) often command *very* high fees—if you can determine who holds the copyright—and some publishers encourage writers to simply rewrite a passage *sans* lyrics rather than put up with the headaches.

PERMISSIONS SERVICES

For projects in which an author needs to seek a number of permissions or is too busy or unable to do the job personally, the help of an editorial service that specializes in this area may be secured. (Many of these firms, of course, offer other services as well—researching, indexing, editing of manuscripts, etc.)

To work effectively and efficiently with one of these services it's imperative to:

- Notify them far enough ahead of time to get the job done—three to six months ahead of the date your manuscript is due was mentioned most often. Allow more time if permission from works published abroad needs to be secured.
- Call in advance to discuss the project.
- Provide complete copies of material requiring permissions, adequate source data—i.e., where it came from, and description of where and how you intend to use it.

Randall E. Greene, who heads an editorial service for book and newspaper publishers in Cynthiana, Kentucky, encourages authors to be scrupulous during the writing process about keeping full and accurate notes on material they plan to quote: "An incorrect listing for a publisher, a missed page number, an incomplete title anywhere along the way can make the permissions process expensive and sometimes unworkable."

Many of these services charge an hourly rate (generally from $15 to $30 per hour and up), though some charge per permission. Phone, mail and fax expenses usually are added on top of these.

LISTINGS

Literary Market Place runs listings of permissions services under Editorial Services. A few are listed below:

All-Media Services
13415 Ventura Blvd.
Sherman Oaks CA 91423
(818)995-3329 (24 hours a day)

Authors/Writers Helpline™ Advisory
Communications Building 102
Middle Island NY 11953-0102
(516)924-8555

BZ/Rights & Permissions Inc.
125 W. 72nd St.
New York NY 10023
(212)580-0615

Catalyst Communications Arts
2241 Boulevard Del Campo
San Luis Obispo CA 93401
(805)543-7250

Editorial Perspectives
918 Church St.
Honesdale PA 18431
(717)253-3008

GREENE Communications®
417 Wilson Ave.
Cynthiana KY 41031
(606)234-3266

Oxnard Publishing Services
13109 Humphrey Dr.
Austin TX 78729
(512)331-1300

Silberfeld Communications
2336-B NW Pettygrove
Portland OR 97210

TRADEMARKS

We'll add a note here about registered trademarks because their improper use by writers routinely raises the blood pressure of trademark holders.

Many trademark holders—the makers of Styrofoam, for example, prefer that you use a generic term—e.g., "expanded foam" in referring to their product. Or, if you insist on having your protagonist use a Weedeater on his front lawn, you'd better be sure to refer to it as a "Weedeater® brand trimmer." The fact that it doesn't have the same flow is of no concern to the holder of that (or any other) trademark. Their concern is to protect and preserve their good name.

An incorrect use of a trademark will frequently bring you a nasty letter from the owner—and it's amazing how they keep track of even obscure publications. But if it's thought the use was malicious, or casts the trademark holder in a poor light (a play on the name "Coke" with drug connotations, for example), you might well find yourself the target of a suit.

For proper spellings of trademarks and their descriptive terms, consult *Trade Names Directory*, published by Gale Research, or the *Standard Directory of Advertisers*, both available in larger libraries.

In addition, the U.S. Trademark Association provides information and maintains a library open to writers on the subject of trademark usage. "Trademarks: The Official Media Guide," and a "Trademark Checklist" are available by writing the USTA, 6 E. 45th St., New York NY 10017. A Trademark Hotline, (212)986-5880, is staffed from 2 to 5 p.m. EST, Monday through Friday, to answer questions.

RESEARCHING FICTION

Fiction writers, as well as nonfiction writers, dig for facts—the facts necessary to set a mood, move the reader into a unique time or place or even, as Truman Capote and others have shown, to be the basis of the story's action itself. Sometimes it's not possible to try out an experience firsthand. John Gardner, who's continued the James Bond series since the death of Ian Fleming, relied on book descriptions of how to fly a particular aircraft when he couldn't find access to a simulator or the genuine aircraft.

And until time travel becomes a reality, writers in historical genres will have to rely on book research. Author Rosemary Rogers confesses to relying on *Timetables of History* to find out what was happening in other parts of the world at the time her characters were "doing their thing."

Obviously, many of the same resources used by nonfiction writers will be helpful to fiction writers as well. Some of these resources may even trigger ideas for stories.

Even for non-genre fiction, adequate research, well used, "gives a texture to your story, a ring of authenticity," says Jack Heffron, associate editor of *Story*, who receives 200 submissions a week for the quarterly literary magazine.

The fiction writer's research must be every bit as careful as that of his nonfiction writing brother or sister, for one false note can jar the reader out of that fragile landscape of words the fiction writer has crafted.

If your story is set in a service station, for instance, the story is strengthened and enriched if the sounds and sights and smells are included — and, above all, accurately portrayed. Editors are scrupulous about details that might detract if they're carelessly or wrongly used. "A good part of my day is spent in the library, checking spellings, dates, and other [factual] details that writers have included in their stories," Heffron says.

Occasionally a writer may have to do research to know what to leave out of a story, as well. Heffron says he once had to determine whether a certain popular fast food chain had a branch in Gary, Indiana. The restaurant was a key locale for a story Heffron was writing about cocaine running in the Midwest. He wanted to make sure the setting was realistic — but not too realistic — on the outside chance the restaurant might sue.

Beware of "over-researching" your story, Heffron adds. "Some authors writing about the '50s or '60s seem to want to drop in every pop culture cliché there is." He advised having someone else read your work before sending it out to make sure the background touches add to your story but don't overpower it.

So how do you accumulate the information for these "background strokes"? We've all read about "name" authors globe-trotting to gather information on exotic locales for their latest novels, but few of the rest of us have the travel budget for such a luxury.

Careful research is the answer, and even veteran writers acknowledge that "doing the homework" is as necessary whether it's your first novel or short story or your fortieth.

Jory Sherman, author of nearly 150 books over a 25-year career, has amassed more than twice that number of reference books on life in the Old West and knows writers who have as many as 1,000 in their collection. To write his westerns and novels of the West, Sherman uses many sources, including interlibrary loan through The School of the Ozarks in Point Lookout, Missouri. (For a description of how ILL works, see the Libraries section.)

Sherman also advises calling, writing or visiting the historical society in the area in which you're interested. These groups have access to obscure books, maps and other artifacts that can add detail and color to your writing, and they frequently publish scholarly monographs. Sometimes their members are experts on rare and interesting subjects and are willing to share information. (Historical societies' libraries are valuable resources as well. To locate these, check out the *Directory of Historical Societies and Agencies in the United States and Canada*, published by the American Association for State and Local History, available at most larger libraries.)

Even globe-trotting authors frequently don't set foot into a new book's setting until they've laid out a groundwork of book research. James Michener, for example, reportedly reads 300 to 400 books on an area before starting a new blockbuster. (For *Texas* he reportedly read 500 books on that state.)

Patricia and Clayton Matthews, a husband and wife writing team who between them have written nearly 100 novels, dozens of short stories, and countless other pieces in a wide range of genres, have logged many miles in their on-site research. But they still frequently sketch out the setting for a story line in advance from their Prescott, Arizona, home. The Matthewses consult travel magazines (*National Geographic* and *Smithsonian* are particularly helpful) and sometimes travel films (larger public libraries frequently have good selections) to scout out the topography, climate and landmarks beforehand.

(Fiction writers who have computers and modems can check out some of these details electronically. See the Database and Resources sections.)

Veteran fiction writers recommend, of course, that nothing beats an on-site visit to check the accuracy of your yarn. Jory Sherman has actually walked in the ruts left in the ground by wagons traveling the Santa Fe trail. Patricia Matthews rewrote the opening to *Love, Forever More* after a visit to Virginia City showed that the initial description she'd written of that locale was off the mark.

There's another reason these travels are invaluable. Visiting old bookstores, the local newspaper office, even tourist attractions can turn up privately published booklets, pamphlets and other source materials not available through conventional research methods. Jory Sherman and Patricia and Clayton Matthews also scour local bookstores and say owners frequently know who—or where—the best "repositories of information" are.

Many fiction researchers take conventional notes on these scouting trips, but others find a small, unobtrusive tape recorder (or, in some instances, a video camera) useful for recording information on landmarks, customs, and especially interviews with locals. The latter can provide "earwitness" accounts of speech patterns, colloquialisms, etc., that can give your dialogue—as well as your plot—the ring of truth. (Remember to keep records and receipts from all such trips—they're legitimate business expenses and are tax deductible.)

Rather than drudgery, research can be a serendipitous event for the fiction writer, turning up unexpected legends, little-known colorful characters, or folklore that can give writing a new twist or spark ideas for further stories, the Matthewses point out. "I've never understood why anyone would want to have a stranger do their research," says Patricia Matthews. "A lot of the story comes from assimilating the culture yourself."

When they're not traveling or at the typewriter, though, the Matthewses are researching all the time. Patricia suggests keeping clip files of magazine and newspaper articles containing news items in your area of expertise (e.g., police procedurals). Even if you're not working on a project that can use that information at the time, a clipping about a new method in crime detection, for instance, might prove useful at a later date.

FIRSTHAND EXPERIENCE

As further seasoning for their stories, some writers like to tell how they've worn many "hats" even for short periods to soak up atmosphere. Mary Higgins Clark sits through "a lot of trials" to get close looks at psychopathic killers. ("They look perfectly normal.") Marion Zimmer Bradley worked as a fortune-teller at a circus for one of her novels. The announcement that you're a writer—and the offer to work free for a couple of days or even a couple of hours—are a combination that many gatekeepers find irresistible.

EXPERT ADVICE

Short of verifying details of your stories personally, you can call on experts on travel, history, technology, etc. to answer questions related to your story. Most people are flattered and willing to expound on their field of expertise, provided you identify yourself as a writer with a legitimate project, do the obvious homework first, and arrange for a mutually agreeable time and way to conduct the mini-interview. Some writers find that a letter with a self-addressed stamped envelope for a reply works just fine, while others swear by the telephone interview. (For hints on how and where to find experts, consult the Resources section.)

But don't overlook friends, relatives and co-workers who may be untapped sources of information. For just the right poisonous plant to describe in one of her novels, for instance, Patricia Matthews called on former co-workers at California State in Los Angeles for help. (She made it clear that the plant was intended for her fictional—not her real-life—spouse!)

NETWORKING

Belonging to writers' groups that specialize in your area of interest also helps, most fiction writers point out. Members of groups such as Romance Writers of America, Mystery Writers of America, Science Fiction Writers of America, and others are generous about sharing information and frequently sponsor seminars, workshops, etc. that touch on special research needs. Their addresses are in the Community of Writers chapter.

FICTION RESEARCH RESOURCES

The Fiction Writer's Research Handbook by Mona McCormick (New American Library) covers some of the same ground we've covered in this section, but delves into a great deal more that is tailor-made for the creative person interested in fiction (e.g., chapters on where to find background on manners and customs, intellectual life and popular culture, politics, language, etc.)

Some of the resources frequently mentioned by fiction writers were:

What People Wore: A Visual History of Dress from Ancient Times to Twentieth Century America by Douglas Gorsline (Bonanza Books) remains one of the bibles in the fiction research field, though many writers have scouted out their own guides to various historical periods. Clayton Matthews recommends the various series published by Time-Life Books (on the Old West, on U.S. history, on seafarers, etc.). Patricia Matthews also favors *Historical Dress in America* by Elisabeth McClellan (Tudor Publishing), who wrote several versions covering various periods in early American life. She also enjoys *A Browser's Book of Beginnings* by Charles Panati (Houghton Mifflin), which describes the "who and when" behind a number of common objects, and uses Avenel Books' *Seven-Language Dictionary* to provide a foreign word or expression on occasion.

ADDITIONAL RESOURCES

The Facts on File Visual Dictionary Series (Facts on File) gives the correct terminology for the component parts of more than 3,000 objects.

Characters in 20th Century Literature (Gale Research) summarizes major works by 20th century authors. It's indexed by author, character and title.

Multinewspapers (P.O. Box DE-W, Dana Point CA 92629) offers international magazines and newspapers.

The New York Public Library Desk Reference contains charts, lists and other compendia representing some of the most-asked questions of the reference desk at that venerable institution. Fun for both research and pleasure reading.

The Regency Companion, by Sharon Laudermilk and Theresa Hamlin (Garland Publishing).

Romance Reader's Handbook, by Melinda Helfer, Kathryn Falk, Kathe Robin (Romantic Times).

What's What: A Visual Glossary of the Physical World, by Reginald Bragonier Jr. and David Fisher (Hammond).

SAMPLE FICTION SEARCH

Suppose you're setting out to write a novel based in modern-day Alaska, but you haven't the budget to permit on-site research. Do you switch your locale to Oregon instead?

You don't have to. With the right research, you should be able to do a pretty creditable job of re-creating the land of the midnight sun without actually being there.

To begin, you might check *Books in Print*. Under the general listing, "Alaska," you'd find *A Geographic Dictionary of Alaska*, published by Shorey Historical Service, *Handbook of Alaska: Its Resources, Products and Attractions*, and similar titles. Under "Alaska, Description and Travel," a promising title is *Faces of Alaska: A Glimpse of History through Paintings, Photographs and Oral Histories*, published by the Yukon Historical Society.

In the General Periodicals Index, the listings under "Alaska, Personal Narratives" turn up many titles from *Alaska* magazine that would describe the lifestyle there. And if you want to weave a topical thread through your narrative, your plot could revolve around the cleanup efforts surrounding the Exxon Valdez oil spill, with many magazine accounts of that event, again listed in the GPI.

That's just the beginning. The point is that the setting and plot of your fiction is bound not by the limits of your pocketbook but by the limits of your imagination — and your willingness to do the research. Remember, the same 500 books that are available to James Michener are available to you.

INFORMATION ACCESS

Those used to dealing with government bureaucracies on a regular basis know that the information controlled by the various agencies is, for a variety of reasons, not always made readily available through conventional indexes, published reports or other channels. And civil servants of a government supposedly of, by and for the people are sometimes reluctant to share public information with the press or even with interested citizens.

For that reason, a quarter of a century ago, the government took steps to ease access to information.

The federal Freedom of Information Act (FOIA), enacted in 1966, was designed to allow public access to records in the possession of any federal agency. The act allowed for nine exemptions of material from FOIA requests: classified material that might jeopardize national security; agency rules which are "predominantly internal in natuᵣe"; information exempted by another federal statute; "trade secrets"; internal memoranda; documents which would invade personal privacy; investigatory records; and two other specialized categories of exemptions involving banking and oil.

The government in the Sunshine Act (generally referred to simply as the "sunshine law"), passed 10 years after FOIA, provides for the right, again with certain exceptions, to attend meetings and gain access to the records of specific federal agencies' governing boards.

Since FOIA, most states have enacted their own access laws involving records and meetings that pertain to the operations of local governments. So the mechanisms are in place to provide for a free flow of information between government agencies and the people to whom they're answerable, right?

Well, right and wrong. Despite amendments to FOIA in 1974, there still remain some serious bugs to be ironed out in the machinery—delays in processing requests and, more seriously, questions on just what constitutes a record under FOIA jurisdiction.

When the original laws were passed, of course, the computer had not yet become the record gatekeeper of the office as it is now and records were most always paper documents or microfilmed copies. The battle is currently on as to whether FOIA covers access to computer files and the law probably will have to be rewritten to govern the computer age.

Until that time, writers will have to cope with the hazy areas of the law and also with delays in processing FOIA requests—a frequent complaint from applicants.

Under the law, an agency is supposed to respond to a properly filed FOIA request within 10 working days, and some do. But many extend the deadlines, and delays of months—and years—are not uncommon.

Some of the delays are the result of poorly prepared request letters—vague descriptions of the materials sought, addressed to the improper person or agency, etc.

Kathleen Edwards, manager of the Freedom of Information Center at the University of Missouri, says many of the callers to the center's FOIA "hotline" at (314)882-4856 (staffed 8 a.m. to 5 p.m. Monday through Friday) are seeking "elementary advice" on what's available through FOIA—and how.

The center, which handles approximately 3,000 calls annually, dispenses information and counsel from very basic FOIA matters to more complex queries—e.g., citing case law to bolster the arguments of writers appealing the denial of an FOIA request.

"The nation's most comprehensive files on freedom of the press and free speech" are housed at the center, Edwards says, and can be used on-site or accessed by phone or mail for a nominal research fee and photocopying charge. The thousand topics covered in the files are far-reaching, from illiteracy on the international front to obscenity rulings on the domestic front.

The way to expedite your request, Edwards advises, is to be as specific as you can in what you request and to whom you direct that request. Check with the agency you've determined has the information you seek and find out the name of the person who processes FOIA requests.

Find out, too, the fee schedule for processing such requests. Under the law, the agency may charge for searching for and copying documents. You may be entitled to a reduction or waiver of the search fee if you will be using the information for a noncommercial scientific, educational or journalistic purpose, or if you can prove that disclosure of the information is in the public interest.

The letter you write should state clearly all of those things:

- That it is an FOIA request for [include the specific name of or specific description of document or documents].
- Whether you are requesting a waiver or reduction of fees—and why—or the maximum amount of fee you are willing to pay.
- Complete addresses on both ends—yours (including a phone number, if possible) and the agency to whom you're sending the request.

Writers used to filing FOIA requests admit that persistence and patience are the most effective tools in prying out information from bureaucrats.

Journalists and others are constantly testing the limits of the FOIA, and the courts are constantly issuing rulings relating to access. Consequently, if you will be using this process frequently, it's wise to keep abreast of current developments on the FOI front. The National Freedom of Information Committee of the Society of Professional Journalists (formerly Sigma Delta Chi) and Gannett News Service annually produce a Freedom of Information Report that includes a roundup of FOI-generated stories and how their reporters got them, hotlines to obtain FOI help, and a state-by-state description of open meetings and records (sunshine) laws. Formerly a tabloid on newsprint, the report is now a special fall issue of *Quill* magazine, the official publication of SPJ-SDX. A copy of the report can be ordered from the Society of Professional Journalists for $3 (plus $2 shipping and handling) by writing P.O. Box 77, Greencastle IN 46135, or calling (317)653-3333.

If you're still confused about FOI requests, a number of other agencies, associations and organizations publish helpful materials.

The Government Printing Office (see the Government Documents section) publishes *A Citizen's Guide on How to Use the Freedom of Information Act and the Privacy Act* ($1.75, order stock number 052-071-00865-9). *FOIA Update*, a quarterly containing news articles on FOIA interpretations, etc., is also available from GPO. Price is $5 per year and order number is 727-002-00000-6.

The Consumer Information Center, P.O. Box 100, Pueblo CO 81002, offers "Your Right to Federal Records," a 25-page booklet (order booklet 462W) for 50¢.

The American Civil Liberties Union has released *Your Right to Government Information, A Basic Guide to Exercising Your Right to Government Information under Today's Laws*, by Christine M. Marwick, $4.95 from Bantam Books.

The Reporters Committee for Freedom of the Press, Suite 504, 1735 I St. NW, Washington D.C. 20006, publishes *How to Use the Federal Freedom of Information Act* ($3 includes tax and shipping) and *Tapping Officials' Secrets* on state open meetings and records statutes ($5). Other publications include a quarterly magazine, *The News Media and the Law* ($20), and *Access to Electronic Records* ($5). The RCFP also staffs a hotline to field FOIA questions: (800)FFOI-AID.

The Freedom of Information Clearinghouse, a project of Ralph Nader's Center for the Study of Responsive Law, consults by phone or mail to provide help to individuals, public interest groups, and the press on FOI matters. The nonprofit organization fields questions on a wide range of subjects, provides research services in some cases, and may even provide litigation support in "significant cases" that might prove precedent-setting. A pamphlet, "The Freedom of Information Act — A User's Guide," is available with a SASE from the Clearinghouse, P.O. Box 19367, Washington D.C. 20036. Phone is (202)785-3704.

DIGGING OUT FACTS WITHOUT FOI

Filing an FOI request is not always necessary for obtaining information. James Derk, an assistant metro editor at the *Evansville* (Ind.) *Cou-*

rier, regularly trains reporters in investigative techniques and says that a helpful exercise is to send a new reporter to city hall, county court or some other agency "and simply to introduce himself or herself to each person in the offices there for a rundown on the types of records they keep."

Derk, a former investigative reporter whose stories have won numerous awards and been followed up by "60 Minutes" and other news organizations, says that the county recorder's office, board of elections and other agencies can be gold mines of information for all types of stories.

"You'd be surprised at the kinds of documents that are kept on individuals, and the broad range of places that they're kept." He once tracked a subject down from a softball roster kept by the city's Parks and Recreation Department.

His tips for a successful "paper chase":

- If you're looking for information on a person, a company, an organization, put yourself in their shoes to determine the best source of information: Have they bought or sold property? Filed bankruptcy? Paid (or not paid) taxes? Any (or all) of these can lead to information sources.
- If you're dealing with government documents, try asking directly without making an FOIA request, but make it clear that you'll file one if necessary. "Sometimes an agency would just as soon not bother with the paperwork required in an FOIA request."
- Again in dealing with the government, try requesting the same information from a number of related agencies (or a Congressman on a particular committee involved with the subject). Since delays are common in dealing with government bureaucracy, if you're facing a deadline, you'll improve your chances if you aim at more than one target.
- Another, somewhat unorthodox, tip which not every writer would agree with: "From time to time, I've asked for a lot more material than I was really after, so that the bureaucrat would call me up and say, 'Look what is it that you *really* want?' and then he'd ship it to me," Derk laughs. "Sometimes it helps to ask for the moon when all you want is a little piece of cheese."

A resource Derk recommends for writers who plan to do a number of in-depth investigations is Investigative Reporters and Editors, a nonprofit organization of approximately 3,000 investigative journalists and editors from around the country. IRE, headquartered at the University of Missouri School of Journalism, offers, besides a network of writers skilled in investigative techniques, these resources:

- *IRE Journal*, a quarterly "how to" for members. (A subscription is included in the $30 annual membership fee.)

- Access to the Paul Williams Memorial Resource Center, a collection of several thousand investigative pieces done by newspapers, magazines, TV and radio (searches of this collection are conducted free for members).
- *The Reporter's Handbook*, a 500-plus page guide covering where and how to find personal records (birth and death certificates, marriage and divorce papers), tax records, credit records, court records. The book is a short course in investigative techniques, as well as a fascinating read, as it's liberally laced with true-life investigations. The price, at this writing, is $24.95 (hardcover for nonmembers) and $21.35 (softcover); for members, it's $19 (hardcover) and $16 (softcover). Add $1.50 for postage and handling.

Also available from the group is *The Investigative Journalist's Morgue* ($20), an index to more than 6,000 investigative stories in IRE's library.

Mailing address for IRE is 100 Neff Hall, School of Journalism, University of Missouri, Columbia MO 65211. (314)882-2042.

RESOURCES

Despite the importance of doing background research in preparing an article, the live interview remains the heart of most writing projects. Unless you have an editor who'll give you a specific lead on who to contact ("Go out and talk to Mrs. Gottrocks about the dog show on Saturday") finding live interview subjects — good interview subjects, not just live bodies — is up to you.

The *Encyclopedia of Associations* is the first place a lot of writers look to find national experts on a variety of topics. But there's one drawback to it, as far as writers are concerned. Many of the associations listed simply don't have the staff — or the resources — to act as information clearinghouses for writers.

There are a number of places, though, that list helpful associations that do provide information. *Instant Information*, by Joel Makower and Alan Green (Prentice-Hall), lists the names and phone numbers of almost 10,000 government agencies, corporations, trade associations, universities and nonprofit groups and other "experts." Grouped by state, these are also indexed by code number, which makes looking them up somewhat awkward, but it's a valuable resource nonetheless.

Matthew Lesko considers himself the guru of low-cost and free information from the government and other sources. (A frequent guest on talk shows, the hyperkinetic Lesko resembles Ralph Nader played on fast forward.) His newest offering, *Lesko's Info-Power*, lists 30,000 sources that provide "answers for every imaginable issue concerning work and play." The book is available for $33.95, plus $4 postage and handling, by calling 1-800-54-LESKO. The information in the book is also updated continuously on-line for subscribers to CompuServe (see the Databases section).

Not as much fun as Lesko's books, but still helpful is the *National Directory of Addresses and Telephone Numbers* published by General Information Inc., 401 Parkplace, Kirkland WA 98033. (800)722-3244; in Washington, (206)828-4777.

Find It Fast: How to Uncover Expert Information on Any Subject by Robert I. Berkman (Harper & Row) identifies government departments and other agencies that are "rich resources" and tells how to mine them most effectively.

Broadcast Interview Source, 2233 Wisconsin Ave., Washington D.C. 20007-4104, publishes *The Directory of Experts, Authorities and Spokespersons*, (202)333-4904. Broadcast Interview also publishes *Power Media Selects* and *Talk Show Selects*, by Alan Caruba, both references full of experts.

Writers looking to keep their long-distance bills down might want to invest in AT&T's *Toll-Free 800 Directories*, available by calling — what else — an 800 number — (800)426-8686. Updated each fall, the volumes come in both a business edition with 120,000 entries and a consumer edition with 60,000 entries.

Speaking of phone numbers, phonefiche, which represents the listings in more than 300 phone books, is available at many larger libraries. It's valuable for finding addresses or for bypassing directory assistance charges.

Monitor Publishing Company produces a library of "leadership directories" — that is, phone books targeted to provide information on reaching the movers and shakers in government, industry, etc. *Federal Yellow Book* covers federal departments and agencies, while the *Congressional Yellow Book* and *State Yellow Book* provide information in those areas. The firm also publishes *The Corporate 1000*, *The Financial 1000*, *Over the Counter 1000* and other yellow books. (These are sometimes available in larger libraries.) For a catalog, or ordering information, contact Monitor at 104 Fifth Ave., 2nd Floor, New York NY 10011. (212)627-4140.

To smoke out resource people to contact you, some writers have successfully tried *Partyline, the Public Relations Media Newsletter*, which circulates to public relations persons in universities, hospitals, professional associations, public relations agencies and businesses large and small. *Partyline* contact Betty Yarmon says the weekly newsletter handles requests from writers for "verified publications." They'll run a brief description of your research needs free of charge and many get good response. Lead time for the newsletter is 10 days to two weeks. Write 35 Sutton Place, New York NY 10022; call (212)755-3487 or fax (212)755-3488.

If you're looking for resource people in your own backyard, veteran writers know of a ready source in most large and medium-size cities — the faculty of local colleges and universities. If you have a question on or need an interview with someone on anything from child rearing to Chinese artifacts, there's generally someone in local academic circles to provide answers — or leads. The public information office of many colleges and universities can generally give you a line on faculty members' particular expertise, and many regularly publish directories spelling out the subject areas in which professors are willing to speak/be interviewed, et al. Don't be shy about calling or writing an academic public relations office with your request. Most are only too happy to help their faculty members get into print.

ADDITIONAL DIRECTORIES

Celebrity Register with listings on entertainment, sports, arts and politics (Suite 300, 1780 Broadway, New York NY 10019. (212)245-1460 or (212)757-7979).

Current Biography, a monthly magazine with background information on people in the news, celebrities and politicians. Bound copies are available at the library.

The Sports Address Book: How to Contact Anyone in the Sports World, by Scott Callis (Pocket Books). Covers all the usual sports and even some of the unusual — horseshoes, martial arts, aerobics, etc.

The Capital Source: The Who's Who, What, Where in Washington (National Journal, Inc.), 1730 M St. NW, Washington D.C. 20036. (202)857-1491.

American Federation of Television and Radio Artists (213)461-7145 or the Screen Actors Guild (213)856-6741. Most actors are registered with one or the other, and they can provide you with a manager or representative's name to contact.

CLEARINGHOUSES/NONPROFIT INSTITUTIONS, ETC.

Organizations, interest groups, etc. whose activities are detailed or described in popular media have an interest in assuring that those descriptions are accurate and complete. Therefore, many have established clearinghouses and other avenues for answering questions, providing expert input and the like for writers, and they can be valuable research aids. Remember, though, that some sources, especially those underwritten by commercial enterprises, strive to present their topic only in a favorable light and therefore may present material that is somewhat biased.

Some helpful sources whose titles are fairly self-explanatory:

Scientists' Institute for Public Information
Media Resource Service
355 Lexington Ave.
New York NY 10017
(800)223-1730 or (212)661-9110 in New York State

National Health Information Clearinghouse
(800)336-4797

EXPERTS ON-LINE

If you have a computer and modem, you have the means of inviting a wide range of live "sources" right into your own home for a personal chat. You might need an expert to flesh out a nonfiction magazine article, a collector of old weapons to answer a question about a detail in your short story, or a fellow romance writer to help iron out a plot problem for your novel in progress.

One way to go about it is to search conventional databases to see who's published the latest article or given the latest speech on your topic and then contact that person by letter or phone. The benefit here is that you're pretty much assured that your expert has sound credentials — or, at least he's stuck out his neck elsewhere in print.

The National Referral Center (NRC), administered by the Library of Congress, was a phenomenal resource of more than 13,000 "information sources" referred by phone or mail free of charge to any writer who cared to ask. Unfortunately, budget cuts forced the closing of the center in 1986, though the NRC Master Database remains for on-site use. Future access to this information remains up in the air. (202)707-1608.

Michael Banks, author of *The Modem Reference*, who also writes in the science fiction field, also suggests that computer bulletin boards and special interest groups (SIGS) are good sources for writers with specific problems or for those who simply want to widen their circle of contacts.

The Law Enforcement Roundtable on GEnie, for example, has individuals with expertise in that field, and can provide quick answers that might take days or months of tracking down by conventional means. And posting a specific question on a computer bulletin board service (BBS) has gotten him answers on a variety of topics, including other leads for experts, Banks notes.

SIGS and BBSs are provided by a variety of computer groups, large and small. The commercial on-line services (described in the Database section earlier in this chapter) also frequently offer their own roundtables, described in their catalogs. Write or call for details.

OUT-OF-PRINT/RARE BOOKS

Writers are sometimes frustrated when they learn that a title they're after is out of print. R.R. Bowker's *Books in Print* carries an "Out of Print/ Out of Stock Indefinitely" supplement that carries listings of out of print retailers and wholesalers (by state), wholesale remainder dealers ("remainders" are those books which make it to the bargain table), and search services — firms which, sometimes for free, will help you find which source around the country still carries your rare or out of print title. Bowker's *American Book Trade Directory*, available at larger libraries, also includes a listing under Antiquarian Book Dealers for tracking down old or rare books.

The Antiquarian Booksellers' Association of America (ABAA) maintains a membership directory of about 450 sellers and buyers of old books, some of whom provide search services for locating old titles. The directory provides addresses and phone numbers for these specialized stores, while indexing them geographically and by specialty (50 Rockefeller Plaza, New York NY 10020. (212)757-9395).

For dealers in your city, check the Yellow Pages under "Book Dealers — Used and Rare." Some of the larger ones (Pomander Books in New York City is one) will help writers track down out of print titles.

OTHER WRITERS

We've made reference before to the benefit of joining writers' groups as a source of quick answers to questions on writing fiction, etc. And, as any satisfied group member will attest, the benefit of having fellow toilers around to celebrate/commiserate with is perhaps the best attribute of membership.

Writers' groups are treated at length in A Community of Writers chapter of this book, but, in terms of research benefits, it should be mentioned that a number of writers' groups maintain reference libraries of varying sizes for use by their members. (Some carry only references that can already be found in any good public library, but many writers like to browse the specialized selection.) A few with reference resources are:

The Writers Room
153 Waverly Place
New York NY 10014
(212)807-9519

The Writer's Center
7815 Old Georgetown Road
Bethesda MD 20814
(301)654-8664

Community Writers' Library
McKinley Foundation
809 South 5th St.
Champaign IL 61820
(217)344-0297

Literary Center
1716 North 45th St.
Seattle WA 98103

The Loft
2301 E. Franklin Ave.
Minneapolis, MN 55406
(612)341-0431

Poets House
351 W. 18th St.
New York NY 10011
(212)627-4035

The Authors and Artists Resource Center (TARC, Inc.)
4001 E. Fort Lowell Rd.
Tucson AZ 85712-1011
(602)325-4733

Van Voorhis Poetry Library
Poetry Society of America
15 Gramercy Park
New York NY 10003
(212)254-9628

Woodland Pattern Book Center
720 E. Locust
Milwaukee WI 53212
(414)263-5001

In addition, The American Booksellers Association Information Center, a collection of books and periodicals about the book industry, is open by appointment at 137 W. 25th St., New York City. Brief reference questions may be answered by phoning (800)637-0037, and The Council of Literary Magazines and Presses (CLMP) has donated a library of 1,600 different literary magazines to the New York Public Library.

Chapter 4

PRODUCING AND POLISHING IT

Transforming an idea from brainstorm to brilliant manuscript takes time, effort and sometimes a careful collaboration between writer and freelance editor, writer and expert, or writer and printer.

To give your project luster and more clout in the marketplace, you can employ a freelance editor who will help you rewrite and polish your work. Or, if you have a track record in editing and publishing, you can offer your services as a freelance editor or co-author to persons needing such help.

As a writer committed to your craft, you should refine your editing skills so you can send your work directly to publishers without the help of a freelance editor. Freelance help, though, speeds up this learning process and enables the editor to earn extra dollars that sometimes are recycled into the freelancer's writing career.

Whether your goal is to find a freelancer or find clients to help, this section will explore the many opportunities. From freelance editing to ghostwriting, from graphic designing to desktop publishing, you'll learn what to expect from these freelancers and how to offer these services.

HELPING HANDS

As a writer/client or freelance editor, you'll be making a short-term or long-term commitment to someone you've probably never worked with before. Such partnerships can affect your professional life and goals, and your partner's—for better or worse.

If you're co-authoring a book or editing an unpublished writer's first book, you need to promote a positive working relationship: thoughtful, helpful and timely responses, and terms and rates that do not take advantage of the writer.

As the writer, you need to give your freelancer carefully prepared material and responses, to trust your freelancer's judgment, and to send payments as promised. As wordsmiths, we work with words, but ultimately we're working with people.

Bestselling author Samm Sinclair Baker, who has written 32 books (16 as co-author), stresses that partners must work together as a team without trying to cheat one another. "My basic rule for a successful and profitable co-authorship is the writer should care more and do more for the well-being of the partner than for one's self."

This advice applies to any editorial partnership.

Your first step as writer or freelancer is to carefully investigate the possibilities rather than jumping into a relationship that you or your wallet can't live with. Ideally, look for a person whom you like, respect or want to help or work with, especially if the project will demand a long-term partnership.

Also it's important to have a signed letter of agreement before you invest time in a project. That protects both you as a writer, freelance editor or collaborator *and* protects your editorial partner.

Letters of agreement prevent misunderstandings and ensure that crucial commitments have been discussed and agreed upon: What will be provided, by when, in what form, at what price and/or percentage, with what exceptions? Who will provide the expenses such as postage, long-distance calls and photocopying? Get these business considerations out of the way so that you can focus on the reason for the partnership.

FINDING A FREELANCE PARTNER

Writers and editors live in big cities and small towns, but where can you find that freelancer who will boost your writing career? And where are the writers who need help?

Consider looking first in your hometown or the nearby city. Even in small cities, you can usually find editors who edit national magazines or professional writers who freelance frequently with New York magazines.

The cost will vary depending upon the credentials of the freelance editor, whether he works from his home or in an agency office, and in what part of the country he lives. In addition, the amount of work your manuscript needs and the amount that an editor charges per hour or per project will affect the final bill.

Most freelancers have a set price for various editing jobs but also will negotiate or vary the price depending on the project. There are no industry-wide pay standards. In fact, associations are prohibited, by law, from recommending standard rates. Freelancers subscribing to the same referral services or organizations may charge more or less than their colleagues. Where the freelancer lives—and the amount of local competition—can affect the rates he charges and, likewise, where you live can affect the rates that you charge your clients.

One of the most cost-efficient ways to receive feedback on an article, story or book chapter—and to get ongoing writing advice—is to take a writing course at a nearby college or community center. Even if the instructor does not edit your work line by line, he can advise you on what a manuscript needs so you will know what type of editor to contact.

During the course, don't hesitate to ask the instructor for more feedback on your manuscript, especially if the instructor assigns letter grades and few comments.

It's important, however, not to abuse a teacher's willingness to help you. Don't expect a teacher to edit your book or additional stories. If you benefited from the teacher's critiques, consider negotiating an agreement with the teacher for additional editing—*after* the course has concluded.

Another way to find people locally who can edit your work is through editors' and writers' associations. Watch for notices about upcoming meetings in your local newspaper or call the editor of a nearby publication to inquire about editors' groups in your hometown. Also consult the Yellow Pages' Business-to-Business Directory under Editorial Services and any freelance specialty that you need.

On the local level, many organizations publish a directory with members' names, media affiliation, addresses and phone numbers, and a monthly or quarterly newsletter—which can provide you with names of area people to contact. (See A Community of Writers chapter for more information.)

Some chapters of Women in Communications, for instance, include a "Services WICI Members Can Use" and "Services WICI Members Can Provide" designations after each member's name. Directories of some groups are often available to members only, so if you are a freelance editor looking for clients, consider joining such an association. Some organizations, such as the Austin (Texas) Writers' League, will match members with local persons and companies needing freelance work, but will also respond to calls from anywhere in the United States.

Some local groups, with limited funding and a goal to help local professionals and companies, limit their referrals to a particular geographic area. The benefit of this for you as writer or freelance editor, though, is that you can phone and meet the person at little expense. Writers and companies who receive referrals then negotiate the terms and cost for each editing project.

In joining editors' or writers' groups in your area, you'll become eligible to be listed in their directories. Another approach would be to run an ad in an editorial organization's newsletter. For some groups, running an ad is a membership privilege, and there is no charge.

In the *Writers Connection* newsletter, for instance, classified ad rates are 75¢ per word with a 10-word minimum and 20% discount for six consecutive ads.

The Writers Connection in Cupertino, California, is truly that for its more than 2,000 members, most of whom are California writers, editors and publishing professionals. The association offers a newsletter, writers' directory, job shop referral service, writers' referral consultation service, resource library, bookstore and seminars.

CONTACTS ACROSS THE COUNTRY

You can find a freelance editor, indexer, translator or co-author by contacting any of a number of organizations. Among them is the American Society of Journalists and Authors' Dial-a-Writer Referral Service at (212)398-1934. ASJA's service matches writers in the United States and overseas with publishers, corporations, universities and individuals who need the assistance of a professional writer or editor.

Clients then negotiate the fee directly with the ASJA member, and there is no charge for a quick referral. Persons requesting an extensive search for a book collaborator or corporations seeking referrals pay a $50 search fee.

To get freelance jobs through the Dial-a-Writer service, you'll have to join the 770-member organization, but not all writers are eligible. ASJA requires substantial freelancing credentials of its members. Most ASJA members are active freelance writers, many of whom have published numerous books, which makes Dial-a-Writer a good source for finding competent freelance assistance.

Cassell Communications Inc., based in Fort Lauderdale, Florida, provides an International Writer Data Bank that helps writers and editorial specialists find one another. Copyediting, ghostwriting/collaboration, indexing, manuscript editing/revision, proofreading and translating are among the 35 writing/editing skills under which persons' names are filed. Phone number is (305)485-0795.

The Editorial Freelancers Association (Box 2050, Madison Square Station, New York NY 10159) provides referrals for freelance editorial services to the publishing and communications industries, but writers can also use this service. Members of this nonprofit organization run by and for freelancers include editors, indexers, writers, translators and proofreaders.

The EFA Job Phone, (212)677-3357, enables you, as a writer, to obtain the names of freelance editors or, as a freelance editor, to receive the names of potential clients.

As an editorial freelancer—especially in the New York City area— consider joining the Editorial Freelancers Association. In addition to the Job Phone, the group provides contacts to members through a bimonthly newsletter, an annual directory, program meetings, educational programs and medical insurance programs.

Another benefit of EFA is a confidential in-house book about members' experiences with publishers, companies and individuals. Members can consult this book in the EFA office to know more about potential clients. As a member, you can contribute (or just benefit) from anonymous specific feedback in the book such as "Don't ever work for this guy because I didn't get paid" or "This is a wonderful person to work for, and they have interesting books," points out EFA Co-Executive David R. Hall.

Payment from some clients can be a problem for freelancers, but is less likely to happen with referral services. Sometimes even companies can take up to 60 days to send a payment. Letters of agreement help to remind partners of the commitment they've made to one another.

To find additional writers' organizations that might direct you toward editorial freelancers or clients, consult the *Encyclopedia of Associations*, the *Book Publishing Resource Guide*, and *Literary Market Place*.

As an editorial freelancer with book publishing references, you can request to be listed in the annual *Literary Market Place*. This comprehensive directory of the American book publishing industry, available in most city libraries, includes an Editorial Services activity index of persons and agencies that offer copyediting, fact checking, ghostwriting, indexing, line editing, manuscript analysis and proofreading.

Literary Market Place lists editorial freelancers free of charge, but it is by no means free to anyone. Potential nominees for the next edition must fill out a detailed questionnaire, give references, and meet the March 31 deadline. References are then checked by *LMP. LMP* listings give each person's or agency's name, address, phone number, and brief description of the services and specialties.

The *Writer's Yellow Pages* (Steve Davis Publishing) also provides listings of publishing specialties, including freelance editors, proofreaders, indexers, manuscript analysts, ghostwriters and collaborators.

Weekly magazines such as *Publishers Weekly* and *Editor & Publisher* include classified advertising sections in which writers can advertise for assistance or editors can advertise for clients.

Writer's Digest, The Writer, and other writers' and editors' magazines also run ads for people looking for or willing to be collaborators, editors or proofreaders. This enables you to contact freelance editors eager to edit and/or proofread your manuscripts.

Another source of freelance help is the Writer's Digest Criticism Service. You can receive detailed advice for improving and selling books, novels, articles, short stories, scripts, poetry, songs and query letters. Professional writers, freelancing for the service, write a detailed critique about the manuscript's strengths, what needs to be changed, and how to make those changes. If your manuscript is marketable "as is" or with slight revisions, you'll receive specific marketing suggestions with the names of publications and editors who buy that type of writing.

Some literary agents (and other individuals) provide a critique of manuscripts for a fee, but this is no guarantee that the agent will represent you or your book. The *Literary Agents of North America* (Author Aid Associates), *LMP*, and the *1992 Guide to Literary Agents & Art/Photo Reps* (Writer's Digest Books) list agents who, in addition to representing books, critique writers' work.

WHAT TO EXPECT FROM EDITORS AND CLIENTS

You can receive a "polish" on your manuscript from a freelance editor in many ways: rewriting, content editing, copyediting and proofreading. Some freelancers provide a critique or manuscript analysis. Knowing the differences between the concepts helps you hire a freelancer suitable to your needs.

"Make it clear to the freelance editor what you expect and acknowledge the editor's expertise," recommends author and editor Kirk Polking, former director of the Writer's Digest Criticism Service.

The freelancer—in response—should be candid about what he can and can't provide on a given project, says David Hall of the Editorial Freelancers Association.

HOW TO CONTACT A FREELANCE PARTNER

To contact an editorial freelancer, send a brief letter of inquiry and a self-addressed stamped envelope (SASE) to the person. In your letter, request information on the services offered and the costs. (If you'd prefer to call first, keep it brief and follow up with a letter.)

Don't hesitate to ask for the credentials of the person who will be editing or evaluating your work. Any freelancer worth his blue ink will have a bio sheet to send to potential clients. If not, go elsewhere.

Look for a freelancer whose work experience and credentials reflect a commitment to the type of material you write. For instance, if you need a children's book to be edited, the ideal freelance editor will have worked for a children's magazine or have published several children's books. The best editors provide specific ways to improve the manuscript so that it is not only grammatically correct but also marketable. To make a manuscript salable, the editor must know the markets to which the manuscript would be submitted.

Also, contact several editors before entrusting your project to a freelancer. This will enable you to survey the variety of services, prices and qualifications of freelance editors.

If you need assistance on a book project, you may want to hire a freelancer first to edit a magazine article or short story you've written — or perhaps edit one chapter only. This is a good way for you to evaluate this editor's helpfulness — before making an expensive long-term commitment.

Analyze the person's ability to communicate the strengths and weaknesses and to show you how to improve your manuscript. A good editor will not only point out what needs to be improved but also will show you how — *on* the manuscript — depending, of course, on whether you've requested editing or an analysis.

As a freelancer marketing your services, you'll be in competition with other editorial freelancers. Writers — the smart ones — will shop around. That's okay. The benefit of this search for you as a freelancer is that potential clients who have selected you will be convinced that they have made a good choice and will be eager to receive your comments.

Some freelancers prepare a brochure that lists their services, prices and credentials. A brochure or carefully designed information sheet can *illustrate* your professionalism. State your policies in writing. One Pulitzer Prize nominee says in his literary consulting brochure: "Because of our dedication to providing the finest in creative consulting services, and our genuine respect for writers and the craft of writing, we will accept no assignment unless we believe we can help the author substantially improve his or her material and thereby enable it to compete in the world of best sellers and six-figure advances." Define for potential clients what constitutes a critique or any other terms you'll use in working with them.

An editor with a national track record generally charges more than that "friend-of-a-friend who was an English major in college," but from the professional you should receive advice to make the manuscript complete and grammatically correct, interesting to read, and marketable. Here's a case where that worn cliché applies — you get what you pay for — unless that casual acquaintance is also an accomplished editor.

Book content editors charge $12 to $50 per hour and more, or $600 to $5,000 per manuscript depending on the size and complexity of the project. If you need someone to rewrite your book, the charge is about

$18 to $50 per hour. Services for a book copyeditor can range from $9 to $22 per hour or more.

Textbook copyediting can earn $14 to $20 per hour depending on whether the book is a technical or nontechnical elementary, high school or college text. Freelance editors of medical texts charge $25 to $65 per hour.

You can expect to pay about $160 for a critique of a book outline with the first 20,000 words. A critique for an article or short story up to 3,000 words costs an estimated $40.

Writer's Market lists a range of payment rates for numerous freelance specialties. Use these guidelines to set your freelance rates or to compare the rates you've received from freelancers.

Ideally, you should employ a freelance editor to hone your skills so that you no longer need this "middle man" to get your work ready for publication. Any freelance editor who convinces you that you will never write a marketable manuscript without this outside editorial help is creating a dependency that will cost you money, time and self-esteem.

You need to master the rules and variations of the language and spot where you can improve a manuscript, or else you'll always be turning over one of the most satisfying parts of writing—the polish—to another person.

The ideal freelance editor explains his changes and will encourage you to become your own editor—even when it costs that editor a client.

PROOFREADERS

In pre-computer times, all published material had to be proofread as a separate stage of the publishing process. Now some in-house editors edit and proofread simultaneously—and they actually proofread the version that appears in the publication—without having to employ a proofreader. Type compositors/printers and publishing houses, though, still employ proofreaders, some of whom are freelancers.

If, as a writer, you want someone to proofread your work, you can hire a proofreader. But with the hourly rate for proofreaders and copyeditors so similar, you can get more for your money by employing a copyeditor who will also correct poor word choices.

Most freelance editors listed in industry directories also offer proofreading services for clients. Some editors, though, don't like to proofread, says Gwen Bish who started Gwen Bish Proofreading Service after working many years as a full-time proofreader of textbooks.

As a proofreader for a printer, you would compare the printer's proofs or galleys against the edited manuscript to identify and correct errors in the typeset copy in addition to making sure that the type and headings conform to the specifications.

Before soliciting proofreading assignments, consider working in-house as a proofreader to learn the expectations of clients and to gain speed and accuracy. Contact area publishers and printers first and consider running a small ad in your hometown newspaper.

To develop a clientele, send a cover letter, résumé, and (optional) proofread page proof with your marks to publishers and printers. Most companies will not respond, but from those that do, you can begin to find proofreading work. When a company is pleased with your work, you'll continue to get calls.

As a freelance proofreader, you can set your own hours, but sometimes to meet publishers' and printers' schedules, you'll encounter long hours and short deadlines. Some companies may want you to work exclusively for them, which you can't do as a freelancer, unless the price is right.

Before you accept a proofreading assignment, ask for an estimate of how long the job will take or how much work is expected within a specific time.

Most proofreading jobs offer a set hourly rate. Freelance proofreaders of books earn $6 to $25 per hour and sometimes $1.50 to $3 per page. If you proofread textbooks, you can earn between $9 and $18.50 per hour. Medical proofreading assignments pay more: $12 to $30 per hour.

"If you're good at what you do, you can really pick the type of books that you like to read," says Bish.

Publishers will usually tell you what they pay. If you have significant credentials, payment may be negotiable. Some publishers give a per-book rate, which will vary from book to book, depending on how complicated or simple the book is.

TRANSLATORS

As a translator, you can specialize in commercial, literary or technical translations, or you can accept assignments in all three specialties. Today, the immediate demand in this field is for translators of technical material.

Depending on the language(s) you know and the type of material you prefer to translate, you need to get your name into the hands of publishers, companies and individuals who need translations.

If you are a translator looking for work, contact the 2,800-member American Translators Association, 109 Croton Ave., Ossining NY 10562, (914)941-1500. The association publishes a monthly newsletter, *ATA Chronicle*, in which members and nonmembers advertise translating services (15 words or less for $10), or place a more costly display ad. The newsletter also provides leads from companies and individuals who need translators.

ATA's *Translation Services Directory*, published every two years, lists translators, their languages and specialties, but to be included in the directory, you must be an active ATA member and pay the annual $50 membership fee.

To find a translator, consult ATA's directory or the *Literary Market Place* directory that lists translators, their languages and specialties. Translators and interpreters are indexed by source and target language.

The Write People agency, Suite 100, 4999 Northcutt Pl., Dayton OH 45414, (513)275-0616, offers translations to and from English in 26 languages and will provide referrals to companies and individuals. Translators with experience can contact The Write People for an application and, pending an interview, might be matched with potential clients.

This agency also has the names of more than 400 freelance specialists on file who can translate, provide technical and commercial editing and proofreading, and promotional writing.

In book publishing, translation rights are one of the subsidiary rights of a copyright owner. A publisher that decides to produce its own translated edition for another language market pays the translation fee and splits the royalties between the original author and translator at an agreed-upon rate. The translator's royalty is a percentage of the original author's royalties, usually 15 to 20%.

Commercial translators charge $115 to $120 per 1,000 words. If you receive a translating project through an agency, you might owe a commission to the agency, an estimated 33⅓%. Government agencies pay up to $125 per 1,000 foreign words into English.

The U.S. State Department, for instance, pays freelance translators $80 per 1,000 words of general material; $86 per 1,000 words of semi-technical material; and $92 per 1,000 words of technical material. For translations from English into another language, you can receive up to 50% more than the $80 to $92 rate.

Literary translators usually receive a per-project fee or about $40 to $100 per 1,000 words for books. Translators of magazine articles can earn $40 to $50 and more for 1,000 words. Payment is negotiable depending on the translator's credentials and the publisher's availability of funds.

If you want to be a literary translator, prepare a translation of a work you feel strongly about. Send this translation sample (a maximum 10 pages) with a letter stating your credentials. "Enthusiasm and concern for a text are what will attract a publisher rather than being there on a list and being competent," says Pulitzer Prize-winning poet Richard Howard, who has translated 150 books.

One way to add to your list of credentials is to write reviews of book translations for periodicals. Your critique of the translation shows your ability to understand language and translation.

INDEXING

Indexers read books and manuals—as do all editorial freelancers—but in a much different way. "When indexing, you are reading to pick out what are the concepts and ideas that someone will need to find and what are the relationships between them," says indexer Alexandra Nickerson, who works for 12 to 15 book publishers.

An index can take a few hours to hundreds of hours to compile.

Whether you compile indexes with index cards and a typewriter or with a computer and commercial indexing software, this freelance specialty demands long hours, adherence to details and deadlines, and a commitment to clients. Because of the constant decisions on entries and cross-references, it's a skill that takes practice and indexing know-how. Book production editors prefer to work with professional indexers.

To market your skills as an indexer, consider joining the American Society of Indexers, 1700 18th St. NW, Washington DC 20009. This group publishes an annual *Register of Indexers* for $15 which lists indexers and their specialties and *A Guide to Indexing Software*, an evaluation of programs for IBMs and compatibles, for $15. (For publications write to this ASI address: P.O. Box 386, Port Aransas TX 78373.)

Even with 25 years of indexing experience, you might write a letter soliciting your service and not receive a response from a publisher. "Word of mouth" among publishers and satisfied clients is the way many indexers get jobs.

Another source for finding indexers or indexing jobs is through colleges that offer library science degrees. Consult directories such as *Degrees Offered by Colleges and Subject* or *Peterson's Guide*. And see the directories mentioned earlier in this section.

An index is generally the responsibility of an author. The author may choose to compile it or ask the publisher to find an in-house or freelance indexer to do it. Often an indexer's fee will come out of the author's royalty.

Some authors over-index. "It's hard to separate yourself from something you've poured your life blood into, and everything is important, but if you put everything in the index it is not useful as a guide to the reader," points out Nickerson.

Indexers occasionally are employed to edit indexes provided by authors—to refine the style. "The author may refer to a topic by one term, and it's the indexer's job to think about the audience and come up with any alternative terms they might be likely to look under."

When you receive an indexing assignment, you'll use page proofs to compile the index. Depending on whether you use a typewriter or computer, you need to submit a typewritten index or a computer printout of the index and the disk.

Payment is negotiable. It depends on the level of difficulty of the book, the comprehensiveness desired in the index, and the size of the page and type. More experienced indexers can command a higher rate of pay. Indexers get paid more for medical books, legal texts and highly technical materials.

You can be paid by the page (page proof, not manuscript page), hour, entry, line or project. There are advantages and disadvantages to each method of payment.

You can earn $10 to $40 per hour or $250 to $900 per book. The fees vary widely depending on the complexity of the project and geographic location of the freelancer.

Some indexers who work with established clients don't require a letter of agreement, but more publishers today are insisting upon them.

As a freelance indexer, insist upon a letter of agreement with authors. If the author submits the page proofs late to the indexer or delays sending the index to the publisher, the indexer can get blamed.

The American Society of Indexers has compiled a sample letter of agreement to help members avoid potential problems. Indexers' agreements should specify the rights acquired (if any), author of the index, credit and editorial approval, subcontracting (whether the publisher will allow the indexer to subcontract the work), payment, delivery of work, and a termination clause.

One potential problem with hiring indexers or compiling indexes is timeliness. Your indexer must know how to meet deadlines. Of course, as the writer, you need to be timely with the promised materials.

When employing a freelance indexer, ask for references and a sample of his/her work. When you have chosen your freelancer, it's important to clearly communicate what you want in an index. Assuming that you were impressed with the credentials of the person you hired, trust your indexer as you should with any freelancer you hire to enhance your work.

COLLABORATION

Whether you dream of producing romance novels, textbooks, or lavish coffee-table books, a collaborative writing arrangement may help you achieve that goal. Today, in nearly every genre, writers are sharing the work load, profits and sometimes bylines that in some cases would not be possible without a two-person team.

Of the 50,000 books that are published each year, it is impossible to estimate how many result from collaborations, but industry sources cite a steadily increasing number.

"Today with the interest in celebrity books, there is a growing need for more people who can talk well to subjects and draw them out and most importantly organize their thoughts well into a book," says John F. Baker, editor-in-chief of *Publishers Weekly*. "Part of being a successful collaborator is to shape a book out of somebody's random reminiscences, thoughts and opinions." Celebrity books, though, aren't the only types of collaborations that you can pursue. There are various approaches that you can use to initiate a collaborative writing agreement and different roles that you can play as a collaborator—with these varying amounts of credit:

collaborator (By Leslie Jones *with* or *as-told-to* Your Name)
co-author (By Leslie Jones and Your Name)
ghostwriter (By Leslie Jones—and no byline for you)

You'll encounter varying amounts of work with each project and, of course, need to carefully explore each collaborative option—the benefits and drawbacks—before agreeing to work on a project.

For instance, collaboration can mean that you'll write the entire manuscript based on your partner's tape recorded dictation and several face-to-face meetings, or that you'll provide extensive or light revision to a manuscript that your partner has written. With a fifty-fifty co-authorship, you and another author would each write, say, eight chapters in accordance with the outline that both have drawn up. As a ghostwriter with a nonwriting partner, you'll assume—while writing—the "voice" of the celebrity, the sports hero, the business leader or politician.

What is important is that you first consider your time, personality, writing goals, interests and financial needs, and then reach a written agreement that will satisfy you, your partner and your publisher.

Bestsellers produced by collaborators—*Iacocca* and *In Search of Excellence*—have brought the concept of collaboration onto center stage. With publishing houses and agents eager to work with collaborating writers, you have the opportunity to carve a niche for yourself in a specialty that writers, working alone, have overlooked.

"The opportunities for writers who can collaborate with other writers, with celebrities, or with experts who don't have the time, ability, or inclination to write, are greater than ever before," report author Hal Zina Bennett and literary agent Michael Larsen in their collaborated book, *How to Write with a Collaborator* (Writer's Digest Books).

If the thought of working with another person or writer scares you, consider the benefits. In some cases, your partner's life experiences or knowledge will be the research that might take you years to collect. An expert in a field—be that person a physician, lawyer, psychologist or teacher—can provide the content of the book while you produce and polish the material and collect additional anecdotes, quotes and facts. Or maybe you have mastered the skill of writing excellent narratives, but struggle to plot a story or invent characters.

The ideal partnership means that both parties bring something unique to the book—a unique story to tell, research and writing ability, knowledge of a topic, access to sources, or a combination of these qualities—in addition to a sincere commitment to complete the book.

There are also numerous drawbacks to collaborating: sharing the profits, receiving a fair share (if you are a writer without a track record—in some cases the writer will get 10%), deciding who has the final word (when both collaborators disagree), and venturing into a long-term arrangement where it's impossible to predict potential problems such as personality clashes.

To help you decide if collaboration is a good choice for you, consider ghostwriting a magazine article first. You can earn $400 to $4,000 for the article and at the same time evaluate your client's suitability for a long-term project. Also, you might decide to expand the topic of that article into a book. That's what happened to author Samm Sinclair Baker. "I sent an article on skin cancer to a leading health magazine, and the editor said he wanted the article, but it would be much more valuable to him and they would pay a lot more if the article were co-authored with a dermatologist," says Baker. "That gave me the idea first to co-author." That project later became a book.

When selecting book topics, choose a subject that excites you exceptionally and has the potential for a big sale, Baker recommends. Otherwise, the collaborators will be working more for their own satisfaction than income *or* may not even get the book into print. Self-satisfaction can be a valid reason for writing a book, but discuss this prospect in advance with your partner: Can we afford to write this book if it doesn't earn any money?

FINDING A COLLABORATOR

The search for a collaborator begins with deciding what type of collaborator your book project demands. Do you need (and want) an expert-in-a-field/collaborator or a writer/collaborator, or an expert/writer/collaborator?

If you have an agent and are interested in actively pursuing a collaboration, tell your agent. Most agents, though, will suggest this possibility to the writer/client if and when there is a suitable collaborator. Today agents often initiate a publishing "package" that includes a writer and an expert or celebrity.

To find a collaborating writing partner, begin exploring many of the leads that you would in finding a freelance editor. Consult writers' and editors' publications and directories, and contact college English or journalism departments. Watch for ads in *Writer's Digest*, *Publishers Weekly* and other trade and association newsletters.

By attending meetings and joining editors' and writers' associations, you can meet potential co-authors (writer/collaborators). That approach will also work if you are looking for someone to write your life story. But don't "pop the question" of collaboration until you know that person and his or her abilities. Realize that building mutual rapport and respect takes time, sometimes many months. If your topic demands immediate action, a writer at your local newspaper or media office could be a potential collaborator.

If you want to collaborate on a book in a particular field or specialty, you'll need to look where these experts work, publish and gather. Consult the local Yellow Pages where professionals are indexed by category. Attend conferences where you can meet specialists in the field that you'd like to write about.

To find contacts in a specialized field, also consult the *Encyclopedia of Associations* and the trade journals of that field. Persons quoted in articles may be willing sources for collaborations. And bionotes at the end of articles sometimes tell you that the article writer specializes in this or that topic.

For additional contacts, consider running a small ad in a field's most respected trade journal: "Published author with M.A. in music willing to ghostwrite or collaborate on book projects. Send details with SASE for response to . . .". Some journals may allow you to run a brief notice at no charge.

To market yourself as a collaborator, contact by letter the person whose story you'd like to write. Say that you would like to discuss *the possibility of* writing an article or book together. If you don't receive an answer within a month, follow up with a phone inquiry. Unless your book idea revolves around a recent now-or-never news topic or trend, don't demand an immediate answer. A potential client may be a decisive leader in his or her field, but extremely careful and hesitant in selecting a collaborator.

In providing information to a potential partner, give your publication credentials and education in a succinct one-page biography accompanied by a cover letter. Any evidence that shows that you've collaborated with other writers or experts is helpful. You might have to convince a potential collaborator to select you over several other contacts.

When you meet this person face to face, you'll again need to decide if you want to proceed. Perhaps you won't like one another's personalities, demands or expectations for the book.

The ideal collaborator will live in or near your city, but more importantly must have the experiences, expertise and interest in the type of project you want to pursue—and vice versa. Assess a potential collaborator's enthusiasm for the project, and the credentials and ability to produce or contribute to a marketable manuscript.

Author Holly G. Miller, who has written 12 books (11 of which were collaborations), believes that choosing the right partner is the most important step in collaborative writing. If you will be collaborating with a writing partner, look for someone with equal writing ability. For instance, with a beginning and long-time writer working together, the more experienced partner will edit the other more often. Also avoid choosing someone whose abilities and perspective are too close to your own. Your collaborator ideally should have different strengths to complement yours.

Collaboration adds more layers of editing to a book and sometimes takes more time even though the work load may be shared. Select a partner who will conscientiously tackle the required and unexpected demands of the book.

Designating one of the collaborators as the leader also helps you resolve potential problems. When a writer and expert-in-a-field collaborate, the expert in writing the book—the writer—makes the best leader. When two writers collaborate, decide which person will play this role.

CONTRACTS AND INCOME

As a collaborator, insist on two signed agreements—a contract with a publisher and a letter of agreement with your collaborator—before you invest considerable time and effort in the project.

While there are few guarantees in any writing project, a contract and advance with a publisher tell you that you're pursuing a marketable project. Whether the book sells 10,000 or 500,000 copies depends on many factors, but, with a contract, the book has a better chance of reaching readers.

Agent and author Richard Curtis recommends that writers have a separate collaboration agreement in addition to a publisher's contract. "Publishing agreements define the collaborators' joint obligation to their publisher, but they don't define their obligations to each other," says Curtis about collaborations in his book, *How to Be Your Own Literary Agent* (Houghton Mifflin).

In a collaborative agreement or a letter of agreement that some authors use, the collaborators define who specifically will do what, for what royalty, hourly rate or per-project fee, within what time frame and with what deadlines, and who will pay for what expenses. Partners should agree in writing and in advance who has the final approval on the finished manuscript and select a person who would serve as arbitrator—editor, agent or attorney—if a dispute arises.

Decide in advance if one or both collaborators' names will appear on the book and in whose name the copyright will appear. Sometimes experts-in-a-field or celebrity collaborators will pay a larger portion to the writer who is willing to forgo the byline. Consider how important that byline is to your publishing goals and then decide whether you prefer to be a co-author or ghost.

How much each collaborator will receive from the arrangement often depends on each person's track record and perceived value in the marketplace. The novelist who collaborated on Donald Regan's White House memoir received one-half of the royalty, beginning with a $1 million advance. "Not many collaborators get paid on that scale," says John Baker, editor of *Publishers Weekly*.

More common today is for the collaborator to receive 10 to 25% of the royalty, while the celebrity collaborator receives the remaining amount. "The publisher is really paying for the name of the celebrity, and that's where most of the money has to go," says Baker. "I'm afraid for all too many collaborators it is a rather unsung and not particularly well-paid job."

Sometimes, though, an unsung job will give you more clout in negotiating later collaborations and books. It is up to you, as the writer, and your agent to insist on a mutually beneficial collaboration for the writer.

Ghostwriters who won't be receiving as-told-to credit charge from $5,000 to $35,000 plus expenses paid at the completion of each chapter or at four intervals: down payment, half-finished, three-quarters finished and completion. Six months' ghostwriting work on a corporate book can earn you $13,000 to $25,000. The hourly rate for a ghostwriter can vary from $15 to $50.

Experienced collaborators recommend that the profits from the royalty and expenses be divided evenly with the writer receiving 50% and the expert-in-a-field or other writer getting 50%. "An equal partnership means equal respect," says Samm Sinclair Baker.

GRAMMAR SERVICES

Newsman Dan Rather has called the Writers' Hotline in Emporia, Kansas. So has Walter Cronkite. Beginning and long-time writers, and anyone too smart to guess about the English language can try this alternative.

A grammar hotline gives you free fast answers to questions on writing, grammar, punctuation, diction and syntax. Some hotlines, though, won't pay the long-distance phone charges, so, if possible, you'll want to find one in your city. *The Writer's Yellow Pages* and a brochure published by Tidewater Community College can help you do that.

As Tidewater teacher Donna Reiss received calls from across the country at her school's hotline, she began compiling a list of grammar hotlines to help callers learn about nearby ones. Her list of 12 hotlines has now expanded into the annual *Grammar Hotline Directory* which includes 60 hotlines and shows that grammar help is "just a phone call away."

Most hotlines are operated by colleges or former teachers as a public service to writers—and the language. "There is no organization of grammar hotlines," says Reiss, director of Tidewater's Writing Center and Grammar Hotline. "There is only the informal connection of the ones I've heard about."

Grammar hotlines have varying policies. Follow the guidelines of the one which you have contacted. For instance, the Writers' Hotline at Emporia State University will accept mail, phone and in-person inquiries, will return long-distance calls, has additional evening hours on Thursday, and has an answering machine in operation when the office is closed.

Tidewater College—which underwrites the cost of the grammar directory—cannot answer grammar questions by mail and asks that callers pay the long-distance charges.

Hotline hours throughout the country will vary, depending on the number of staff members. Some are open during school hours and closed during summer and term breaks. Few hotlines are open in the evenings, but if you live on the East Coast, you can call a West Coast hotline for an answer later in the day. Some hotlines have 24-hour answering machines and will return your call as soon as possible.

To get the most from a hotline, have the question or manuscript in front of you when you call. If you read the sentence slowly to the hotline assistant, he or she can then suggest the correct grammar, punctuation or word usage. Faculty members, graduate students and former teachers who staff phones generally will answer technical, mechanical and grammatical questions, or refer you to reference librarians or appropriate sources when they can't answer your question.

Some callers will contact several hotlines about a difficult question. Hotline veterans applaud this approach. "Calling for corroboration is another sign of the professionalism of the writer, not a sign of ignorance or weakness," says Reiss.

When you call a hotline, asking one or two brief questions is the best approach. If you have numerous questions or paragraphs of material, the hotline volunteer might recommend that you seek an editor who can read and mark your manuscript. Remember that the hotline volunteer is at a disadvantage because he or she can't see your manuscript over the phone. Don't expect a hotline volunteer to edit an entire document or proofread your work.

Be patient when you call a hotline. Sometimes, at college writing centers, the hotline assistant will be helping someone in the office and you might have to call back.

Most hotline assistants will do what they can to answer your question. Some programs require that staffers look up the answer in two sources before giving the answer. Most hotlines try to give immediate answers, but will arrange to call you back if they need to find an answer.

Mail inquiries can take one to two months, but first call the hotline to make sure that it will respond to mail requests.

Here are a few grammar hotlines. To get a complete list of hotlines, send a self-addressed envelope with one first class stamp to Tidewater Community College. Sending a SASE is also the best approach if you are soliciting information from a hotline that accepts mail inquiries.

HOTLINE LISTINGS

Grammar Hotline
Tidewater Community College
% Grammar Hotline Directory Request
1700 College Crescent
Virginia Beach VA 23456
(804)427-7170

Open Monday through Friday, 10 a.m. to noon; afternoon hours vary; reduced summer hours

Grammar Crisis Line
Ball State University
The Writing Center
Muncie IN 47306
(317)285-8387

Open Monday through Thursday, 9 a.m. to 8 p.m.; Friday from 9 a.m. to 5 p.m. From May to August, open Monday through Friday from 11 a.m. to 2 p.m.

Grammar Hotline
Northeastern University
English department
Boston MA 02115
(617)437-2512

Open Monday through Friday from 8:30 a.m. to 4:30 p.m.; summer hours vary.

Grammarphone
Amarillo College
Amarillo TX 79178-0001
(806)374-4726

Open Monday through Thursday, 8 a.m. to 9 p.m.; Friday, 8 a.m. to 3 p.m.; Sunday, 2 p.m. to 6 p.m.

National Grammar Hotline
Moorpark College
Moorpark CA 93021
(805)378-1494

Open from September through June, Monday through Friday from 8 a.m. to noon.

Grammar Hotline
Emporia State University
Emporia KS 66801
(316)343-5380

Open Monday through Thursday, noon to 4 p.m.; Wednesday, 7-10 p.m.; Tuesday and Thursday, 8-10 a.m.; Thursday night, 7 to 10 p.m.; Sunday, 4-6 p.m.; summer hours vary.

WORKING WITH ARTISTS, DESIGNERS AND ILLUSTRATORS

Let's forget about the words of your manuscript for a minute. Picture your manuscript's message. What images would best illustrate and enhance what you're writing?

That's how artists, designers, illustrators and photographers approach their work. While you focus on the words, the visually oriented person sees the images, their placement and other design aspects. Thank goodness, because while we struggle to find the best words to convey a message, the artist is working to visually enhance that message or, in the case of a novel, to capture the atmosphere.

If you are self-publishing a book or newsletter, you can act as your own art director or hire one. Of course, much of the advice we discussed about editorial freelancers applies to working with illustrators and designers: Respect and understand their talents, use good common sense and communicate.

The type of artist you hire depends on what you want to visually depict, and in what medium. Do you want a fine art painting with carefully placed titles or a bold words-only cover for your book? Do you want pen-and-ink line drawings or photos to illustrate a how-to process in Chapter 3? Or maybe your newsletter needs a distinctive nameplate or logo. These are just some of the decisions that an artist/designer can help you make.

Before you hire a specialist in one type of artwork, though, research the vast variety of graphics that will complement your work.

A careful scan of *Artist's Market*, especially listings in the Book Publishers, Magazines, and Newspapers & Newsletters sections, will show you the artistic skills that art directors look for. Some of these techniques—say, calligraphy or charcoal pencil drawing—you might prefer for your publication or book. In graphic design books, look for various techniques, styles and effects. The *Art Directors Annual* (Art Directors Club, 250 Park Ave. S., New York NY 10003) for instance, showcases outstanding work in one volume. Photocopy and collect your favorite styles.

Next, talk with several graphic designers who can show you a wide choice of art/design possibilities within your budget. Most designers won't charge you for the initial consultation. Usually, at first meetings, designers will show you their portfolios, ask you about your prospective project, and discuss some general approaches and prices. Show examples of the designs you like so the designer won't have to guess, but also be open-minded to the expert's suggestions.

To find a designer who specializes in the type of publications(s) you wish to produce, consult local and national directories of artists, designers and illustrators. Some source books focus on artists and design agencies in geographical areas: the *New York Gold* book (New York artists), *Chicago Creative Directory* (Chicago illustrators and designers), *Madison Avenue Handbook* (New York City area agencies), *The Work Book* (California designers and artists), and *Creative Source* (Canadian source book). Some directories include artists, designers and illustrators throughout the United States: *American Showcase*, *Creative Black Book*, *RSVP* and, for design firms, *The Design Firm Directory*. *Literary Market Place* also lists artists and art services.

If the visual design of a publication is a new venture for you, explore local sources first, especially in small cities. That enables you to meet face to face with potential designers/artists.

However, with fax machines, overnight delivery services and the advantage of putting what you want/expect in writing, you can still work effectively with an out-of-town designer. This is particularly advantageous if you live in a large city but can't afford the cost markup of metropolitan design firms.

The best designers—for self-publishers on a budget—will suggest cost-effective ways to add variety and "color" to your pages without using the expensive four-color process, unless your book's topic demands it.

Design specialists charge various rates, depending on the complexity of the project. Some charge an hourly rate plus expenses (including a markup on services which they have subcontracted on your behalf—for example, camera-ready resin-coated pages). Most work on a per-project basis and charge expenses. You can spend between $300 and $5,000 for your book's interior design and between $500 and $3,500 for the cover. The design of a masthead and cover for a magazine can cost between $500 and $2,750.

Page design programs, like Xerox Ventura Publisher or Aldus Page-Maker software, enable you to decrease long-term design costs, but do not guarantee that you'll produce graphically dynamic products.

If you'll be wearing the designer/art director's hat and don't have extensive graphics training, consider hiring a designer as a part-time consultant. For $45 to $90 per hour, a designer can review the prototype or sample pages that you've prepared and provide suggestions on how to enhance your graphic approach.

As you determine the design format for your publication, begin looking for artists who specialize in the type of artwork you want. Local galleries and sidewalk and library art shows enable you to browse until you find a technique or style that you really like. Attend art shows at nearby colleges. Young artists are eager to establish a reputation, and most would work hard for the opportunity to have their work in a book, newsletter or magazine.

Martin Colyer's *How to Find and Work with an Illustrator* (North

Light Books) provides excellent advice not only on finding illustrators but also on getting the results you want.

When you have selected an artist/designer/illustrator, you need to provide specific "guidelines" so that person can best enhance your writing: the manuscript(s) to accompany the graphics, samples or rough sketches of what you want and a letter of agreement or contract outlining the terms and what needs to be done. New York attorney and author Tad Crawford has written a series of books to help writers and artists negotiate contracts: *Business and Legal Forms for Authors and Self-Publishers*, *Business and Legal Forms for Graphic Designers*, *Business and Legal Forms for Fine Artists* and *Business and Legal Forms for Illustrators* (North Light Books).

The terms will vary depending on whether you're contracting for several illustrations or whether you and the illustrator will be collaborating on a book. If you and the illustrator will be collaborating on, say, a children's book, you will probably share the work load. In such a case then, you wouldn't be assigning illustrations; as partners, you and your artist would discuss the needs of the book and responsibilities to one another.

Artists, designers, and illustrators will be especially concerned about retaining the copyright and ownership to their work and appreciate receiving credit for illustrations. *The Artist's Friendly Legal Guide* (North Light Books), *How to Protect Your Creative Work* (John Wiley & Sons) and *Make It Legal* (North Light Books) will help you understand this complicated subject. "The Business of Art" section in *Artist's Market* also provides guidelines.

Jean S. Perwin, an attorney specializing in intellectual property law, tells artists that "although retaining ownership of the copyright gives you the legal right to prevent someone from taking reproductions of your work, the contract should spell out clearly what is being bought and sold."

When you negotiate a price and the rights for artwork, you'll suddenly understand why magazine editors—whom you've encountered while freelance writing—want to purchase all rights. It's easier for you to commission an artist on a work-for-hire basis and own all rights to the artwork, but that's the same thing publishers say when they buy all rights to your writing. You'll have to resolve this ethical dilemma for yourself. Be sure, whatever you decide, you specify the rights purchased in your letter of agreement—and the price—in addition to terms that will make your relationship mutually beneficial.

Experienced artists/designers/illustrators will want the following areas addressed in the contract or letter of agreement: method and timing of payment, copyright and reproduction rights, termination and cancellations, artistic control, insurance and delivery charges and expenses.

The money-motivated self-publisher can draft one-sided agreements, especially with new artists or photographers who don't understand the consequences, but then the cycle of abusing creative people continues; the self-publisher perpetuates what he might be trying to escape from.

If you are assuming the role of the art director, assigning the artwork and illustrations as soon as possible is the best approach to ensure a careful job and allow extra time for unforeseen delays and revisions. Some design firms have a traffic manager who directs the flow of work to various specialists to meet all deadlines, but most freelance artists, working alone, juggle their own projects. Most freelancers encounter the "feast or famine" problem of having too much work or not enough at a given time. As you interview prospective artists, inquire about their turnaround times. Does the artist use a computer or drawing board to create and change images? How long does it generally take for the artist to re-draw or re-design a project? Is there an extra charge for immediate turnaround?

An important guideline in working with artists or any vendor is to build extra time into your publishing schedule for each step, but be firm in expecting deadlines to be met.

Computers have revolutionized the design field—giving designers, illustrators and publishers more options and flexibility than ever before—but the efficiency of computers has also led to misconceptions. Software sales materials suggest that users can instantly create a document with graphics. True, but ideas and concepts, expressed in words and art, take time to develop and refine.

In some cases, computers have reduced the time and graphics costs, but just because a designer uses a computer does not mean designs will cost less. Flexibility is the big advantage with the equipment on the designer's desktop. A designer can change the typeface or move an illustration from column one to column two with a touch of the mouse.

Keep in mind, though, that all graphics work, illustrations and photos have a market value, regardless of the time it took to create them. If an experienced book designer is able to create and output a jacket design in two hours, he or she will most likely charge the going rate for a cover in the specific market: $300 to $3,500.

"It's unfair to just estimate how long the execution will take because they're going to have to set aside time to plan and to conceptualize the piece. Also their talent is worth something, too," points out Susan Conner, who edited four editions of *Artist's Market*. "Time isn't the only element."

The complexity of a project, the skill and experience of the artist/ designer, the turnaround time and rights will affect the prices you'll have to pay. One drawback for you as a small publisher or self-publisher is that you'll be competing with commercial publishers for the services of artists and designers. Some designers, however, will accept a lower profit margin when the project has a limited market value, such as a small town's history or a church's recipe book. That won't be the case if your book, magazine or newsletter has national or international potential.

"Everyone is in the business to make money, and you have to realize that and if they can charge you $70 an hour and you're willing to pay for it, they'll charge that amount," says Deborah Dent, president of Willow Design. "That doesn't mean they're being unfair; they're probably priced just the same as most graphic design firms."

Working with young artists can benefit your first-time publishing efforts *and* the artists involved — if you can provide additional guidance and be patient about small mistakes that might occur because of inexperience. And if you are willing to provide a learning experience for a college artist, the graphics side of your book or publication could become a two- to three-month nonpaying internship for the student assigned to your project. You would have to follow the guidelines required by the specific art school, but in most cases your willingness to work with a student will provide you with valuable and inexpensive graphics assistance.

Professional designers often use the Graphic Artists Guild's most recent *Handbook of Pricing & Ethical Guidelines* to determine the costs for specific projects. To get a range of prices, study the publishers' entries in *Artist's Market* — you'll see what publishers are paying artists, designers and illustrators. For instance, Pocket Books pays by the job, $800 to $4,000, for illustrations, preferably paintings and color washes. The University Press of America pays $175 to $250 for cover assignments. *National Geographic* magazine pays $3,500 for inside color illustrations and $750 for black-and-white illustrations. On the regional level, for instance, *Phoenix Home & Garden* pays $35 for inside black-and-white illustrations and $250 for color.

When you've hired an illustrator for your project, arrange to review the early drawings and then allow the person to work in his own way. "If you know that artist's style, then you're going to have to have a certain element of trust, but then you also need proof that they understand what the concept is," says Conner.

Allow artists the freedom to do what they do best, and your words — on well-designed pages with evocative graphics — will look as they never have before.

Following is a list of organizations that you can contact for more information about artists, designers and illustrators.

LISTINGS

American Center for Design
Suite 500
233 E. Ontario
Chicago IL 60611
(312)787-2018

American Institute of Graphic Arts
1059 Third Ave.
New York NY 10021
(212)752-0813

Graphic Artists Guild
11 W. 20th St.
New York NY 10011-3704
(212)463-7730

WORKING WITH PHOTOGRAPHERS AND STOCK PHOTO AGENCIES

Whether you're a self-publisher, a magazine journalist or a technical writer, you may need the services of a photographer.

When photos will accompany a manuscript you're writing or publishing, you have three choices: hire a photographer to shoot the photos, lease photos from a stock photo agency, or shoot photos yourself. All three demand careful scrutiny because obtaining photos is not as simple as you offering, say, $25 per photo.

Most photographers consider their time, expenses, how you will use the photo, and for how long when setting fees. That person is like you when selling a manuscript — the photographer offers specific rights for a particular price. Most photo buyers prefer exclusive rights to a photo, but with this exclusivity comes a much higher price.

To understand the photo market from the photographer's perspective, read *Sell & Re-Sell Your Photos* and *How to Sell Your Photographs and Illustrations* (Writer's Digest Books). You'll see why photographers are reluctant to immediately quote a set price.

Three of the most economical ways to obtain photos are to shoot the photos yourself, acquire the services of a friend with competent photographic skills, or contract with a stock photo agency. With each of these options, the cost, responsibility to the photographer, and the professionalism can vary.

If your writing projects constantly demand photos, consider developing your own photography skills. With a photo course and practice, you can produce competent photos. This approach especially works well when magazines offer no additional payment for photos or when you want exclusive rights to the photos without having to pay the high cost. *Photographer's Market* (Writer's Digest Books) provides a list of photography workshops across the country. On the local level, colleges and community education programs offer classes and workshops.

If you're designing pages and shooting photos for a book or newsletter, you can ensure a more professional end product by seeking a graphic design consultant. "There are certain visual trends happening in the marketplace," says *Photographer's Market* Editor Sam Marshall, noting that designers are the most reliable consultants on these trends. "There's nothing worse for a book, especially a self-published book, than to look like it's 10 to 20 years behind the times."

With an hour or two of intensive advice, you can learn current design trends, avoid amateurish mistakes, and get tips on how to add good variety and composition to your pages and photos. You can pass along this advice to your photographers—whether that photographer is a friend or professional. The advice from a $45 to $90 per hour consultation could be of lifelong value to any publication you produce.

The ask-a-friend option to acquiring photos has both benefits and drawbacks. You know the trade-offs here. Of course, if you're getting amateur photos for an affordable price, you're getting exactly what you pay for. A stock photo agency then becomes your best option.

"What is making stock photography so important to many buyers is that it is less expensive and time-consuming than hiring a photographer or trying to find a photographer who has the exact image because the stock agency acts as a clearinghouse," says Marshall.

The stock agency provides one-stop shopping for you as the newsletter publisher or book self-publisher who might need a variety of photos. The agencies can range from a one-person operation to firms that represent 50 to 150 photographers. At small agencies, you might get more personal attention, quicker service and a lower price. But you might not have the more comprehensive selection of a large agency to draw upon.

Photographer's Market lists some 175 stock agencies—from the perspective of the agency which acquires images from photographers—but it will show you the variety of stock agencies.

The Picture Agency Council of America (4203 Locust St., Philadelphia

PA 19104, (215)386-6300) is an excellent way to locate stock agencies and be assured of their reliability. The council's member agencies have signed a Code of Ethics to ensure fair business practices in dealing with photographers, clients and other agencies. PACA members agree to keep adequate records of each image's sales history, to avoid bribery and deceptive advertising, to honor all client confidentiality requests, and to protect photographers' copyrights.

Photo researchers will ask numerous questions when you call a stock agency. Your answers will help them determine what types of photos you need and how you will use them. Consider and decide what you want before inquiring about a stock agency's images: Horizontal or vertical? Color or black-and-white? People in the photos (and of what age, gender and ethnic background)? Do you need space in the photo where you will superimpose words? Also be open to suggestions. "Remember: your stock agency is a partner in the creative process," says the *Guide to the Best in the Midwest Stock Resources*, compiled by 13 stock photo agencies to showcase their services.

All stock agencies want to know whether an image will be used on a cover or in inside pages, whether it will be quarter, half or full page, and whether you're using it in advertisement or editorial space. The press run and circulation of your newsletter or book are other crucial questions upon which agencies determine their fees.

A photo can cost $110 to $165 or more for a quarter page depending on how many you buy. A full-page photo can cost $225 to $300 — or several times that amount. The photographer will usually get 40 to 50% of the amount (before taxes, marketing and other fees) with the other half going to the agency.

Some agencies will charge you a research fee of $65 to $125 or waive that fee when images are leased. There might also be a holding fee if you keep the images from 30 to 90 days without leasing or buying them. Find out specifically the policies of the agency you plan to work with. Also inquire about an agency's specialties and select one that has a substantial collection of images in your field. For instance, Geoscience Features Picture Library (6 Orchard Dr., WYE, Nr. Ashford, Kent TN25 5AU U.K.) specializes in earth science and natural history images. Historical Pictures Service, Inc. (921 W. Van Buren, Suite 201, Chicago IL 60607, (312)346-0599) offers an estimated 3 million vintage images.

"Know what you want or have a good idea before you call, and don't go on a fishing expedition," recommends John Patsch, co-owner of Journalism Services, Inc. "And allow some time."

Involving a stock agency at the outset of the project gives researchers more time to locate specific images you need. Some agencies will also arrange for photos to be shot if none fits your project. With extra time, you can use both approaches, acquiring some photos from a stock agency and assigning others to a photographer of your choice.

When hiring the services of a photographer, look first in your city. Scan the Yellow Pages' section on photographers and check area publications for photo bylines. Local editors', photographers' and art directors' clubs will usually recommend photographers. Directories published by photography organizations are excellent sources, although the self-publisher on a budget might not be able to afford the services of higher-priced professionals.

The American Society of Picture Professionals (%Comstock, 30 Irving Pl., New York NY 10003) for instance, issues a membership directory every two years that provides information about each member and is cross-referenced by region and company names.

When you call a photographer, one of his or her first concerns is to establish the terms of copyright and usage with you. He will want to know some of the same information that a stock agency does: How will the photos be used? What is the press run and circulation?

To arrive at a price for photos, most photographers will use a three-point formula that includes a basic shooting fee, expenses and usage. A photo for a nationally distributed book with long-term shelf life will cost you more than one for a local newsletter. Overall, photographers are selling a product and a service in addition to a one-of-a-kind image that can be marketed over and over again.

"Most photographers will want to avoid surrendering the copyright to their image, and people who don't work in the industry on a daily basis assume that when they pay a photographer, they own the picture," says Sam Marshall.

Unless you have purchased exclusive or all rights to a photo and can prove this in writing, you will owe the photographer for any second printing or subsequent uses.

Major magazines will generally go to the extra expense of offering assignments to photographers because they want unique photos precisely tailored to articles. But newsletter publishers and book self-publishers can usually save money by buying onetime rights.

As the publisher of your own magazine, newsletter or book, weigh the advantages and disadvantages of each approach. And if you need photos for a manuscript/photo package to submit to a magazine, you have the additional option of collaborating with the photographer in a fifty-fifty partnership. Then you'll follow many of the guidelines of a writing collaboration and can hammer out an agreement to fit both partners' creative and financial needs.

If you need historic photos for histories or biographies, contact organizations or even families with unique photos in their files. Historical societies, archives, churches, schools and private foundations have varying policies and prices for photos. Your best approach here is to call or write for this information. If you encounter reluctance to share these photos, offer to credit the photographer or organization *and* emphasize how important it is that readers have the chance to see the photos.

The professional photographers' organizations below can provide valuable insight and leads. Some of these groups have local or regional chapters and can provide details on local photographers, workshops and price ranges.

LISTINGS

> **Advertising Photographers of America (APA)**
> *578 Broadway*
> *New York NY 10012*
> *(212)807-0399*

> **American Society of Magazine Photographers (ASMP)**
> *205 Lexington Ave.*
> *New York NY 10016*
> *(212)889-9144*

> **National Press Photographers Association (NPPA)**
> *Suite 306*
> *3200 Cross daile Dr.*
> *Durham NC 27705*
> *(919)383-7246*

THE BUSINESS OF PUBLISHING

For centuries, writers have turned over their manuscripts to somebody else who decided how the words would be arranged on pages and how the pages would be bound. Writers wrote. Typesetters set type. Publishers published. The book's creator had little choice or control.

Today, however, technology has merged these roles, and you have a choice: You can control how your words appear in print. You can now be the writer, typesetter, page designer and publisher, depending on the time and funds that you are willing to invest. You can use desktop publishing as a final pre-press step in producing newsletters and tabloids *or* as a stepping stone to becoming a self-publisher or small-press publisher.

DESKTOP PUBLISHING

Desktop publishing gives you the tools of a publisher in your own work space. With a computer and a variety of accessories that we'll be discussing here, you can design the pages of a book, magazine or newsletter, and design charts, brochures and calendars. With word processing software, you no longer have to pay a printer to typeset your manuscript because you do the typing. With desktop publishing software—and here's where your role really expands—you decide and lay out what text and art will appear on each page. "Art" in this case means any visual element that a publisher uses to enhance your text: titles and chapter headings, charts, drawings, photos and lines that add a unified look to each page.

With these professional capabilities in your office or home, you also have the option of renting desktop time to companies and writers at a cost that is affordable for them and money-making for you. But before hiring out your desktop equipment, you'll have to assume the initial costs—which brings us back to the issue of how and if a desktop system will benefit you as a writer.

It's like buying a car. No one but you can decide what's best for you. Study computer catalogs first, but realize that photos and brief descriptions are only the beginning of your research. Books on desktop publishing, such as Michael Kleper's *The Illustrated Handbook of Desktop Publishing and Typesetting* (TAB Books), enable you to carefully decide which desktop options best suit your needs. Computer magazines frequently discuss the pros and cons of various desktop approaches. And to get specific answers to your questions, talk with people who are using desktop publishing equipment. Most people love to talk and give advice, and you can learn what works and what doesn't.

One misconception about desktop publishing comes from its name. Desktop software can give you the technical power of a publisher, but to actually publish your manuscripts, you have to develop the reputation, know-how and savvy of a publisher.

Desktop publishing provides the pre-press steps of typesetting and layout, and self-publishing takes the desktop-produced pages, has them bound, and then proceeds to market and distribute the book. While desktop publishing software can assist you in producing sales materials and brochures for your book, and in keeping your financial records and mailing lists, self-publishing takes the work from the desktop into the marketplace where your book then competes with other self-published, commercially published and subsidy-published books.

To start at the ground floor of desktop publishing, you need a microcomputer, a word processing software program and/or page layout software program, a printer and training on how to use them.

Consider the degree of proficiency and professionalism you hope to achieve, and then the products and prices. Price, of course, will depend on the decisions you make in the previous areas.

PROFICIENCY

Imagine, for a moment, tubes of paint and the artist's canvas. From them, and the interaction with the artist, they can produce an ineffective muddle or a museum masterpiece, depending on how proficient the artist is in using the materials. The same is true for the computer and TV-like monitor that become the desktop publisher's "canvas."

Used effectively, a desktop system can produce a book or newsletter that looks like one from a top New York publishing house. But the system doesn't have a mind, like you, so it needs to be told what to do. That's why proficiency and training are so important.

Unlike writing, graphics training is not a prerequisite of most high school or college programs; most writers never imagined that they could do their own graphics work or could own typesetting equipment like a publisher.

A proficiency in knowing what goes where in a book and on a page is crucial. Unfortunately, the *ability* to choose what you want on each page does not guarantee that you will make the best choices.

Betty Wright, director of the National Association of Independent Publishers (P.O. Box 850, Moore Haven FL 33471, (813)946-0293) sees 400 to 500 books that small press publishers and self-publishers submit to the group's annual contest. Sometimes a book topic will be a good idea, but the book will be poorly planned or manufactured—for instance, no index or bibliography.

If you resent spending your writing time as an art director and book designer, then desktop publishing will not be your best option. Don't, however, immediately rule out this possibility. The time you spend on the graphics side of the writing business will decrease as you become more efficient with these tools. You'll learn to think like an editor who must envision an entire publication's art and words.

James Ferguson, general manager of Personal Publishing Centres (9402 Towne Square Ave., Cincinnati OH 45242), believes that knowing the graphics side can actually help in the writing of the book.

Writers and companies—with and without desktop capabilities—rent time at his Personal Publishing firm for various stages of the publishing process. At offices such as PPC, you can keyboard your own text at $25 per hour. For $45 per hour, you can do your own page design at one of the PPC workstations.

To avoid graphics that won't enhance your writing, you must learn how to use the sophisticated computer software and how to design an effective publication. Courses on these topics aren't as plentiful as writing classes, but today we're seeing more of them and also one-day workshops on desktop publishing. The costs of training will vary greatly depending on the sponsor and format of the classes. Whether the desktop training is offered at the keyboard or in a meeting room with one computer on display will affect the price.

Workshops can cost as much as $100 to $200 per day or as little as $35 when a nonprofit group offers a workshop for its members. Micro Center, a computer department store in Columbus, Ohio, offers seven-hour courses for $98. The center also holds free two-hour seminars on choosing desktop publishing and word processing software. Word processing and page design instruction at commercial training centers can cost as much as $40 to $60 per hour.

If you already have desktop expertise and credentials to prove it, consider approaching writers' groups and community education programs about teaching such a course. Writers will be grateful, and you can earn $10 to $60 an hour or as much as $350 per day, depending on the sponsoring group's budget. Some desktop publishers will conduct a workshop for a nonprofit group—at little or no stipend—to establish contacts in the city.

Also the excellent step-by-step guides to desktop publishing—both from the computer perspective and from the graphics perspective—provide an inexpensive way to learn desktop publishing.

Proficiency in any field demands a commitment of time and resources. If you don't have them to give now in your career, don't rush into desktop publishing. In this competitive business, a poorly designed document will shortchange the years you've spent learning to write.

As you'll see, the commitment and cost of desktop equipment make it feasible only for people who will use the equipment on a continuing basis.

PROFESSIONALISM

How proficient you are in using the software and in making effective design choices will determine the "professionalism" of your book, magazine or newsletter. No one likes amateur productions. Readers don't know how to design books, but they can spot flaws that mark it as amateur: too many typefaces, no consistent visual "look," or borders around pages of text.

At the *Writer's Market* office several years ago, writers would call to complain about "magazines" that were typewritten, photocopied and obviously produced at the kitchen table. They were sorry that their work had appeared in such a publication. "It looks like a church bulletin," said one writer.

Today, that happens less frequently. As the cost of computer equipment has decreased, individuals and small groups committed to publishing books or newsletters can afford desktop equipment to give their publications a professional look. And desktop users who understand how to use the equipment to the fullest get the best return on this investment.

THE PRODUCTS

Apple Computer, in 1984, made the publishers' domain more accessible to writers by pairing a Macintosh personal computer with PostScript software and the Aldus PageMaker page layout program. Other computer firms have joined the race to attract computer users to their word processing, page design and graphics software.

Most computer specialists recommend that you find the software features you need and then find the microcomputer that will accommodate them. If you have a microcomputer, however, then your primary concern is finding desktop software that is compatible with your current hardware.

"There's really nothing magical going on in this whole process—it's understanding how the software works and what kind of hardware you need to make it work," says MacMillan Graphics owner Gregg MacMillan.

A Macintosh microcomputer with Aldus PageMaker software is generally the best choice if you want page design capabilities with speed, user friendliness and flexibility for newsletters, magazines and sales brochures. Publications ranging from *USA Today* to writers' newsletters use Macintoshes.

IBM-compatible microcomputers can also be used for page design and graphics, and have excellent business applications software that can help you handle the business side of your book, magazine or newsletter. PageMaker can also be purchased for an IBM-compatible system.

If a writer contacts the National Association of Desktop Publishers for advice on book publishing software, executive director David Stein will recommend the Xerox Ventura Publisher, a desktop publishing program created for long documents. Ventura Publisher will work on an IBM-compatible PC with a 20 megabyte hard disk and processing unit.

The popularity of various computers shouldn't be your only criterion for selecting hardware and software, but that factor enables you to find more people who can discuss options and newfound problems.

The National Association of Desktop Publishers, for instance, offers a forum for education and information exchanges through 11 user groups: IBM PC User Group, Apple Macintosh User Group, Aldus Page-Maker User Group, Letraset Ready, Set, Go! User Group, Xerox Ventura User Group, Quark XPress User Group, Adobe PostScript User Group, Linotype Linotronic User Group, WordPerfect User Group, Microsoft Word User Group, and the Self-Employed DTP User Group.

You can even join these groups for $40 without becoming a member of NADTP. Members stay in contact electronically through the GEnie On-Line Network, mail and phone. NADTP can also refer you to specialists with a particular software who can provide you with more information.

Consider exploring some of the programs that NADTP members use—Letraset Ready, Set, Go!, Quark XPress, Adobe PostScript, WordPerfect, Microsoft Word and WordStar. Also some page-design programs today, such as PageMaker and Ventura Publisher, contain word processing capabilities that will save the first-time software buyer from having to purchase both word processing and page-design programs.

To adapt your word processing computer to a page layout program, you'll need to purchase some additional hardware: a mouse, a cursor-moving device; expanded random access memory (RAM); a graphics board and a hard disk. For optimum performance you may want a windows program and an accelerator board.

If you're trading your typewriter for a new computer with desktop capabilities, consider the Mac Classic with at least a 40 megabyte hard disk drive. There are numerous microcomputer brands and less expensive clones of the name brands, but with a lower price you sometimes get little technical support and no warranty. Some computer companies offer the option of purchasing a service contract that enables you to make a specified number of calls for step-by-step instruction and troubleshooting. If you have no computer experience, track down the store in your area with a reputation for answering questions and following up on requests. Don't hesitate to ask local writers where they buy their computers and desktop equipment.

Another major decision that you'll have to make is about the printer. You can use an inexpensive dot-matrix or daisy-wheel printer to proof-read your work, but for the final output of your camera-ready copy, you generally need a printing resolution of 300 dots per inch (dpi) up to 2,470 dots per inch. A $2,000 laser printer will give you 300 dpi; the $70,000 Linotronic 300 will give your type 1,270 dots per inch and artwork, 2,470 dpi.

A bottom-of-the-line laser printer is a good investment for a writer because, with 300 dots per inch, you can print camera-ready copy as a self-publisher and also produce attractive query letters.

Plan to spend an estimated $1,300 to $1,500 when you buy a laser printer with a 300 dpi or higher resolution.

As a desktop publisher, you become responsible not only for designing the pages, but also for producing the camera-ready pages which the printing company will work with. "The quality of the original prototype that you create will have a large impact on the ability of the printer to create a quality product," says Clifford Weiss, director of publications for the Printing Industries of America.

To produce a professional prototype and book, most writers will pay service bureaus $3 to $15 per page to output camera-ready pages. That approach saves you from purchasing the $20,000 to $70,000 phototype-setting equipment that publishers can afford. The other option is to use 300 dpi page or even daisy-wheel-produced copy. The output won't look like pages of a commercially published book, but you'll have saved an estimated $300 or more.

PRICES

What desktop publishing will cost you depends on what equipment and capabilities you need. And with each capability that you add to your desktop repertoire, you'll incur additional costs. For instance, if you want to turn your black-and-white newsletter into a color magazine, you'll need software designed for color and a color monitor. For some computers that can be an expensive change; for others the conversion is not possible.

Purchase of a desktop publishing system costs an estimated minimum of $3,300. That would include an IBM-compatible computer or a Mac Classic, $300 for word processing and page design software, and $1,500 for a printer.

If you don't want to invest in desktop equipment now, you can continue to watch for new developments in the field and more affordable prices.

"What people are going to see is that things are going to get less expensive—with more competition—less expensive at service bureaus, less expensive to buy software and hardware ... and [you'll see] better resolution from printers and probably see a time when service bureaus are needed less and less [for self-publishers' documents]," predicts Stein.

ASSOCIATIONS

Association of Desktop Publishers
P.O. Box 881667
San Diego CA 92168-1667
(619)428-4285

National Association of Desktop Publishers
1260 Boylston St.
Boston MA 02215
(617)426-2885

SELF-PUBLISHING

When you have mastered the craft of desktop publishing, you have the ability to more effectively self-publish books, newsletters and magazines. Writers have always been able to self-publish by hiring a printer or operating a small printing press in the basement, but the finished product usually lacked the polish of a commercially published book. Today you can control many of the pre-press steps and ensure a professional product.

If you've decided not to invest in desktop publishing equipment, however, you still can self-publish your work. You just contract for each of the pre-press services: typesetting, page design, layout and cover design.

The most difficult part of self-publishing, though, is the "publishing," not the printing of the book. Printers are accustomed to following specifications, and your book will have the qualities—dimensions, paper, ink, binding—that you specify in the contract.

When you take your book into the marketplace, however, there will be little predictability. Advertising, marketing, distribution (through bookstores and/or direct mail), and travel expenses for you can yield good or disappointing results, but in either case will cost you time and money.

Despite the drawbacks of self-publishing, most writers venture into this hands-on approach because established publishing routes have said "no" or didn't offer enough flexibility. *Huckleberry Finn, What Color Is Your Parachute?, Ulysses* (James Joyce's version), and *The Elements of Style* began their literary lives as self-published books.

You might have an excellent book that caters to a narrow market, causing a commercial publisher to doubt its salability. Or you might want to earn more than the standard 6 to 15% royalty and retain more control over the editorial or visual content of the book. Fulfilling the dream of seeing your writing bound between a bright cover or professional advancement are other reasons writers are self-publishing.

The economics of publishing and self-publishing can be discouraging, though, no matter which avenue you choose and how much money you have.

A New York publishing house invests thousands of dollars per book and thus carefully selects books, usually with a focus on each book's marketing potential. Commercial publishers generally want a book to retail for about eight or nine times the first-run production costs.

"The reason that the publisher gets to make all of those decisions and be nasty about what the title is going to be and what the cover looks like and even the rewrites is because he's footing the bill," says Mary Bold, publisher of Bold Productions. "It boils down to who's putting out the money."

Bold, also the author of *The Decision to Publish*, turned her interest in producing newsletters into a small press that bears her name and uses desktop publishing to produce books and newsletters. She budgets $5,000 to $10,000 per book and has a seven-title book list.

While she has survived many of the self-publishing hurdles, she sees writers who aren't so lucky. Conducting seminars on self-publishing and desktop publishing, Bold sometimes sees participants' poorly printed books that do not conform to book buyers' standards. Another major stumbling block is approaching distributors.

Writer's Digest Books Editor Nan Dibble agrees. "The bottom line is always distribution; that is the hard part," she says. "If you cannot reach your potential readers with even the news that your publication exists, then you have to have a large basement and be prepared to have it filled for a long time."

To give you an overview of self-publishing, we've divided the process into eight stages. Of course, each stage demands a series of carefully researched steps. You'll need to invest a minimum of $3,000 to $4,000 (not counting desktop equipment) or more if you spend money on desktop equipment, color photos, hardcover binding, magazine ads, etc. Some of these stages, although not specifically geared to self-publishers, are also included in Chapter 5.)

THE DECISION TO SELF-PUBLISH

Unless you have definite reasons for wanting to avoid commercial publishers, consider sending your book manuscript to publishers. With this approach, your book gets published without you having to invest thousands of dollars. *Writer's Market*, *The Writer's Handbook* and *Literary Market Place* list publishers; *Writer's Market* and *The Writer's Hand-*

book detail the submission policies and the types of books each publisher specializes in.

A commercial publisher assumes all steps of the publishing process for the right to collect 85 to 94% of the revenues. You can continue doing what you do best: writing.

When you decide to self-publish, you assume not only the writing/editing responsibilities but also the business concerns. You are responsible for the bills, no matter how few books you sell.

Give your manuscript and your writing the benefit of one to two years of circulation among publishers. Attend writers' conferences where book editors are speaking, and investigate small and regional presses, and even self-publishing co-operatives.

If these contacts don't lead to a book contract, ask yourself: How is my book different from and better than those already on the market? How does my book contribute to the knowledge of readers? (You wouldn't want to invest thousands of dollars in a book with a flooded market or in a treatise that demands extensive revisions to make it marketable.) Finally, is the book worth publishing?

If your answer is yes, then self-publishing will be your best alternative. Self-publishing works best when you've written a nonfiction book geared to a specific audience. This option gives you targeted mailing lists and specialized outlets (conferences and newsletters, for instance) for your book. A mainstream novel or book of poetry, on the other hand, would be bought by a general audience—with resulting expensive mass-market mailings. These books are not good candidates for self-publishing.

YOUR BOOK PROPOSAL AND MARKETING PLAN

When you've decided to self-publish a book, you need a detailed book proposal and marketing plan to steer your efforts. It's easy in the busy-ness of producing a book to delay the more distant steps, such as applying for an ISBN code and contacting book distributors, that will be vital to the sales of your book.

"Ninety percent of the promotion of a book should take place before printed copies exist," recommends Richard Morris, executive director of COSMEP, the International Association of Independent Publishers.

You'll need to work simultaneously at several self-publishing stages and to tackle the marketing and distribution while still making editorial decisions.

Marilyn and Tom Ross's *The Complete Guide to Self-Publishing* (Writer's Digest Books) includes an excellent "Publishing Timetable" to show you what to do and when. Likewise, publisher and author Dan

Poynter provides "Your Book's Calendar" in *The Self-Publishing Manual*.

EDITING YOUR BOOK

No matter how well you write, your book will benefit from the careful reading by an editor—both content editing and copyediting. This person can bring an objectivity to your manuscript that you can't. A good editor can spot inconsistencies, inaccuracies and grammatical problems. For instance, author Jim DeBrosse, in his novel *The Serpentine Wall*, implied that Dave Parker was a Cincinnati Reds player; the copyeditor at St. Martin's Press recalled that Parker was a Pittsburgh Pirate at the time in the novel. You need this kind of editorial watchdog that self-publishing does not provide.

As we mentioned earlier in this section, you can hire an editor on a per-project basis. This will increase the cost of your book, but it will also ensure that the contents within your expensive covers maintain a consistently professional quality.

As more and more writers self-publish their books, it is easier to find someone who also needs an editor. By joining writers' groups and associations devoted to desktop publishing and self-publishing, you increase your chances of meeting someone who might serve as your editor. Of course, such an arrangement should be carefully approached. Does the person have a knowledge of your book's topic—to be able to spot inaccuracies? Will the person be able to assess the book's organizational and grammatical problems? Will your partner be available to edit your book to fit your publishing schedule, and vice versa?

If you choose this more cost-effective reciprocal approach, though, be sure you and your partner thoroughly discuss the demands of editing one another's books. One book could be 160 pages; another could be 600 pages. Prepare and sign a letter of agreement, stating what services you will receive and provide, to ensure that you and your partner will be compensated by one another's editing services.

PAGE AND COVER DESIGN

Page and cover design, if used effectively, can enhance your book in several ways: providing visual clues to each page's content, directing the reader's attention to important elements, and creating a tone or atmosphere compatible with the words. That process is crucial on each cover and page.

As a writer, you know the importance of a tantalizing first page to snag the reader's interest. This obsession with hooking the reader—when you become the publisher—begins with the cover. To compete with commercially published books, your book needs a professional cover. Most writers believe, you can't judge a book by its cover, but professional and consumer book buyers do this every day. Glancing at the cover and title, they'll decide whether to read the back cover or flap copy.

The cover protects and sells your book; it is one area of book production that you don't want to skimp on. A graphic designer will charge from $300 to $3,500 for a cover design, but you'll have a professional "marquee." The cover's artwork can also be used in your book's promotional materials and catalog, assuming you have negotiated this use with your illustrator/designer.

Book covers may use a photograph or an illustration, coupled with the title typography, or may include only title typography. A trained designer can advise you on which approach will produce the effect you want. For instance, how-to and business books look fine with type-dominated covers but a coffee-table book, cookbook or visually oriented topic would be best packaged with artwork and type on the front cover.

Your book's page layout can be done entirely on the computer or done with a combination of computer typeset copy and pasteup. But first (and preferably before the editing stage), you need to select your book's design. What typeface will you use for chapter headings and the text? Will you use upstyle (all words of a heading using capital letters) or downstyle (only the first word and proper nouns being capitalized in a heading)? Will headings be centered or flush left (aligned with the left margin)? Will you justify the right margin or have a ragged right margin? A quick scan of the books on your shelves will show you a variety of approaches.

Most importantly, follow a standard book format rather than guessing what belongs on what page, especially for the introductory material. Books such as *The Complete Guide to Self-Publishing* and *The Self-Publishing Manual* give you step-by-step advice on format.

MANUFACTURING AND PRINTING

Another important decision that you'll make as a self-publisher is who will print your book. For some self-publishers, the choice is easy—they are adamant about a book manufacturer rather than a printer. Other self-publishers of chapbooks, short-run books or academic manuals take them to quick printers in their neighborhood. And another option is the commercial printer who uses metal plates to print large print runs and has the capability to produce books with spines (the flat narrow strip between the front and back covers).

Marilyn and Tom Ross recommend that self-publishers work with a book manufacturer. Because book manufacturers specialize in books, they have the know-how and equipment to best accommodate your print run. For instance, a manufacturer with a Cameron Belt Press or Compu-prep can save you about 20% on your printing bill.

John Kremer's *Directory of Book, Catalog, and Magazine Printers* and *Directory of Book Printers* will help you in your search for a printer as will *Getting It Printed*, by Mark Beach, Steve Shepro, and Ken Russon. *Literary Market Place* lists book manufacturers and finishers.

To get printing bids and quotes, you'll need to develop a specifications sheet for your book. The prices will vary greatly. When Mary Bold sent 28 spec sheets to printers, she found that some bids were six times higher than others. Don't assume that your neighborhood quick printer will provide the best service, quality and price. Sending spec sheets is the self-publisher's way of shopping around. Sometimes a printer 1,000 miles away can offer a better price, even when you add several hundred dollars' worth of shipping charges. Ask printers and book manufacturers for a list of recent customers and books they have produced. And before signing a contract with an out-of-town firm, check with the Better Business Bureau in that area.

One of the most difficult questions at this stage is how many books to print. You can get significant volume discounts for larger print runs which will lower your per-unit cost, but don't let this "bargain" prompt you to order more books than you can distribute. Unless you've received pre-press orders on books or have a ready market for your books, order from 1,000 to 2,000 books. "Nine times out of 10, you've got the wrong title, the wrong cover, or the book is missing something," says author and publisher John Kremer. "If you've only printed a few copies, you can make a change more quickly. You don't have to live with your mistake for 10,000 copies."

Kremer, also the chairman of the Mid-America Publishers Association, recommends a 1,000-book print run for first-time publishers. That will leave you with a smaller printing bill and more money for marketing.

As your sales and publishing savvy increase, you can usually schedule a second printing in three to five weeks.

PAMPERING YOUR BOOK
(PROMOTION/ADVERTISING/MARKETING/PUBLICITY)

Advertising in *Publishers Weekly* and book trade magazines is the most efficient way to reach reviewers and book buyers, but also the most expensive and not practical for the first-time self-publisher. A full-page black-and-white ad in *Publishers Weekly* costs more than $3,000. A sixth-of-a-page ad costs more than $1,000. Even commercial publishers struggle to keep down advertising costs.

There are cost-effective ways, though, to get attention for your book — if you're willing to research your book's specific market and actively promote the book. For instance, three-line classified ad rates in trade journals and newsletters can start at $5 per insertion.

News releases alert print and broadcast editors to your book. They might not use your 400-word release word for word, but it can provide background information upon which the medium will prepare its story. If you can find an angle, or reason, that makes the release of your book extremely important for the audience of a publication or station, you'll be on your way to this free form of advertising. For instance, the human interest story of 88-year-old Helen Hooven Santmyer and her novel, *And Ladies of the Club* got nationwide media attention; print and broadcast editors were touched when the Book-of-the-Month Club unanimously voted to include this unknown author's book as a main selection.

Numerous marketing/advertising outlets exist. One-thousand and one, if you ask John Kremer, author of *1001 Ways to Market Your Books*. Books like this and *Marketing Your Books*, by Marilyn and Tom Ross, show you step by step how to do your own marketing.

You also have the more expensive option of hiring a marketing consultant with book publishing credentials. Marilyn and Tom Ross's book consulting firm, About Books, charges a onetime launch fee of $1,800 to $3,400 for developing a custom marketing plan and promotional materials for the book's specific audience, and for contacting distributors and wholesalers.

You can locate marketing professionals in *Literary Market Place* and the *Book Publishing Resource Guide*. A specialist with a track record in your type of publication is your best investment if you don't want to do your own marketing.

Because promotion and distribution are ongoing problems for publishers, numerous books have been written on the subject, and publishers' trade associations frequently address these problems in their newsletters and conferences.

Membership in trade associations places you in the company (and pipeline) of publishers. COSMEP, for instance, exhibits members' publications at the annual conventions of the American Booksellers Association and the American Library Association in addition to holding its own conference on publishing topics. For a $50 annual membership fee, you receive a monthly newsletter with advice and leads for publishers with a noticeable slant toward marketing information.

The American Booksellers Association, the Publishers Marketing Association, the National Association of Independent Publishers, and the Mid-America Publishers Association likewise give members publishing leads, slanted toward an organization's membership. For instance, the American Booksellers Association's more than 6,000 members include small and conglomerate book retailers. The Publishers Marketing Association focuses on marketing.

Regional bookseller and publishers' associations provide additional outlets. The *Book Publishing Resource Guide* can help you find associations in your state, such as the Book Publicists of Southern California or the New York Regional Booksellers Association.

Marketing approaches can range from interviews on radio talk shows to point-of-purchase sales displays in bookstores. You can even start your own small advertising agency to receive advertising discounts. Before trying any of these approaches, however, learn more about them from books, seminars and industry professionals. Some have disadvantages such as printing a Christmas catalog for a specific year (the unused material could not be merged with other sales promotions).

Not starting to market a book early enough can be a major problem for self-publishers. Marketing review copies need to be sent four to five months before a book's publication date.

DISTRIBUTION

The distribution stage is where most self-publishers fail. A book, magazine or newsletter might be excellent in content and form, but if you can't get it into readers' hands, your efforts in the preceding steps will have been wasted. Also, the momentum and scope of your promotions will lay the groundwork for the type of distribution you will use.

You can approach major bookstore chains, but do so with prepared sales materials, and plan frequent mail and phone follow-ups. Some of the large bookstore chains include Barnes and Noble, Bookland, Crown Books, B. Dalton Bookseller, Doubleday Book Shops, Follett College Stores and Waldenbooks Company, Inc.

If you are fortunate enough to sell most of your print run to a major chain, though, remember that the stores can return the books if they aren't selling and request a refund. For this reason, don't immediately consider those books sold and order a second printing. You can generally get a book manufactured in three to five weeks, so don't risk having unsold first- *and* second-run books.

"Getting a book in a bookstore is not selling a book; a book is not sold until a customer buys the book from the store and does not return it," says COSMEP's executive director.

Independent non-chain stores provide an excellent outlet for self-publishers. Their buyers don't have to abide by corporate rules, and they can be more receptive to local authors and the reading habits of their customers. One of the most efficient ways to get your books into stores and libraries is through distributors and wholesalers. But you have to contact wholesalers and distributors at least six months before the publication date.

With a distributor, you would sell your books on its consignment basis and receive payment 90 days after the sale. Wholesalers will buy your books outright. Realizing that you can't call on every book buyer in person, most self-publishers must use these approaches. Distributors that cater to various markets—bookstores, libraries, schools, religious market, etc.—increase your chance of getting books into readers' hands.

One surprise to new self-publishers is that distributors and wholesalers will not pay the cover price for books. Many expect discounts as large as 40 to 50%.

Direct mail provides an excellent approach to marketing self-published books. Readers, in response to ads or publicity, send a check and fee for postage and handling, and you ship the book. To help you figure every cost and what percentage of response you need based on your selling price, *Mail Order Selling Made Easier* includes a break-even work sheet.

Your best approach is to use a combination of distribution methods to reach professional and consumer book buyers.

Another cost-effective way of self-publishing your book is to produce and distribute copies as you receive the orders. By photocopying the laser-printed page prototypes and then binding the printed pages in response to several orders, you can avoid printing too many copies. This option, though, will only work with mail-order distribution to periodic demands, say, when you address an audience that might afterwards want to purchase your chapbook or manual.

Nan Dibble did this with her *Acquainted with the Night Series* (a fanzine of fiction with characters from the TV series "Beauty and the Beast"). Her first print run was 500, but as fans of "Beauty and the Beast" see her one-inch $5 ads in fanzines and order a copy, she'll be able to print the 200-page 'zine as needed. This practice will also work with poetry chapbooks, scholarly monographs, cookbooks, or any type of book that does not demand a factory-bound cover.

WRITING AND ACQUIRING OTHER BOOKS

When you have found your readers and niche in the marketplace, there is no reason to stop with one book. And if you've been publishing a magazine or newsletter, it might be time to spin off a book on the same nonfiction topic. If your books have inspired readers to refine their art or archery skills, or their awareness of people or the stock market, they will want *more*. You can then write similar books or find authors whose books will enhance your list.

At some point, though, decide if you wish to work mainly as a publisher or author. You can do both, but writing another book when you should be writing news releases can water down your talents for both crafts. Decide which areas you are best at and consider hiring part-time employees to handle day-to-day tasks such as shipping book orders and answering the phone.

Self-publishing a book (and establishing a sales track record) sometimes gives that book a better chance of being sold to a commercial publisher, thus enabling you to turn over your publishing responsibilities to a publisher while you continue writing.

If you want to turn your self-published book into the cornerstone for a small press, you'll need to acquire additional books (written by you or other authors). By compiling a book catalog, you can simultaneously "sell" all of the titles when readers inquire about a book. Small press experts estimate that a small publisher needs a minimum list of four books to maximize the costs of operation.

Distributors and wholesalers will be more receptive to a self-published book if you have a line of books. That way, if they must return a book that isn't selling, you can offer them a credit toward another book from your list. Wholesalers are often afraid that the self-publisher won't have the available cash to make the refund.

As you progress from one stage to another, you'll be learning new tricks for future publications—whether you continue self-publishing, writing or combining both crafts.

PRINTERS AND TYPESETTERS

Unless you're accustomed to working with printers and typesetters (the human kind), you'll be sailing into uncharted waters and into the printer's triangle. Quality, service and price comprise the triangle.

Printers attempt to offer quality, service and a good price to customers, but when you want, say, high quality and fast turnaround time, then the price will increase. If you want to decrease the price part of the triangle, quality and service will suffer. "You can usually get two of these three things," says MacMillan Graphics owner Gregg MacMillan. "Which two of these three are most important?"

Only you can answer that question, but in the competitive marketplace, you'll want to carefully weigh the quality of the printing that you're buying. Paper texture, weight and durability will affect the life and appearance of your book, magazine or newsletter.

Thumb through several books on your shelves. Compare the feel of each book's pages. When you find several paper types that you like, use these samples to show a printer what you want. He can then advise you on the advantages and disadvantages of various paper stocks, and price.

"Make sure when you come in for your initial meeting that you have a good idea of how you want the concept in your mind translated to paper," says Minuteman Press Vice President Edward Breyer Ryder IV. "That saves your time and saves the printer's time."

Also you need to decide whether a quick printer or commercial printer, or combination will best cater to your publication. That will generally depend on the type of book you plan to produce. For example, many quick printers can print and bind a softcover spiral-bound manual but do not have the facilities to produce a clothbound book with a spine even though they could print the pages. You would need to ask the print shop if such a service were available or could be subcontracted.

One of the major differences between quick printers and commercial printers is the equipment they use. Commercial printers produce a metal plate which makes possible large print runs, whereas quick printers usually use non-impact printing. You can find both quick printers and commercial printers listed under Printers in the Yellow Pages; bookbinders are listed under the heading Bookbinders.

There are several nationwide chains of quick printers that provide easy access to the printing process. PIP Printing, for instance, has more than 1,100 independently owned outlets in 47 states and 75 outlets in the United Kingdom and Canada. Minuteman Press has more than 1,000 independently owned franchised locations across the United States and in the Canadian provinces of Nova Scotia, Ontario and British Columbia. Kinko's, the Copy Center, has more than 500 locations in the United States and Canada. These companies offer toll-free numbers for customers needing to know the nearest location; however, a quick glance in the Yellow Pages will give you that information. Locally owned printers in your own town can also provide a wide range of services.

Minuteman franchises, (800)645-9840, offer black-and-white and color printing, typesetting, design and layout consultation, and binding services. Between 40 and 50% of the Minuteman outlets offer a desktop service where you can bring your book on disk to be printed on a 1,200 dots per inch printer similar to those used by New York publishers.

"Some of our owners believe desktop can reduce their actual typesetting costs and other owners, a proportionate number, say that it does not yet offer the same degree of sophistication," says Ryder.

That's why it is so important to talk with printers before you rush into a contract. Find out what services each outlet offers and then decide which one can best meet your book's needs.

That is also true for PIP Printing, (800)421-4634, where 662 outlets offer desktop publishing services. With PIP's LookSmart Desktop Publishing program, you can bring your typed book or newsletter on disk, or the outlet can provide typesetting for you. Prices will vary from market to market, depending on the services you require, but generally the desktop rate ranges from $50 to $60 per hour.

Kinko's Copy Centers, (800)933-COPY, have early morning and late night hours, are open on weekends, and many of the outlets are open 24 hours a day, seven days a week.

Your costs will vary depending on what services you need from a printer and what each outlet charges. For example, at Kinko's Garden Street location in Ventura, California, word processing costs $12 per page. To have 1,200-1,800 dpi prints made will cost $9.95 per page, and $7.95 for each additional page.

Your working relationship with a printer can begin at various stages depending on how much of the work you have already completed. Some printers will even accept handwritten material, but you can decrease your printing costs by providing typed material or, better yet, material on a disk.

Find out how much extra a printer will charge you for typing from a handwritten manuscript. You'll usually find that it will be more cost-effective to have your manuscript typed before you approach the printer, preferably on an IBM-compatible or Macintosh disk.

Even the most inexpensive IBM-compatible or Macintosh-compatible word processor will save you significant typesetting charges. And if you plan to write on a long-term basis, the word processing capabilities alone will pay for themselves. For each extra step that a printer must complete, there will be a charge.

A nationwide average shows that typesetting and printing of a camera-ready page will cost about $28 per page whereas the cost of outputting a camera-ready copy of your typed document is $6 per page.

Whether you or a hired typesetter type your book, make sure that there is only one space between each sentence. Two spaces between a sentence — which typists included in the pre-computer days — will appear as gaping holes in your typeset galleys. Also decide if you want a line space between each paragraph. Two touches of the return button will leave a line of white space between paragraphs. If a book page designer must delete these spaces, you'll have to pay for this avoidable step.

If you are compiling a directory for your writers' group, remember that the group's database of members can be flowed into a page design program, such as PageMaker, without retyping the names and specialties. "It's not only time-saving, but it's more accurate," said MacMillan, who did that for a chamber of commerce directory.

Quick printers are an excellent outlet for writers who need fast short-run printing and in-house binding. Some printers will even store negatives and mechanicals at no charge. Again, you'll want to compare stores in your area for the one that best fits your schedule.

PIP Printing estimates that 1,000 copies of a two-color self-covered (80-pound paper cover) book of 50 pages would cost $2,026.05 or $2.03 per copy. That same book and quantity with 250 pages would cost $7,843.55 or $7.84 per copy. When you order 2,000 copies of the book, the per-unit cost decreases to $1.64 for a 50-page book and to $5.94 for a 250-page book. Two-thousand copies of the 50-page book would cost an estimated $3,289.60; the 250-page book would cost $11,874.60. Five-thousand copies of the 250-page book would cost an estimated $23,967.75; with double that amount of copies, your printing bill will be more than $44,000. Of course, printing costs vary from company to company and from market to market and depend on the specifications you want. One drawback of quick printers is that they don't print trade books as frequently as book manufacturers or commercial printers. Most quick printers do not have the facilities to bind a book with a spine, although some will arrange to have the bindery work done elsewhere.

To get a list of book manufacturers and printers, consult *Literary Market Place*, the *Directory of Book, Catalog, and Magazine Printers* and the *Directory of Book Printers* (Ad-Lib Publications).

Because printing/manufacturing costs can be two to six times different in price, you'll want to get estimates from numerous firms. Next, request a price quote from two to three vendors whose prices and policies seem to best fit your project.

There are numerous ways that a printer/manufacturer can save you time and money. Delta Lithograph Co., a book manufacturer in Valencia, California, shares this advice with self-publishers in two brochures, *21*

Ways to Save Money on Your Next Publication and *12 Ways to Improve the Turnaround of Your Next Publishing Project.* The staff there is friendly; they follow up on requests and will send you the brochures if you call (800)323-3582 or (800)223-1478 in California.

To give you a general idea of book manufacturing costs, Delta inside sales representative Ara Norwood estimated that an 8½×11, 320-page hardcover book will cost an estimated $7.62 per book for 2,000 copies.

A 96-page (5½×8½ inch) trade book with a four-color cover and perfect binding would cost $1.90 per book for 2,000 copies. That same book would cost an estimated $1.03 per book when 5,000 copies are printed.

If you provide page negatives stripped to Delta's specifications, the manufacturing would cost $1.56 per book for 2,000 copies or 89¢ per book for 5,000 copies.

Two thousand copies of a 192-page trade book would cost $3.73 per unit if you provide the camera-ready pages. With page negatives that fit Delta's specs, the price drops to $3 per unit.

Most self-publishers produce pages on their laser printers or pay a service bureau to produce resin-coated pages. A printer then will produce negatives of those pages which in turn will produce the printing plates. You can save the $3 to $15 per page cost of resin-coated pages by requesting that your service bureau produce negatives. This is a frequent approach for advertising agencies and graphic designers, but rare among self-publishers.

If you try this approach, however, make sure that your service bureau and printer compare specifications for the pages and negatives. Reshooting or restripping the negatives could be more expensive than resin-coated pages.

Carefully investigate and compare printers. Their work will make your work look more professional or brand it as an amateur product. Also realize that if you cut costs on paper, ink or binding, your printer is not at fault. "In the printing industry, the final quality that you get is the result of what you want to put into, what you need out of it, what your readers expect, what your readers will demand, and what you *perceive* your readers to demand," points out Clifford Weiss, director of publications for the Printing Industries of America.

One problem that self-publishers often encounter is the lack of clout with printers. Printers will sometimes delay the work on a onetime book project to accommodate regular customers or print brokers representing self-publishers. Build in extra time in your publishing schedule to allow for possible printing delays.

Overruns by printers can also alter your careful plans — and budget — depending on the company's overrun policy. Most printers cannot guarantee an exact number of books and impose on you a 5 to 10% overrun range. You will be billed for extra books (within the company's specified range) or receive a credit for the books not printed. This is a standard practice among printers; allow for a higher printing bill or fewer books within the range.

Whether you contract with a quick printer, commercial printer or book manufacturer, consider that firm a partner in your creative process. The printer gets to do the final polish, and then your book or newsletter is ready. Finally. Now you can really pamper your project: Promote, advertise, market, and enjoy what you've worked so hard to accomplish.

LISTINGS

Kinko's Service Corp.
255 W. Stanley Ave.
P.O. Box 8000
Ventura CA 93003-8000
(800)933-COPY

Minuteman Press International Inc.
1640 New Highway
Farmingdale, NY 11735
(800)645-9840; New York residents, (516)249-1370

PIP Printing
27001 Agoura Road
P.O. Box 3007
Agoura Hills CA 91376
(800)421-4634

Chapter 5

SELLING IT

NEWSPAPERS

THE DAILIES

Newspapers use freelance writers to a greater or lesser degree depending on the size, budget, locale and preference of the particular newspaper, as well as a host of other factors worth investigating on a case-by-case basis. Unlike magazines, just about every city has a newspaper—sometimes more than one—and they usually look for local writers if they need to supplement their staffs, so it's wise to focus close to home in making inquiries. (Sunday newspaper magazines may be the exception to this rule; see Weekly Magazine Sections later in this chapter.)

To make the initial contact, target the editor of a particular section. Newspapers usually assign their editors to different "beats"; at smaller papers, one editor may cover several beats, but they still are charged with writing, assigning or gathering the material for those areas—entertainment, business, science, health, and so on. Newspapers divide these sections up in the manner that works best for them. You can find a list of newspapers according to geographic location in the *Gale Directory of Publications* (see Daily Newspaper Listings at the end of this section).

Query the section editor by phone or by letter. At larger newspapers it's less likely an editor will want to talk extensively on the phone, but you can at least introduce yourself. If you freelance for other markets in the area and can drop the name of a colleague or mutual acquaintance, so much the better. With this call, you are basically inquiring about the editor's need or interest in using freelance in general. You can offer to follow up with a letter detailing your credentials and perhaps suggesting some story ideas—unless the editor asks you to elaborate on the spot. The editor is more likely to be interested in your writing credentials than your story ideas, so be prepared to supplement your interest with evidence of previous writing credentials. Clips from other newspapers or those on similar topics will carry the most weight.

If you can't get initial telephone time, don't pursue it. Begin with a query letter that includes your credentials and references—a few clips are a big plus—and perhaps a story idea if it's something that you are in a unique position to write about.

All things being equal, an editor would rather assign a story to a writer he knows, if not someone on staff. Newspaper editors tend to keep fairly tight editorial reign on the ideas that form the content of the newspaper. They're not as hungry for ideas as they are for reliable and talented journalists who will come through when they're in a time or staff crunch. So concentrate more on making initial contact and on proving your reliability than on inundating section editors with endless story ideas. That's not to say that once you're in your ideas won't be appreciated—they will, and may even be used—but to think that you will break into the market on a story idea alone is probably a waste of time and energy.

John Lux, associate features editor at the *Chicago Tribune*, describes his dealings with freelancers—and what he says is true for many papers in cities of Chicago's size, or even those a little smaller:

"There's no central clearinghouse for freelance writers or story ideas, which is where a lot of freelancers go wrong; they will write a general query to a 'features editor' of the *Tribune*—which tells us right off the bat that they have no idea how the *Tribune* works and they've never even read the paper. These letters usually end up in the trash can . . .

"How the *Tribune* and how almost every other major paper works is that individual editors edit feature sections, and you have to tailor a query to the individual editor. It's a big waste of time to paper the country writing query letters to various papers that you haven't even read."

The *Chicago Tribune* has 17 feature sections and the majority of the freelancers are doing local reporting because, as Lux points out, "We are a regional paper, rather than a national paper." Like other papers, editors do not encourage unsolicited manuscripts but will respond to queries fairly quickly. "The shorter, the better—and the writing counts," Lux says.

On smaller papers such as the Louisville *Courier Journal*, a local writer might have a better shot at making personal contact with an editor because networking is always easier in a medium to small city.

"We publish freelance stories with some regularity," says Features Editor Greg Johnson. Writers who live in the area come in and describe what they're interested in, he says, usually bringing samples of their work. (It's always wise to call before going in to see an editor, so you can schedule a time that won't interfere with deadlines.) Though Johnson rarely will give a definite assignment to a first-time freelancer, he often looks at stories on speculation.

When an editor promises to look at a story on speculation, you've succeeded in arousing some degree of interest. The editor can't make any promises but can at least assure you of a fair read, and you have a better than even shot at getting published. After one or two on-spec successes, you're more likely to get called with an assignment the next time.

An on-spec assignment is definitely a step in a positive direction, though it still requires a gamble on your part. It means you are being asked to complete the story without any formal assignment or guarantee that it will be used. This means no kill fee (a percentage of the full fee guaranteed a writer on assignment if the story ends up not being used).

Newspaper editors don't give even on-spec assignments lightly; it means they believe your story—and you—are worth the chance. They just want the odds to be in *their* favor, so if it turns out to be a bad gamble, they haven't lost anything. Of course, for your part, you will have lost both time and money, so you have to decide if the possible payoff of a new client is worth the investment of time on your part.

Johnson has some additional advice for would-be newspaper free-lancers: If you're trying to interest an editor in a freelance feature story, "see what the newspaper is investing a lot of effort in and (therefore) probably wouldn't need your help in"—then see if you can offer them something not likely to be covered by someone on staff.

A few subjects in particular surface as areas in which many newspapers are long on interest level but short on talent. Freelancers are used, if at all, more heavily in travel sections in many papers. In larger cities, opportunities may be more widely available on the entertainment beat. In cities with an active night life even a large newspaper doesn't always have the staff to cover everything going on. As an adjunct to that, home entertainment is a new area editors are interested in exploring, since more and more people are choosing the "couch potato" route over the "paint-the-town-red" avenue. Writers who have some knowledge about the technology and variety of home entertainment products and services are in an area still short of good writers, some editors say. Other specialties include gardening, art and antiques, and food. And the area of health and fitness remains a never-ending source of interest. If you can spot and document a trend early, you're at a distinct advantage.

Once you've made a successful contact for newspaper freelancing, editors will tend to call you repeatedly when the need arises. In the newspaper business, the need for reliability usually outweighs the desire for "new blood." Newspaper feature writing follows a more standard, more established style than magazine writing and must serve a mass audience. For the most part, newspaper editors come up with the ideas—that's what they're hired to do—but if you can write well in appropriate newspaper style, and you prove to be both available and dependable, it's possible to become part of a "stable" of freelance writers the newspaper calls on with some regularity.

That's the good news. The bad news is the pay is not great, so you better be doing this for supplemental income only—or as one freelance outlet among many if you're trying to make a full-time living as a free-lancer. The most you'll be paid for a single article is about $300—$150 to $200 is the norm in most cities, with some assignments such as a record or movie review running in the $25 to $75 range.

Newspapers don't always have the staff they need but development of syndicated services and wire services have led to a decline in the use of freelancers. A wire service is a cooperative news service that has the right to reprint any local news stories or photographs that originate with member papers. Most newspapers are paying members of Associated Press (AP) or clients of United Press International (UPI), the two major such services—but there are many others. What it means in practical terms is that the daily newspaper in your city has access to hundreds of stories every day that are written for other newspapers around the country.

An assistant managing editor at the *Columbus* (OH) *Dispatch*, Shirley McNeely, explains it this way: "When you're already paying for material, and there's so much good material and you know it has already been through editors at the other end, you're saving a lot of time and effort" by selecting material from a wire service.

On the other hand, *Denver Post* Travel Editor Mary Ellen Botter says, "If you use (wire service material) as a steady diet, then you just regurgi-tate what everyone else is doing, and there's no originality, no surprise."

The travel beat can be an exception. Travel stories are widely available to editors through the wire services, but they're not always the stories local papers are looking for. Catherine Watson, travel editor of the *Minne-apolis Star-Tribune*, points out, "Every freelancer ever born wants to write about Paris, but they don't want to write about Wisconsin." Half of her paper's readership travels internationally, and half does not. It's the half that doesn't for whom they seek articles about places to go on a two- or three-day weekend and what to do there.

"It's almost impossible to get good regional travel writing," says Wat-son, "and that's true throughout the Midwest."

So for freelancers living in almost any area of the country between the two coasts, exploring out-of-the-way vacation spots or day trips may be a good way to get a foot in the door of the travel section of your local paper.

At the same time, editors tend to be very careful in assigning travel pieces to freelancers, and even more so in accepting unsolicited travel articles from people whose names are not familiar to them. This area has a large potential for abuse. Some people claim to be travel writers, expecting perks either from a restaurant, hotel or travel agent hoping to lure customers with the expected "free advertising" — or they naively hope that they can get a newspaper to pay them to go somewhere and write about it.

The reality is that few papers have the budgets to send freelance writers on location for a story, and even fewer writers have the resources to take on this kind of expense on their own. Editors are understandably wary that writers who have been treated to a trip will write less than objective articles. Most newspapers, underbudgeted for travel, also must make do with wire stories even when they'd like to expand their regional travel focus.

This is where an enterprising freelance writer can step in. You may be able to submit a travel piece on spec — say you're an avid camper and you submit the definitive piece on off-the-beaten-track campsites in your area. If you can suggest a piece that interests a fair number of the paper's readers and doesn't strain the travel editor's budget, there's a good chance of getting published and paid, perhaps with a modest budget to cover expenses as well.

In any case, the key to successfully freelancing for newspaper dailies in your area involves narrowing your focus. Cultivating a personal relationship with an editor is recommended often by editors at daily newspapers. "Find one editor to get attached to, have a primary relationship, and build on that," says Jim Davis, assistant managing editor/features at the Philadelphia *Inquirer*.

The other piece of advice offered almost as often is "find a speciality." Perhaps better than "find" would be "have" — that is, concentrate on an area you know well. Often an editor will look at a writer's background because most writers freelancing for newspapers are doing other things as well. It may be a full-time job in business or another profession (some people in law and medicine, for example, just like to write and publish) or it may be devotion to an art or volunteer community work. That other interest or field of expertise can easily be the hinge that swings you into an editor's field of vision. A classic example of this would be the drama professor at a local college who freelances reviews of local theater productions, mainly for the free tickets and the satisfaction of publication. If you're a generalist it's going to be difficult to compete for space in the entertainment section with someone in the community who's got the credentials for this particular area. You may be just as able and willing to cover theater, but you're probably going to have more success if you capitalize on your *own* expertise.

This kind of thing—"serendipity publication"—probably happens more often in newspaper writing than any other freelance market. There are many stories of the right people and subject coming together with the right editor at the right time. Sometimes people cross over from another medium (having a radio show or teaching a cooking class that's very popular) or expand another role (say, as a management consultant with a strong reputation in the business community).

You've read about the unofficial expert in thrift shops who "just for fun" or "to try her hand at writing" completes the definitive story on this subject, writes it well, and gets published. The editor thinks of her for another consumer-oriented piece; she completes the assignment on time with a minimum of rewriting necessary. Before too long, she's a regular freelancer for the paper. I don't know if this particular woman exists, but there are stories about people like her. Sometimes, if the writer has a little bit of savvy, some guidance from someone with more experience, or just a healthy dose of ambition, she may end up self-syndicating, especially if she is able to generate several stories on the subject.

If you're good, you *can* be "discovered," or more likely, you can take pains to *get* yourself discovered. It is worth bearing the following caveat in mind while pursuing freelance opportunities in the newspaper business: In some areas—for example, television writing or book publishing—the odds may be long, but the rewards are great. In newspapers, however, there *is* a point of diminishing returns because the monetary rewards are limited. So if you're not having any luck at a particular daily paper, or with newspapers in general, turn your attention elsewhere—there are plenty of other writing opportunities out there.

DAILY NEWSPAPER LISTINGS

Editor & Publisher
11 W. 19th St.
New York NY 10011
(212)675-4380

This publisher of a weekly trade magazine for the newspaper industry also has annual directories of newspapers and syndicates.

Gale Directory of Publications, Volumes I and II
(formerly Ayer Directory)
Gale Research Inc.

Book Tower
Detroit MI 48226

This directory is available in the reference section of most libraries and must remain in the library. Volume I (Catalogue of Publications) supplies information on newspapers, including the name, address and phone number; date of establishment; frequency of publication; printing method; physical description (number of columns per page, column width and depth); circulation, and a few names — generally the publisher and business manager or circulation manager. Volume II (Indexes and Maps) lists the section editors by name and telephone number, cataloged geographically.

Selected national and regional newspapers:

Atlanta Journal-Constitution
72 Marietta St. NW
Atlanta GA 30303
(404)526-5151

The Boston Globe
135 Morrissey Blvd.
Boston MA 02107
(617)929-2000

Chicago Tribune
435 N. Michigan Ave.
Chicago IL 60611
(312)222-3232

Cleveland Plain Dealer
1801 Superior Ave. NE
Cleveland OH 44101
(216)344-4600

Columbus Dispatch
34 S. Third St.
Columbus OH 43216
(614)461-5000

Denver Post
Media News Group
P.O. Box 1709
Denver CO 80201
(303)820-1010

Detroit Free Press
Knight-Ridder, Inc.
321 W. Lafayette Blvd.
Detroit MI 48231
(313)222-6400

Houston Chronicle
801 Texas Ave.
Houston TX 77002
(713)220-7171

Los Angeles Times
Times Mirror Square
Los Angeles CA 90053
(213)237-5000

Miami Herald
One Herald Plaza
Miami FL 33132
(305)350-2111

Minneapolis Star-Tribune
425 Portland Ave.
Minneapolis MN 55488
(612)372-4141

The New York Times
229 W. 43rd St.
New York NY 10036
(212)556-1234

The Philadelphia Inquirer
Philadelphia Newspapers, Inc.
400 North Broad St.
Philadelphia PA 19101
(215)854-2000

Pittsburgh Press
P.O. Box 566
34 Boulevard of the Allies
Pittsburgh PA 15230
(412)263-1100

San Francisco Chronicle
The Chronicle Publishing Company
901 Mission St.

San Francisco CA 94103
(415)777-1111

The Washington Post
1150 15th St. NW
Washington DC 20071
(202)334-6000

WEEKLY MAGAZINE SECTIONS

The caveat that there's not much money in freelancing for daily newspapers does have an exception—but there's also a catch. The exception is the Sunday magazine section which, though technically part of the newspaper editorial hierarchy, is usually run more like an autonomous magazine. The catch is that contributors to those publications are often hustling the magazine freelance market as well as looking to the newspaper for work.

Although the fairly average pay results in some freelance turnover in the dailies, there is more steady competition for the Sunday magazines. The competition can be pretty stiff, too, particularly for the better-quality and better-paying magazines. And even if you do sell a piece, you're not as likely to become a regular as you are on your local daily newspaper.

Magazines in general—and the ones published by newspapers are no exception—tend to vary their writers. They are generally more willing to take a chance on someone they haven't used before—particularly if the writer's credentials and portfolio are solid. This is good if you're the new writer and not so good if you're trying to get steady work. Don't rely on these magazines for steady work—unless it's the magazine published by the newspaper daily you're already writing for. Regard the better-known Sunday newspaper magazines as long shots, something to aim for but not rely on.

The positive side is that these magazines often depend heavily on freelance writing and they are also more likely to open the door to a writer outside their immediate area. And, as mentioned earlier, payments can reach $1,000 to $2,000.

Some of these weekly magazines have an editor-in-chief who is responsible for the content of the magazine and may rely on freelancers almost exclusively. That editor may or may not be the same person who runs the features section of the daily. The magazine has a production schedule similar to a monthly magazine but much tighter because it comes out weekly. The magazine staff usually plans several issues ahead and works on numerous issues simultaneously—each at a different stage in production.

Some of the larger magazines do have staff writers and some may use reporters from the paper, perhaps deciding that a particular story originally slated for a section instead belongs in the magazine.

In evaluating newspapers as a freelance market, here is a useful generalization: At larger national and regional papers opportunities for freelancers are probably best in the various sections. The magazine usually has a staff of writers and when they go outside, they tend to look for "name" people who are accomplished in their fields or are magazine writers with a specific focus. For these papers, contact the individual section editors as discussed before. At smaller papers in smaller and mid-sized cities, freelance opportunities in the daily paper are likely to be more scarce, so you should check out the Sunday magazine; it may rely largely on freelancers.

A third group consists of just two magazines, one or the other of which appears in a good many of the Sunday newspapers across the country: *Parade* and *USA Weekend*. Some newspapers rely on one of these magazines alone to be their Sunday magazine and some include a local publication as well. *Parade* and *USA Weekend*, which consider themselves weekly magazines and not supplements—as they are sometimes referred to—both use freelance writers, are open to writers outside their immediate publication area, and pay top-of-the-line fees to their writers.

Parade's headquarters is in New York, but Managing Editor Larry Smith insists that writers can come from all over the country "because we like those different points of view. We make it a point to look for people without 'contacts,' and we try each year to publish some. Last year we published two or three articles that came in over the transom."

While acknowledging they are very receptive to new writers, Smith admits that "the essence of successful freelancing is contacts." He reiterates the importance of writers becoming familiar with the magazine and recommends that freelancers "try to develop contacts with individual editors at particular magazines."

As important as contacts may sometimes be, "the other key to successful freelancing," says Smith, is still "coming up with good ideas." *Parade*'s audience is the entire country, and so while a subject has to be specific and interest the individual reader, it must at the same time "cover the entire spectrum of the reading audience in America."

Parade is included in 320 newspapers with a total circulation of 33 million. They figure their readership is twice that because, on average, there are two readers for each copy of the magazine.

"When you're writing for that many people," Smith says, "it's not like you're writing for the Sunday newspaper." It's more like writing for a magazine, though even most national magazines have a narrow audience that can be considered a subset of the "American reading public."

If you can sell your idea in a two-paragraph query letter, the reward could be a fee in the $1,000 to $2,500 area as well as probably the largest audience for your writing possible.

When freelancing for these magazines, remember that while your story must have current relevancy, it also must have "a sense of timelessness," because issues are planned several months in advance of publication.

USA Weekend also uses freelancers — about 70% of the magazine is freelance-written. Associate Managing Editor Amy Eisman says they use a lot of writers from Los Angeles because they are heavy on entertainment coverage. Again contacts *are* important and often "one good freelancer suggests another," she says. Local writers in the Washington, D.C. area have an advantage: They are more likely to make the contacts through social events, and they can stop by the office to meet with an editor personally. But Eisman offers some concrete tips for potential contributors: "Write in a magazine style, not a newspaper style," she says. "Look for a high-profile hook on a story; have a sense of humor; be creative and not predictable."

It's also important, she says, for writers to feel comfortable talking with editors on the telephone, to be able to communicate their ideas, and to be willing to take direction and be edited or rewritten to fit the style and tone of the magazine. As Quincy Jones advised his musicians on "We Are the World": Check your egos at the door.

Again, a paradox inherent in writing for mass market publication exists here: While you do need to be distinctive in your style to capture the attention of the editors, you also need to gain access to the widest possible reading audience, which ultimately requires a certain uniformity in style for these publications.

If you can do this, you might make up to $2,500 for a cover story "of broad-based interest to baby boomers."

Eisman says "good credentials and good clips" are key here. For all the difference between these two high-end magazines and the average regional daily newspaper, they do have one thing in common: Once an editor finds a good writer, that writer's name won't be forgotten.

Also considered high-end markets, but in a different class are the following Sunday magazines: *The New York Times Magazine*; *The Los Angeles Times Magazine*; *The Washington Post Magazine*; *Boston Globe Magazine*; and the *Chicago Tribune Magazine*. Even the typeface on their flags is the same—each a variation on the Old English typeface which connotes authority born of tradition.

These are important Sunday magazines: Their audience may be, to some extent, regional, but also includes a wider geographical focus and perhaps a more sophisticated or more educated reader.

These magazines can be as difficult to break into as any of the more prestigious national monthly magazines. Most of the editors have been in the business for a long time. They know a lot of good writers who are publishing regularly in nationally known magazines, and many of them are competing with one another for space in these Sunday newspaper magazines.

The freelance writer who has the best chance of breaking into a magazine such as *The Los Angeles Times Magazine*, for example, is someone who is an accomplished reporter and has some good clips—perhaps with a glossy city magazine, another major metropolitan newspaper or even a quality trade magazine. *The Los Angeles Times Magazine* admits to having a Western or California bias, according to Senior Editor Susan Brenneman, even if it's subtle. She described the magazine's direction as "stories that have a West Coast angle but national importance." They also look for stories that are "reporting with a featury take," stories with "a lot of different subtexts," and "as much color as possible."

Where these magazines differ from the newspapers that spawned them is that they aspire to a "level of depth that a newspaper can't take," Brenneman says.

Editors at these magazines often spend a lot of time reading other magazines, and if they see a byline on an article they like, they'll seek out that writer. But it's worth knowing that a good magazine clip can go a long way—and payment for an assigned story can run as high as $3,000 in some cases.

All of these magazines get a high volume of mail. Linton Weeks, editor of *The Washington Post Magazine*, says: "There are so many good ideas and so many good writers with good ideas … I'm of the school that believes the cream rises to the top. If you've got a good story and can tell it well, it'll see print."

The Washington Post Magazine tends to look for more of a local angle too. It works in close partnership with the newspaper's feature section, and the magazine enjoys a special relationship with the reporters on the other sections of the newspaper. Despite having a pool of hometown reporters, a staff of writers on board, and a stable of freelancers to draw on, Weeks says he's "always on the lookout for good writers."

If you're outside the region, you better have a good reason or a good method for contacting one of this group of magazines: an inside connection, a good angle on a story that is tailor-made for that publication, and some superhuman persistence and optimism will help.

It may be wiser to look close to home at Sunday newspaper magazines. Many of the dailies publish a strictly regional magazine — though often you have to search through piles of look-alike advertising supplements to locate it. These magazines pay an average fee of about $250, depending on the locale, and vary widely. (Some, such as the *Pittsburgh Press* magazine, pay a top rate of $100, while the *Miami Herald's Tropic* may go as high as $1,000.)

These magazines are tuned in to regional topics, so if you can write well and come up with good ideas, persistence usually *will* pay off in this area.

The writing found in this type of publication varies widely; it can range from mediocre to excellent, depending on the individual magazine editor's ability to attract and pay good writers. You'll have to judge the writing of the magazine in your area for yourself and determine just where you fit in. You may consider it a coup to see print in the magazine, or you may not even want to bother with it at all.

Tom Shroder of *Tropic* magazine says he looks for "superlative writing skills. We're looking for people who can both report excellently and turn it into really excellent writing. There are some people who are great reporters and who can't write, and some people who are great writers who can't report, so when I see that combination of talent, I really go out of my way to nurture that."

Freelancers also may find that many newspapers now include a weekly supplement appearing during a weekday that focuses on community news, people and events in the neighborhoods around town. These are good places to get a foot in the door, particularly if you can alert the editor to newsworthy people in the community.

ALTERNATIVE WEEKLIES

Another kind of weekly publication in the newspaper field is in a class of its own — the alternative weekly. *Writing A to Z* (Writer's Digest Books) describes these as tabloids distinguished by their urban readership, concern with urban issues, and political liberalism. They are the offspring of the underground papers of the 1960s but many have grown in size, in budget and in readership, and they are frequently the best place to get in-depth coverage of cultural events in the region, particularly events outside the mainstream ballet, symphony and theater activities.

Some, such as the *Village Voice* in New York, have very specific policies regarding the use of freelancers and staff writers, based on a National Writers Union agreement. Many regular freelance writers have a formal contract with the paper—and the *Voice*, therefore, is not an easy place for an outsider to break in. Others, such as the *Chicago Reader*, operate more informally: Editors actually make no assignments. A portion of the paper is staff-written, but editors look at everything that comes in and publish what they like best. Besides the *Reader*'s staff of writers and stable of regular contributors, it has also published freelancers on a one-shot basis only and has some once-or-twice-a-year contributors.

Payment for a feature may be $700, though the maximum can go to just over $1,000. A four- or five-page record review may net a writer $80.

Who are the contributors? Generally, people who are freelancing for other publications around town, some of whom have full-time jobs which may or may not be writing-related. The same is true for the *San Francisco Bay Guardian* which pays rates from $40 to $300.

Many of the alternative weeklies publish writer's guidelines and will send them to you when you send a self-addressed stamped envelope. Because each of these papers has its own quirky preferences, it's worth reading the particular paper and getting guidelines before querying with your story idea.

NEIGHBORHOOD WEEKLIES

Suburban papers, city neighborhood and rural weeklies also use freelancers, but the pay is usually minimal. Many nonstaff contributors are beginners looking for an opportunity to gather published clips for their portfolios. These papers are *excellent* ways to do exactly that, and if you *are* a beginner, you can't find a better way to get published and make contacts for your future endeavors.

Freelancers must make mental notes of the people they meet in all contexts—you never know when a chance meeting in one place can catapult you into a successful meeting or new freelance contact in another. File all this information, whether longhand or on computer disk, and collect business cards. If you are committed to working freelance, develop a long-range plan and then be willing to swerve from it. Build a career out of the best possibilities you have for steady work—and look at the high-end assignments as "gravy." Even more than for people who work in a single office or for a single company, the lines between friends, acquaintances, colleagues and mentors can be quite blurry for the freelance writer. It's useful to make this work to your advantage—and it begins as early as your first assignment.

WEEKLY NEWSPAPER AND MAGAZINE LISTINGS

See Daily Newspaper Listings for *Editor & Publisher* and *Gale Directory of Publications* information.

Writer's Market
1507 Dana Avenue
Cincinnati OH 45207

Writer's Market has listings by category. You'll find a selection of newspapers and newspaper weekly magazines listed in the section called "Regional," alphabetically by state.

Sunday magazines:

USA Weekend
1000 Wilson Blvd.
Arlington VA 22229
(703)276-6445

Parade
Parade Publications, Inc.
750 Third Ave.
New York NY 10017
(212)573-7000

Washington Post Magazine
The Washington Post
1150 15th St. NW
Washington DC 20071
(202)334-7585

Chicago Tribune Magazine
435 N. Michigan Ave.
Chicago IL 60611
(312)222-3232

The Los Angeles Times Magazine
Los Angeles Times
Times Mirror Square
Los Angeles CA 90053
(213)237-5000

The New York Times Magazine
229 W. 43rd St.
New York NY 10036
(212)556-1234

Plain Dealer Magazine
Plain Dealer Publishing Co.
1801 Superior Ave.
Cleveland OH 44101
(216)344-4500

Tropic Magazine
The Miami Herald Publishing Co.
1 Herald Plaza
Miami FL 33132
(305)350-2111

Pittsburgh Press Sunday Magazine
The Pittsburgh Press Co.
34 Boulevard of the Allies
Pittsburgh PA 15230
(412)263-1510

Note: The "alternative" weeklies listed below are all members of the Association of Alternative Newsweeklies. That organization publishes a roster that lists all its member papers, but it has no central headquarters, only a rotating governing board that rotates its headquarters as well, depending on which paper's editor is presiding that year. Any of the newsweeklies listed below may be able to send you a roster upon request, or at least direct you to the proper office for additional information.

The Village Voice
842 Broadway
New York NY 10003
(212)475-3300

Chicago Reader
11 E. Illinois St.
Chicago IL 60611
(312)828-0350

San Francisco Bay Guardian
520 Hampshire St.
San Francisco CA 94110
(415) 255-3100

Boston Phoenix
126 Brookline Ave.
Boston MA 02215
(617)536-5390

East Bay Express
P.O. Box 3198
Berkeley CA 94703
(415)652-4610

L.A. Weekly
2140 Hyperion Ave.
Los Angeles CA 90027
(213)667-2620

SYNDICATION

Syndication is a highly competitive field for a writer to enter, and there are no guarantees about how much money you can make. This will depend on whether the syndicated material is sold to a few papers or, in the best-case scenario, to many papers nationwide – and beyond. Examples of successfully syndicated columnists are Abigail van Buren, Dave Barry and Art Buchwald.

A column that is likely to be picked up for syndication must be unique, both in content and in voice, and it must have breadth enough to generate ideas for material on a regular basis.

A syndicate's choices are as unpredictable as the changing and tricky tastes of the American reading public. A column can also work in one part of the country and not in another. Syndicate representatives rely a great deal on their newspaper contacts to steer them in the right direction: They need to know what the newspaper editors see as trends and what the newspapers are looking for to interest their own particular readership.

"What I specifically look for is a niche ... something that would appeal to the masses that isn't already being done," says Dennis Allen, vice president and editorial director of King Features Syndicate.

If you are writing a regular column (also called a "continuing feature"), you may want to take a shot at syndication by sending your work for review to one of the syndicates. *Editor & Publisher*'s annual directory of syndicated services lists addresses, telephone numbers and key staff. *Writer's Market* also lists syndicates. Although its listings are not as extensive as *E&P*'s, *Writer's Market* offers more comprehensive information about the 50 or so listed.

Columns should be 500 to 750 words on average, although some are as long as 1,250 words. Send a half-dozen samples with a cover letter; you can submit simultaneously to other syndicates but be sure and let each organization know what you are doing, as a courtesy. Of course, if you should have the good fortune to come to a working agreement with one syndicate, let the others know immediately of the change in status.

Payment is usually split fifty-fifty between the writer and the syndicate, and can vary in amount, depending on what the newspaper pays for the column. It could be as low as $8 or as high as $100 per piece. While the tradition has been that the syndicate owns the writer's material after the point of sale, more and more syndicates are beginning to follow the example set by the innovative Creators Syndicate in letting the columnist retain copyright.

For a columnist on the staff of a newspaper, syndication is considered by many the zenith because he is reaching the widest possible audience for his work and getting paid over and above his regular salary. If you are freelancing a column for a local newspaper, selling to a syndicate gives you some assurance of steady work, a little measure of security.

Besides keeping in close touch with newspaper editors at conventions, meetings, and through informal networking, syndicate representatives scout newspapers around the country on a regular basis. Recently, Words by Wire, a relatively small outfit, picked up a story from an alternative weekly in California, the *Chico News and Review*. In this case, it was a "one-shot," a story with "really good information" about home canning that had, according to representative Kathleen Currie, "a rather fresh angle" that she thought would appeal to "organic gardening types." Syndicates sell these single articles as well as columns to newspapers they think are in the market for a particular kind of piece.

But Currie cautions writers not to bank on syndication even if they are "really good writers," but to establish a track record before sending work. For every 15 proposals she gets in the mail, there may be one that is usable. At Creators Syndicate, four submissions were accepted one year—out of 7,000 received.

But if you write a column that is really different—or you have the time to market single articles to syndicates as a regularly scheduled part of your work week—you may want to give it a shot. Some syndicates will try to sell unpublished work to newspaper markets, acting as a broker for the writer's material. You have nothing to lose but time and some postage.

Dan O'Toole, who handles one-shots at the Los Angeles Times Syndicate, says "a syndicate is not the place for a freelance writer to start. Smart freelancers know that if they get that article published somewhere first, so that they get some up-front money, (they can then) look at syndication as icing on the cake . . . a way of squeezing some extra revenue from the piece."

Some writers choose to self-syndicate, contacting newspaper editors on their own, and retaining control of their material and a full percentage of the fee. Sometimes writers self-syndicate as part of a long-range plan to interest a larger syndicate, one that can take on wider distribution and marketing of the work. In any case, self-syndicated writers agree it is not easy. According to one now-retired self syndicator of a column on auto racing, to not only write but also be involved in "the mailing, the advertising, the promotion . . . you've got to be a one-man game."

Fred Flaxman of Flaxman Features is one inspirational success story for those determined to syndicate without the help of the "big guys." Based on his own success, he says, "There are still editors out there who read unsolicited material from people they've never heard of." But he also warns that spending all that time on marketing can be a good way of procrastinating in your writing.

Flaxman had a full-time job as vice president of a public television station outside of Chicago and started writing "almost as a hobby." He started out as a journalist before succeeding as an executive in the broadcasting field. He regularly stayed late at the office while his wife took an after-work yoga class and began writing humorous columns that he thought would fill a void in newspapers. ("When you're writing humor, you don't have to be an expert, you just have to be funny," he notes.) Flaxman tried his writing out on friends, who responded positively.

Then he began the "real test," as he calls it—sending the work out to editors. Though successful in his own field, he had no contacts in the newspaper business, and he sent his work out cold to *The Wall Street Journal* and *The Washington Post*, among others. His theory was "start at the top and work my way down." He also contacted a syndicate, but the syndicate wasn't interested—then, much to his surprise, his pieces were accepted by his first-choice newspapers. Once he had gathered a few impressive clips, he decided to see if anyone would take him on a regular basis. He approached a local newspaper chain in northern Illinois which purchased rights to his self-syndicated column "Unconventional Wisdom."

Before too long, Flaxman had won a prestigious first-place award for his writing from the National Society of Newspaper Columnists. It encouraged him so much he decided to leave his job and accept a full-time newspaper job, leaving Chicago for California. He calls his experience "beginner's luck," but clearly it was the combination of talent and persistence—and yes, luck.

So before you venture into the world of syndication, honestly assess your body of work so far and your willingness to keep plugging away even in the face of rejection. "No matter how good your things are, you're going to get enough rejections to wallpaper a room," Flaxman says. And, finally, ask yourself the Clint Eastwood question, "Do you feel lucky?"

SYNDICATE LISTINGS

A comprehensive list can be found in the annual *Editor & Publisher Syndicate Directory* (11 W. 19th St. New York NY 10011).

Chronicle Features
870 Market St., Room 1011
San Francisco CA 94102
(415)777-7212

Creators Syndicate
Suite 700
5777 West Century Blvd.
Los Angeles CA 90045
(213)337-7003

King Features Syndicate, Inc.
235 E. 45th St.
New York NY 10017
(212)455-4000

Los Angeles Times Syndicate
Times Mirror Square
Los Angeles CA 90053
(213)237-7987

New York Times Syndication Sales
130 5th Ave.
New York NY 10011
(212)645-3000

Tribune Media Services, Inc.
64 E. Concord St.
Orlando FL 32801
(407)839-5600

United Features Syndicate
200 Park Ave.
New York NY 10166
(212)692-3700

Words by Wire
Suite 24
1500 Massachusetts Ave. NW
Washington DC 20005
(202)745-4958

RADIO AND TELEVISION

RADIO DRAMA AND COMEDY

In the good old days before television, radio was *the* home entertainment venue: It offered a wide variety of drama and comedy programming and was considered a writer's medium. In the last 40 years, television has overtaken radio as an entertainment medium and the latter has remained strong by emphasizing an alternative identity rather than a competitive one with television. Radio holds its own by programming that consists primarily of music and news.

However, there is still *some* original drama and comedy in radio programming. And while radio relies on staff support almost entirely, freelance writers can sometimes find a home for their writing — creative or commercial — in the small market of radio entertainment.

In his recent collection of essays, *Writing in Restaurants*, the playwright David Mamet reminisces about his earliest memories of radio, first as a listener and later as a writer for the medium. He calls radio a "great training ground for dramatists." Because radio drama is relatively inexpensive to produce, he says if the American theater has hopes of being reborn, "radio would be a good place for it to happen."

Whether such a rebirth can or will occur remains debatable, but there are a number of people who devote their time and energy to some aspect of radio drama production and who say that the vital signs for this dramatic form are good.

This is not an area to get into for the money. It is, rather, strictly a labor of love, a creative venture. Most of the money for such projects comes from the same sources that fund other fine arts endeavors — government or state grants (which have only been shrinking in the last decade), corporate or private donations, and the like.

Commercial radio has shown almost no interest in radio drama; public radio is the place where just about all radio drama is broadcast — and public radio has its own problems staying financially afloat. What usually happens is a radio production company works in concert with a public radio station, sometimes using the radio's technical facilities gratis, and ultimately finds a home for the work that is produced. If a production company has some funding, an honorarium is paid to the scriptwriter, the actors and the director, and sometimes an attempt is made to compensate the radio station for the use of their facilities. More often everyone is donating talents and resources toward the cooperative creative effort.

Jon Hughes, who heads up the three-year-old Radio Repertory Company in Cincinnati, has produced a 13-part radio drama series that is expected to air on a local NPR station and later be uplinked for national broadcast. After receiving some grant money, Hughes put out a call for scripts, advertising through the Associated Writing Programs newsletter and using a mailing list from a Missouri writing workshop. He received about 100 queries and suspects that a good deal of the publicity was word of mouth. He sent out a set of writer's guidelines and sample pages of the preferred format and read all scripts that came in. Hughes, who teaches a workshop on radio drama writing, reminds writers that a sense of the dramatic, an ability to handle natural dialogue, and a good sense of story are the main ingredients for success in this medium. He emphasizes that "two seconds of dead air is an eternity on radio."

Target the program you want to write for by listening to locally produced programming (check newspaper radio listings to find out what is broadcast, when and where). This is an informal and somewhat esoteric community of writers, so begin networking with people associated with public radio and the drama community in your area. Again, radio drama is more closely aligned with *drama* than with commercial *radio*, so talk to people in local playwriting groups and check out the drama department of local colleges for people in this field. If you become involved with local theater productions you also may be instrumental in the evolution of new radio drama production. This is an area ripe for innovators, and strong on creative control, if not exactly high-end moneymaking.

For more information on the art, craft and marketing of radio scripts, see *The Complete Book of Scriptwriting*, by J. Michael Straczynski (Writer's Digest Books).

If radio is still your calling, but you want to concentrate on the more commercial avenues, the short form comedy market is an area to explore, particularly if you have a comic bent. If you've ever heard those 60-second (or less) parodies of songs and commercials that sometimes appear on commercial radio stations, you are listening to something that a freelance writer may have earned $50 to $200 for writing. There are a dozen or so companies that sell these "products"—fake commercials, song parodies, "interactives" (interviews between the disc jockey and a celebrity impersonator), and other features—to radio stations which may not have the time or the resources to produce this material in-house.

This is a growing market, according to Andy Goodman, president and general manager of American Comedy Network (ACM) in Bridgeport, Connecticut. ACM, in business for seven years, is considered the granddaddy of these services.

"We're always looking for good new writers," says Goodman. He adds that, while there is no *lack* of material being submitted, *good* material is harder to find. Their writers come from varied backgrounds and include people who work in all aspects of radio from sales to production, writers in print media, and stand-up comedians who want to pad their incomes between club dates.

The best place to look for outlets for short form radio writing is an industry magazine called *Radio and Records*, where a "Marketing" section lists services looking for new material (see Radio and Television Listings).

Writing for television is potentially one of the most lucrative areas for a writer—and one of the toughest to break into.

In this section, we divide the television broadcast market into four sections for ease of discussion—though there is certainly some overlap in all of the areas: the "big three" network stations, independent (local) television stations, cable broadcast stations and public access.

TV NETWORKS

The most important thing to understand about writing for network television shows is that the networks rarely deal with writers directly. Unless your Uncle Ralph is a major executive (and even then you still have to go through the usual channels), there are no doors to bang on at NBC, CBS or ABC where you won't be immediately directed elsewhere. That "elsewhere" is the production companies. Network executives work with producers in a relationship that mimics that between the producer and the writer: unstable, unpredictable, erratic and market- and ratings-driven. Furthermore, the television industry is extremely collegial, and the work itself is not as singular as writing in other media normally is—rather it is very collaborative in nature, some might argue to a fault. If you're serious about succeeding as a writer in this business you must be sociable and probably hyperconfident—but not falsely so. Finally, you will probably have to relocate to California where the television center of gravity is.

But if you are a beginning scriptwriter, you can do all your groundwork wherever you are. And if most scriptwriters live in California certainly they were not all born and raised there. In fact, it would be foolish to move to California in the hope of writing for television with no contacts, no interest shown in your work, and no experience dealing with the people who run this show. Years of preparation in the craft itself are necessary before you need begin to think about the practical aspects of competing in the marketplace. That means your work is to learn how to write a perfect television script—whether it is for an episodic half-hour or one-hour television series or movie-of-the-week (known as MOW).

You will need to have at least two scrupulously honed scripts to send out to an agent or a producer, and you may have to write a half-dozen drafts or separate scripts before your sample scripts are ready. You prepare by watching and studying television, particularly the show you want to write for, by reading and taking workshops in your area and by writing. And writing. And writing.

When you're pretty sure you've got a really solid MOW script or a great episode of, say, "Night Court," you can send your script out to a production company or an agent. An agent is the better bet and is highly recommended by people in the business. You don't *have* to have an agent, but it frequently works to your advantage. Besides the obvious—the contacts that an agent has in the industry—there is another reason producers are wary of unsolicited, unagented material. The networks are extremely cautious—some people use the word paranoid. Lawsuits occur frequently in which a writer claims a network used an idea without giving due credit or monetary compensation. The networks claim that similarities in ideas, even in scripts themselves, are very common; producers concur, and thus go to great lengths to protect themselves against litigation. Most production companies won't even read an unsolicited script unless it is accompanied by a release form (which can be obtained from the company in question) that protects them against a lawsuit should they reject your work and end up developing a project that, in your opinion, has similarities. Producers, therefore, prefer to work with agents who are known quantities to them.

If you have talent, and if you've been working hard to develop that talent, you should be able to get an agent with a little persistence. The Writers Guild, with headquarters on both the East and West coasts, will send you a list of its signatories for $1.25. Agents on this list indicate if they will consider new writers, if they will consider writers only as a result of references, or if they will take letters of inquiry only.

You can send out a lot of queries or send your script to a lot of agents, but if you can get a personal recommendation, you will probably have better luck, says Kerry Cox, publisher of the *Hollywood Scriptwriter* newsletter.

"If it's a family friend, an aunt twice removed, fine. Search your family tree and find somebody (who) knows somebody, so you can say 'take a look at the first three pages . . . If you think there's some promise there, read it,' " advises Cox.

It is *not* necessary to be a member of the Writers Guild to sell a script to a producer. A producer can hire any writer he likes, but if that writer is *not* a member of the Guild, he or she is required to become a member immediately after selling that script. Usually the writer's contract will stipulate this, and frequently the terms of the contract include payment of Writers Guild dues as well.

Once you have an agent, you're a step closer to breaking in – but you still have a long way to go.

Producer Alan Wagner (NBC's "A Family for Joe") says even when a script sparks a producer's interest, it's rarely bought outright. Usually it's used as a sample script – something representative of the writer's potential.

"It's rare in television anywhere that any of the end users is going to buy a finished product. The only time they buy a finished product is in a very, very, very few instances where a major 'name' writer has 'spec'd' something, or [when a new writer] has so caught the spirit and tone of the characters in a series that their spec script is 100% right," says Wagner, executive vice president of Grosso-Jacobson and head of Alan Wagner Productions.

"The usual procedure is that the end user looks at the script and will decide if this writer either understands the program and can write episodes for it, or he or she is a terrific writer and maybe we ought to get some other ideas and explore it."

Kerry Cox sheds some additional light on this from the perspective of the writer. He begins by stressing that the writer should have at least two of those "first" scripts.

"What happens is – and this happened to me in the early going – is that you come up with your first (script), and you're inspired, and it's 'great' and you want to get it out there. So you send it out, and the first thing that happens is – *if you're lucky* – you get *the call*. They say, 'This is really good, we like it, you've got a lot of talent. *Can you send us anything else you've done?*' . . . And maybe you've had some other ideas in your head so you quickly hack something off that's no good whatsoever and you send it out there and forever destroy your reputation with that particular agent or whatever. (This) happens to a lot of people. So you're going to have to be able to say 'Yeah, as a matter of fact, I've got another script, and I've got several ideas I'm working on right now as well. Let me send you the second script and see what you think.' And *it's got to be as good as the first.*"

The ability to "pitch" an idea is a very important part of the game in television as well, so the writer who is great with words on paper but a disaster in face-to-face interaction with people is going to have a very tough time. The importance of this verbal medium — "pitching" — reflects the role of collegiality in the television business and, as Cox says, "It helps to have a good personality."

These presentation skills — which include not just a facility with words but an ability to think quickly on your feet — are crucial. Writers must further understand that even when a script is purchased, by the time it is rewritten by an assortment of other writers, producers, directors and actors, they may not recognize the original script. This is to be expected in television writing; projects are not written so much as developed. This is very different from the experience of a book author. Even writers who are grateful and appreciative of the work of a good editor are surprised to hear an editor say "Great book, but I think we need to rewrite the ending."

"The writing of comedy is the *most* collegial of all forms," asserts Wagner. A comedy is assembled by a complex hierarchy of eight to 10 writers per show, on average — beginning with the writer-producer who created and wrote the pilot, an executive producer and chief story writer, and a line of writers under that graded on levels of seniority. When a show is fairly new, the scripts are mostly written by staff writers. After a show has been on the air for a while and established a track record, it's more common for the staff to look at scripts that come in from outside. So when targeting a show to write for be sure and select one that has been around for a while.

This inevitable system of collaborative creativity has proved to be too much for some writers to handle and so it may be worth reflecting on whether you have the necessary personality characteristics to work in the television business. In addition, writers should decide early on whether to pursue comedy or drama ("There's a great deal of suspicion of people who cross over — that's a rule of thumb.")

"Many people have themselves removed from the system because of (this) excess of collaboration," says Wagner, citing examples of industry gossip where writers or producers left a project due to "differences in creative control." Those who stay, he said, must be "tenacious" and "hardskinned."

Cox reminds writers who are determined to break in and stay in television writing that "the main thing is to retain flexibility and remember that, as a television writer, you're a hired gun. You have to deliver what the show wants, not necessarily what you want. So when you go in and pitch your idea and they start changing it around, don't be protective and defensive, but rather go with the flow. They're not trying to make the show bad, they're trying to make it good. So go from their viewpoint and help them make the show better."

Of course the assumption here is that the writer has faith in the producer's vision. And here is the crux of the matter: television is a producer-dominated, not writer-dominated, field. Most television writers, therefore, have as their goal to become writer-producers, giving them much more control over the final product.

If you have an agent, have some contact with people in the business, and perhaps have your scripts read, *then* you can consider yourself as having a proverbial foot in the door. It's still a long hard road to getting your work produced, however.

If you are pitching ideas, you may have an idea bought—but there's still no guarantee you will be hired to write the script. Yes, it's certainly nice to make the $5,000 or $10,000 on an option, but if you're a writer you will not ultimately be satisfied with that. This is where having an agent negotiate deals for you can sometimes be useful in giving you leverage. An agent's advice may vary, depending on the particular circumstances. You will have to decide, though, if the advice is working for or against your best interests.

One New York writer, having interested a producer in her MOW story idea—which amounted to a scene-by-scene treatment—had an agent that, in her words, was "hanging tough." The agent didn't want her to sell the story without a guarantee that she would write the script since that's where the money is made. The producer finally convinced the writer, in this case, that "you can't hit a home run unless you get up to bat" and the writer decided to sign the contract, overriding her agent's advice. This particular story has a happy ending: The story was optioned and a few weeks later the writer got the go-ahead to write the script.

There are several lessons illustrated here. One, sometimes it becomes necessary to take a chance. Two, your agent is your *co*-pilot; don't abdicate total control of your career. The agent was not trying to hold back the writer's career—he would have had nothing to gain from that. But he knew the industry game: It's not until you sell a *script*, not a *script idea*, that you gain any credibility in the business. He wanted to hold out, but the writer took the chance. It could have turned out differently: A story can be bought, and then the producer can hire another established writer to flesh it out—and get the credit and the money. The writer with the original idea is back to square one then.

Scripts can be written and rewritten, with several writers hired and fired anywhere along the way, and still never get produced. And writers can be "bought off," thrown off the project or offered "step-deals" where the producer can cut them off at any point in the development and bring in other writers. Writers, for the most part, have very little control until they get to be writer-producers—at which point you begin battling with the network for control.

"Every studio has a room filled with turnaround scripts," says Wagner. These are scripts that may not turn out well, or as expected, or aren't needed as the producer's or the network's needs change, or that the studio has difficulty casting. After a certain amount of time the rights revert back to the producer or the writer or some kind of joint arrangement of ownership. But the point here is that even selling an idea *and* writing the script is no guarantee of a successful production.

However, Wagner says, "Once you've gotten produced and had a small modicum of success, the escalation is very rapid from that point on." But he concedes, "the first years are hellish."

You really have to want it. And you have to be prepared to sweat over a perfect script whose destiny may only be to get you an agent or an invitation to pitch ideas or an assignment to write yet *another* script. The irony is that the first script can end up gathering dust over the years even as your career takes off. You can't get bogged down in sentimental attachments to your writing when writing for television. Writing is more craft than art in this business; you need to be a fountain of ideas, ready to develop or discard them at someone else's whim. Writing and polishing those first scripts for television should probably be considered more of an investment in your future, as writer Lydia Wilen terms it.

Wilen, who works in partnership with her sister Joan Wilen in New York City, displays the kind of tenacity needed to survive and thrive as a writer in the television industry.

"You've got to get the scripts out there. *You* have to get out there. You have to talk to everyone who will listen—you never know where (an opportunity) is going to come from. You have to constantly remind them: I'm a writer, and I'm looking for work. You just have to keep pushing yourself so much."

Asked what she would advise aspiring scriptwriters, Wilen gave a surprising response but with absolute conviction: "Don't let anyone read your script who isn't in a position to really further your career. That's very important. Everyone's a critic—and that's a very dangerous thing. What happens is, you write something, you give it to someone who is 'so bright'—you give it to your English teacher, or to someone you really trust, and they start making you crazy. It doesn't *matter* what they say, whether they love it or they hate it—it doesn't matter. What they may not like, a producer may absolutely love."

This is advice worth reflecting on, though not every writer will be able to—or want to—follow it. Feedback is very important to most of us, after all. But Wilen maintains that if your friend or teacher doesn't like the script—and worse, tells you so kindly—"it's very damaging to your soul and you'll never like that person again." And so what if the person *does* like the script? "It's an ego boost, but it's not worth it." When all is said and done, the fact that the person likes the script has no practical value to you. She maintains a strict rule for her own work: Don't give the script to any person not in a position to buy it.

And what about living in New York? Is it the next best thing to living in California for an aspiring television writer? Wilen says it's tough. The competition is tough because "writers love living in New York," but "it's rough to be in New York and expect the California production companies to use you." Once you're well established, you can live anywhere, she says. But you have to establish yourself in Los Angeles for a couple of years. So the word on living in L.A. seems to be that television writers have to put in some time there. You don't want to go too soon, and you don't need to stay there forever. But you can't avoid it completely. As Wilen points out, L.A. is a company town: Almost *everyone* has a friend or relative, or an aunt twice removed who is in "the business."

INDEPENDENT AND PUBLIC TELEVISION STATIONS

Although NBC, ABC, CBS—the three major network stations in the United States—dominate the television industry, they are certainly not the only stations on the air. Even before cable TV expanded the broadcast alternatives, there were other independent television stations, particularly in the larger cities. But opportunities for writers are almost nil unless you are hired to be on staff. Programming is created internally most of the time—as in the case of public TV—or purchased as prepackaged material by many independent stations whose lineup consists primarily of reruns from old network shows.

Speaking for a Cincinnati public television station, WCET Senior Vice President Jack Dominic said a station such as his might occasionally work with freelance writers in a number of ways, perhaps "to flesh out an idea that is already created and developed" or more likely "to create copy for various campaigns, (such as) on-air fund-raising."

"Most public television stations out of the 200-plus in the country do very little actual production. They serve more as a conduit of materials coming from a national source," said Dominic.

As for locally produced programs in the smaller markets, he added: "These materials are created internally by producers mainly because programming at that level is very, very underfunded, and there just isn't additional funding available to bring in someone else to collaborate."

The other avenue for writing for television is through advertising, discussed in the Word Markets section of this chapter. The employer in these cases would normally be the advertising agency hired by a company who has purchased television airtime to advertise a product.

CABLE TELEVISION

The advent of cable television has provided subscribers with alternatives unheard of just two decades ago: 64 cable channels is standard, and 600 or more is possible if you have a satellite dish. Programming for these new channels is still in the earliest growth stages. The most popular stations are the movie channels (HBO, Showtime, etc.), music stations (MTV, VH-1), and programming for children (Disney Station, Nickelodeon). The Turner Broadcasting System includes TBS, TNT, Cable News Network (CNN) and CNN Headline News.

Liz Bennett, development coordinator for TBS, says "brand new original made-for-TV movies will be emphasized more over the next couple of years." TBS prefers to receive proposals or treatments sent through an agent or attorney, and TNT absolutely will not look at any unagented or unsolicited work. TNT is also expanding its original programming, and as of this writing has approximately 600 original manuscripts logged in its computer. These will be looked at by a reader within the company who then writes "coverage"—a plot summary plus a subjective assessment of the strengths of the idea. The best scripts are brought to a weekly development meeting where the executives discuss and possibly fight for any of the scripts they feel passionate about. Usually a quarter of the week's submissions makes it to the weekly meeting and the ones selected out of that grouping go to network President Ted Turner for final approval.

Scripts come in from all over the country, not just from script-savvy writers on the two coasts, says Serena Misner, assistant in the original programming department. Writers are not expected to follow a certain format: Some people send in treatments, some send in letters.

"Naturally, the more well thought out it is, and the better written it is, (the) easier (it is for an executive) to make a case for it" to the powers-that-be, said Misner.

Jay Mulvaney, director of programming at Nickelodeon, primarily a children's television network, says that using freelance writers can often be cost-effective. However, as you might expect, that's not necessarily great news for the writer. A writer may get $150 for a short script, but you'd have to be working pretty closely with the program to really understand how to write for it successfully.

"We have philosophical underpinnings to everything we do," says staff writer Tom Hill. "Most of our scripts are bought from a small group of writers (who are) mostly local people."

Those writers interested in writing for cable programs should not approach this as a "market" en masse, but should concentrate on each individual program. Watch the program and become very familiar with it; you should probably have a genuine enthusiasm for the kind of programming offered if you intend to be a writer for that program. If you *are* enthusiastic, persistent and you're good, you may eventually convince those looking for writers for the show that you are one writer they've been waiting to find.

Mulvaney, in fact, likened the search for good writers to panning for gold. The consensus is that there is no lack of material, but quality material is another story. Mulvaney says he goes to comedy clubs and film festivals to search for promising writers and material.

Writing for television means either relentless dogged pursuit of the high-end—writing scripts for television movies or episodic shows—or exploring what might be called piecework for the various cable stations. Movies aside, your method should include focusing closely on the particular show or program that interests you and trying your hardest to be original while still making sure that your writing conforms closely to the style and tone of the show as it exists. This can be a very fine line to walk, but if you think you can walk it, you certainly could be the gold that buyers are mining for.

PUBLIC ACCESS

Finally, the newest opportunity for writers who want to test and perhaps expand their capabilities in television writing: public access television. In more than 1,000 cities in the United States, public access television is a noncommercial, nonprofit venue for citizen-produced programming of every conceivable kind. Typically, church groups and educational or community organizations have used the airwaves to promote their beliefs or publicize their concerns, but there has also been a growing interest in creative programming by anyone and everyone with a hankering to produce a talk show, a comedy show or their original dramas and documentaries on videotape. Most public access stations offer training in video production—including hands-on experience—either for free or for a nominal fee. Many also have staff to offer assistance as you plan and produce your program.

This is not a commercial venture but rather a place to learn about writing for television production if you've never had any contact with this medium—and you can learn while offering your services to any worthwhile organization you may want to promote. You may attach yourself to a production already in the works, or you may organize your own crew and plan your program from scratch.

Typical programming on public access may include a videotaped board of education meeting, a panel discussion on issues facing city council, a production of a Cub Scout talent show, minority- or ethnic-oriented programming, video art, a documentary. The programs may be recorded on location or in the public access studios, shot live in one take (for example, if you are shooting a play that you've been rehearsing for weeks), or shot out of sequence and edited for airplay, or any combination of these. You might be working with a crew of four or five people, each responsible for an aspect of production (audio, lighting, cameras, etc.) or you might be the entire crew yourself.

However you decide to proceed, public access television is a marvelous opportunity for the writer who has been working primarily in the print medium but would like to experiment with "air words." Once a show is complete, you are guaranteed a venue for your work—something we wish we could say after completing a written work for print media. In fact, normally each show is aired six to 10 times during a month.

You will be asked to sign a contract before training and using public access resources that says you will not profit monetarily from any production done on the premises or through using the station's equipment, but there is no objection to your using the tape or a copy of it as part of your résumé or portfolio for other potential clients.

RADIO AND TELEVISION LISTINGS

For a list of literary agencies, send your request plus $1.25 to:

Writers Guild of America-East
555 West 57th St.
New York NY 10019-2967
(212)245-6180

or

Writers Guild of America-West
8955 Beverly Blvd.
Los Angeles CA 90048-2456
(213)550-1000

To order a copy of the *TV Producers Directory*, write to:

DVE Productions
Suite 304
3017 Santa Monica Blvd.
Santa Monica CA 90404
(213)281-7637

A good trade publication is:

Hollywood Scriptwriter
1626 N. Wilcox #385
Hollywood CA 90028

(One-year subscription is $39; six-months, $20)

For information on radio markets, check out the following magazine:

Radio & Records
1930 Century Park West
Los Angeles CA 90067
(213)553-4330

$235/subscription, goes to radio stations, record stores, some bookstores

For nationwide listings of cable TV, consult the *Cable Programming Resource Directory*. This may be available from your local library, or contact:

National Federation of Local Cable Programmers
P.O. Box 27290
Washington DC 20038
(202)829-7186

WORD MARKETS

Words are everywhere we look—and someone has to write them. Freelance writers have an endless number of markets, from the most obvious and conventional such as magazine writing to the vast array of businesses and products that require brochures, newsletters, customer letters, catalog copy, advertising, signage, software manuals and contracts, as just a few examples. Even the wording on utility bills and product warranty labels was planned, written, approved and paid for by someone, somewhere.

The magazine market itself extends far beyond the high-end, well-known "glossies" such as *Esquire*, *Redbook* or *Vanity Fair*. Go into any good bookstore and you will find hundreds of specialty magazines in every field imaginable, many of which rely on freelance writers with regularity. If you're aiming for freelance magazine writing, buy the ones you'd like to read—or write for—and send out query letters to the managing editor (who will route it to the appropriate reader on staff) as often as you have good ideas. Make sure your idea is well thought out and described briefly and energetically in an engaging query letter—and send one or two of your best published clips if you think they will improve your chances of getting an assignment.

Newspaper or other magazine clips are best, if you've done these already. If you're crossing over from another field, rely on the strength of your idea and letter rather than send irrelevant pieces such as media kits, brochures or technical articles. If you've targeted a couple—or even a half-dozen—magazines that you'd like to publish in, send queries as often as you have ideas, especially if you get any kind of encouragement at all. Some writers draw encouragement from any kind of response at all—even "thanks for sending, but not at this time" on a form postcard. (If an editor specifically requests that you stop sending letters because you're way off-base, it's time to look elsewhere.) The point is, persistence and familiarity pay off. Even unsolicited mail is still handled by a person, not a computer. An editor "programmed" to be skeptical of unsolicited ideas can reprogram herself pretty quickly if the right idea crosses her desk.

Also be aware if you're intent on freelancing for magazines that the array of magazines distributed to retail outlets are *not* the only magazines that employ freelance writers. There are thousands of trade and specialty magazines in businesses, nonprofit organizations and professional organizations around the country. Some may use only staff writers or contributions from professionals in the field only; some may not pay very well but any can open doors to other opportunities. You can find these publications listed by subject or by geographical location in the *Gale Directory of Publications, Writer's Market, Standard Rate and Data Service* directories and *The National Directory of Magazines* (Oxbridge Communications).

Again, target specific magazines if you have a good reason or relevant background for contributing to that particular magazine. Sometimes it's worth a phone call to inquire if the magazine publishes writing from freelancers; if you happen to be a professional in a given field, you're a step ahead. Often, for example, professional journals publish book reviews—and if you have the credentials and the idea, you may tap into something steady. In addition to book reviews and article writing, some publications need copywriters and editors for various departments.

CORPORATE WRITING

More than ever, the kinds of assignments a company is likely to farm out to a freelance writer can be unpredictable and varied in category and scope. Manufacturing companies, health care and other service industries, nonprofit organizations of every type and retail businesses are finding that hiring freelancers cuts overhead costs, as well as hefty health, unemployment and other benefits. In addition they can hire freelancers only when needed instead of hiring an employee who may be idle during slow work periods.

Sandra Burgess, who left a position handling internal publications for a Detroit hospital to go out on her own as a freelancer, has gathered from researching the trade publications in her area that "the use of freelance writing for a variety of purposes is expected to increase substantially in the next 10 years or so." Her observations and conclusions were borne out repeatedly by freelancers and employers alike who have been tracking this trend over the last 10 years. Burgess, who is well connected to a Detroit freelance network of her colleagues, notes that the auto industry there—a mega-employer—is included in these rough statistics, hiring freelancers for projects ranging from public affairs to video production.

To become part of this network, call all writing-related professional organizations in your area and join the active ones. Women in Communications, the Public Relations Society of America, the International Association of Business Communicators, the Society for Technical Communications, the American Society of Journalists and Authors—all or some of these national organizations may have branches in your area. Most of them publish directories of their members, often listing the member's place of employment. This gives you an automatic contact, especially if you've involved yourself in the social networking system these organizations encourage—with people who may hire freelancers or who can direct you to the person in their company who does.

Take a look at the business community in your area: Who are the 10 or 20 biggest employers? Your local business newspaper can give you this information. Keep your eyes and ears open for listings of all kinds; search them out in business newspapers as well as those provided by the Chamber of Commerce or tourism bureau and collect directories of every stripe. Brainstorm in your local library where there are directories published for a variety of fields, often indexed geographically, including the *Encyclopedia of Associations* and a directory of directories. (See listings at end of this section, as well as the Researching It chapter.)

Heighten your awareness of the social and economic community in which you live. If there's a big university, are there professors or departments frequently struggling to write grant proposals? Some must publish articles or even books regularly in order to compete for a tenured position—and getting their research material into acceptable written form may be the biggest chore in the world for them. But be forewarned when working with independent private clients instead of companies: Get everything in writing. It doesn't have to be formal; a simple letter of agreement will do the trick. Just have in writing your agreement about the nature of the work, deadlines, fee payment and schedule.

If there is a large food industry, think about the needs of related businesses like supermarkets and restaurants—what are *their* communication needs? Almost every city supports a telephone company (AT&T is a virtual city of communication needs, and they *do* use freelancers); insurance, banking and real estate firms; utility and transportation companies of various kinds; computer or other engineering-related manufacturers; department stores and smaller retail businesses; and a host of museums, social service and religious affiliated agencies. All of these organizations communicate, by print media at the very least, to the public and often to other individuals or groups.

The kinds of materials that may require a writer's professional expertise with language form and content include press releases, brochures, newsletters, internal and external magazines, proposals, speeches and catalog copy among the obvious—and new home descriptions, appetizing menu selections, program notes, and employee orientation manuals, to name a few that are less obvious.

To get an idea of just how far you can take this game of "who needs writers?" try this exercise: Take a conscious look around you today at written copy, wherever you are, beginning with what's right in front of your eyes—a calendar that has photo captions; an advertisement on the back of a cereal box; a button or T-shirt with a cute slogan on it—and continue throughout the day, wherever you are. Don't overlook the flyers posted on telephone poles by a local theater company, signs on the backs of benches or high up on billboards, and your own mail, especially your direct (also called "junk") mail. These were all written by someone, somewhere, who spent hours with pen or keyboard and presumably collected a nice paycheck for his trouble.

Of course not all of these were written by freelancers, but it's safe to assume that any of them *could* have been. There is no communications area left—with the possible exception of top-secret government agencies—that exclude work-for-hire as a possibility. Notice I didn't say that every company hires freelancers; some do not, even as a matter of policy. But policies can change; what is done by a staff person in one company may be done by a freelancer in another.

It's not practical for you as a freelance generalist to be a one-man or one-woman band, hiring yourself out for *any* kind of writing, anytime, anyplace and for anyone. You will cheat yourself and your employer if you attempt to do this. Writers are like doctors; specialization is the key. To get anywhere you need to focus your energies. So the question is who or what do *you* focus on—and how do you get the work?

ADVERTISING AND PUBLIC RELATIONS

One way is to target the kind of company that depends on writers and may frequently use freelance writers: advertising and public relations firms. These are the experts to whom many companies turn for help in developing their various communications-related projects. In fact, if you go to a company on your own to vie for a freelance assignment, you may compete against agencies for an assignment. But for now let's look at how to get an assignment *from* such a firm, and what the advantages of selecting this route actually are.

The biggest advantage—once you've made the connection—is that the agency finds the clients; all you have to do is complete the work. This can be attractive if you tire of freelance hustling, especially if you can become a regular in an agency's stable of freelancers. You may assure yourself a steady source of income, and if it's a quality firm, you enhance your own reputation by association.

If you already have some experience with a specific kind of assignment (you've designed and written brochures in your last job) or you're well grounded in a certain area of expertise (you're a volunteer or a past employee in an organization that caters to senior citizens) *sell yourself* as an expert in this area. If you do your job well, the agency can be persuaded not only to see you as someone they can use for a certain kind of assignment or project, but they may also see you as a subtle selling tool to bolster *their* client base in the area of *your* expertise. In other words, if you are well known in the retirement home community and doing work for Agency X (which has been trying to attract clients from a health care industry in your area), you become doubly attractive to the agency. But it's up to you to make sure the agency views you in this way. They won't know if you don't tell them.

And you have to tell them who you are succinctly – don't overload potential ad agency employers with words. They probably value language that cuts to the chase. Anne Schrup, who frequently hires freelancers to work with her on accounts for the Minneapolis firm of Yeager, Pine, and Mundale says, "I don't want the traditional résumé. I want your name and phone number and area of expertise right up front. I want to know who does media relations and who does special events . . . who you've worked for before."

Sounding an optimistic note along with her forthrightness, Schrup adds, "I would say that anyone who wants business in this market – if (he's) a professional and good at what (he) does – can make a living in this business. The key is marketing yourself, and you have to know what it is that you do. If you get in with a client, he will discover that you do other things. Just get in there."

But do you need to sell your services to big agencies to get work from big companies? Not necessarily. Many companies, because they must produce a large volume of what some call collateral material, still find themselves in need of freelance help when the work load gets heavy. These pieces – from a postcard or brochure to a direct mail piece – are used to advertise the company to the public as opposed to an internal publication for employees only. Sometimes a company will be looking for someone who can shepherd a project from conceptualization to production; other times they may only need simple copywriting done – but done immediately.

It's not necessary to be very familiar with the company itself if you know what you're doing or you know your subject. Says Pat Mead, creative projects director at Minneapolis's Carlson Company: "Sometimes it's good to get someone who doesn't know everything, but knows a lot about the one thing you need written about." She too cites a trend of companies "not having all that kind of talent on board, but (rather hiring) the expertise you need for a particular project."

Ford Motor Company in Dearborn, Michigan, is one of those large companies that has a lot of communications professionals on staff and so doesn't ordinarily need the kind of service an agency would provide, says Howard Sieloff, manager of the creative services department. When hiring freelancers, Sieloff looks for "a proven performer," whose previous work is "of a high level, highly regarded." In addition, he deems "a sense of confidentiality and security" to be crucial, so take note: When showing your portfolio to one company, don't inadvertently betray the confidences of internal communications of another company that are either still in progress or not meant for outside viewing.

The person to contact at some of the larger companies may go by any number of titles. It may be a director of publications, of corporate communications, or of public relations. If the company has a sophisticated operation, it may have borrowed the term "creative services director" from the advertising industry, particularly if it uses both print and audiovisual media. Sometimes the word marketing will be in the title; other times that word will lead you into the wrong department altogether. It depends on the kind of company. If in doubt—and especially if you're cold calling—a well-placed phone call to the personnel or human resources department will probably get you the name of the appropriate department, staff person and title.

Sieloff, who pursues freelance assignments in addition to working a full-time job, says "There's a lot of freelance writing in corporate America—which is where the money is." He reminds his colleagues that they need not only writing, but marketing skills as well. "In order to get the business, you've got to get out there and chase it hard. It takes tenacity, perseverance and self-confidence."

Dennis O'Connor of Shamrock Communications in Covington, Kentucky, likens his small, fairly new, shop to a freelance business and offers some good advice to freelance hopefuls, particularly for the advertising and public relations business: "Attend as many business-type trade shows as possible; create some kind of flyer and handout that you can give to people that serves as a marketing piece. It can be as simple as a résumé or [as elaborate as] a four-color brochure. A lot of times all you have to do is give out a business card, work with the handshake, talk to people."

To identify new businesses, especially small businesses that may be in need of your services but are not big enough or established enough to hire a full-service agency, O'Connor recommends calling the Chamber of Commerce and asking them to update you or send you material on small businesses. Scout local business newspapers or the business section of daily newspapers to identify companies that have just applied for vendors' licenses. Then send them a personal or form letter to generate interest in what you have to offer. If you can be specific, so much the better.

New businesses, says O'Connor, often don't give much thought to professional marketing. "They hang their sign up and open their door and wait for business to come in. Of course that doesn't happen. You have to let people know you're there."

This is where the enterprising freelancer can step in, letting the retailer know you're there to help him let his potential customers know that he's there.

If high-profile aggressiveness is the key in some businesses, it may not be the appropriate style for every freelancer and some employers appreciate a lower key. Particularly when networking among social services, arts and educational agencies and the nonprofit sector generally, personal reputation, civic and community connections—along with a reputation for results—may weigh in a little more heavily than they do in businesses, where the bottom line is emphasized. Of course it's sometimes tricky to draw lines between where public relations leaves off and advertising/marketing begins—today more than ever.

Hospitals are a case in point. In the last 12 years, almost all hospitals' public relations departments have become marketing communication departments as federal cutbacks and product line competitiveness have forced hospitals to walk a financial tightrope—while producing more written copy. Hospitals have had to cut costs dramatically and it's no coincidence that hospitals have increased their use of freelancers to supplement or take the place of in-house employees. It's a simple matter of cost-effectiveness.

Many arts organizations are suffering from a similar fate, but even more so because fund-raising for the arts is lately more of a hard sell than fund-raising for hospitals. Still, the educational and social service functions of many organizations require writers who can write for media (press releases, media kits), communicate ideas that may often be complex (explanation of a disease, billing instructions) or sensitive (education about care of the mentally ill or aged) to varied consumer audiences. Sometimes harried executives must balance their responsibilities to inform the public (annual reports), keep employees satisfied and informed (internal publications), and please their own top brass (who may delegate a corporate history written consistently with the company's projected image).

Some organizations have a department they call public affairs where much of this kind of work is done. One director of marketing and communications for a major real estate firm also reminds freelancers that "practically every corporation of any size that has senior executives has speech writers." Executives don't hire speechwriters the way a politician might hire a speechwriter. Someone from public relations is usually assigned to do the job. It may be something *you* can do a few times a year along with numerous other assignments, so if you find you have a particular knack for it, serve it up as an area of expertise.

The trick in such a case is the confidentiality question. It makes some people uncomfortable to think that their leaders—community or corporate—are speaking words that flow from someone else's pen, even if the words are designed to mirror their thoughts. You may need to clear this with the people for whom you write speeches. Consider the case of Peggy Noonan, former President Ronald Reagan's speechwriter. Even the former president's detractors agreed that his speeches contained some of the most well-turned phrases in American political history. Reagan's term is over, of course, but Noonan's talent can find another home.

The usual methods of networking through individual colleagues as well as professional associations, combined with cold calling, will help you locate the jobs you seek. But whether you are approaching an agency, a company or an individual, it's always wise to use each previous experience as a way of opening doors ahead.

TECHNICAL WRITING

Even specialties have specialties within them. Technical writing is seen these days as a freelance specialty—so much so that there are not only separate professional organizations for technical communicators, there has also been a proliferation of certificate and degree programs in technical writing. Gayle Schindler, as associate communications specialist in the Document Design Center of the American Institute of Research in Washington, D.C., describes technical writing as "putting complicated information into plain language in an understandable form." Pam Ecker, a technical writing instructor in Cincinnati, expands on that definition by calling it "writing that is primarily designed to inform, to instruct, and sometimes peripherally to persuade."

By far the biggest area for technical writers is in the computer industry, though Schindler cites a wide variety of possible technical writing assignments, including preparation of customer letters (an insurance company may have 50 different letters to compose) utility and phone bills ("there are a lot of bad form writers out there," observes Schindler), owner and user manuals for cars, insurance benefits packages, contracts ("some states have 'plain language' legislation that requires contracts and insurance policies to be written in plain language"), and franchise documentation (writing the forms needed for franchising a business).

Another big area, says Schindler, is product liability: This involves writing manuals and instructions for equipment that is dangerous and writing warning labels for which there is "a whole specific system." This is a huge market, says Schindler, "and a whole new area; companies often need to do this both to reduce accidents and at the bidding of their lawyers who say 'we need manuals we can defend in court.' "

But the biggest market for technical writers is definitely computer software and hardware manuals. Writers who can bridge the gap between technicians and engineers who design the things and the customer who buys and uses them are still in high demand.

Technical writers themselves often shy away from the term "freelance writer." For some reason, it seems to have negative connotations in their business, as if to be freelance is to be not quite legitimate. (All freelancers usually run into this attitude sooner or later, so it's not only confined to the engineering field). But for whatever reason, they tend to be known more often as independent contractors or consultants.

Christopher Juillet, an independent contractor from Ann Arbor, Michigan, heads up a new subsection in the Society for Technical Communications designed specifically to meet the needs of the growing number of independent writers in the technical field.

Juillet says that there are as many ways for writers to enter this particular industry as there are people entering it, but he emphasizes that "you don't need an engineering background." He explains the growth in this area in this manner: "Some engineers can write very well, but more of them are not as practiced in the science and art of writing technical material that non-engineers can understand. They're doing their jobs by being engineers. To describe clearly an engineering process does not necessarily require an engineering degree. It requires the inclination to be able to do it. Maybe it requires the ability to step back and not be so close to the problem. (Maybe) it's better *not* to be an engineer."

Pam Ecker's experience differs somewhat: "The strongest need is for people who have the most advanced knowledge of computer systems. (The people) who combine knowledge of programming language with the knowledge and ability to write about it will demand the highest salaries." She concedes, however, that within the broad field of technical writing, "there are still opportunities for the literate generalist . . . the good writer who is a quick study."

There are a number of ways to locate these jobs, besides word of mouth, as you build a reputation for good work. If you're cold calling large companies, you'll want to contact the manager of technical communications or manager of documentation. There are also a number of contracting agencies that act as liaisons between the companies' needs and the people looking for work. These agencies can be found in your local Yellow Pages under Engineering Consultants and are also listed in several directory-like periodicals with listings (see Word Market Listings), have been around since World War II. They used to be strictly for technicians and technical professionals. Only recently have they begun to find that technical writers are much in demand by these same companies, and the writers are out there as well, looking for work.

SETTING FEES

Fees can vary widely for the freelancer exploring word markets. Sometimes a fee will be based on an hourly rate set by you or by your employer. Sometimes it's based on a per-project estimate. Hourly wages can vary—employers and writers alike have quoted a range of $15 through (rarely) $90 an hour, with the average freelancer hovering in the $20 to $40 range. Business or the private sector pays more than the non-profit sector. Experience counts, and so does previous salary history. It's a good idea to set an hourly rate for yourself that you feel comfortable quoting when asked, but be prepared to be flexible. Some employers will tell you what they're pay rate is; others may ask what you charge. If they ask, they generally don't like you to be evasive or wishy-washy. It's not very professional to show uncertainty in this area and often, if they're asking, you can feel free to quote your high-end fee. In the meantime, do some research in your area to find out what the going rate is for different jobs. Colleagues in most cities will be helpful, and you can raise or lower your rate depending on your own experience and comfort level—and how competitive you feel you need to be.

Whether you're writing a videoscript for an employee orientation, a grant proposal for a doctor trying to get funding for his latest research, or working on just the right 10 words for what retailers call point-of-sale signs, someone has probably done it—or something like it—before. Join associations, contact colleagues, and remember that people are usually flattered when you ask for their advice. Feel free to be equally generous with counsel when it's your turn. Remember that the person who solicits or offers advice today may offer you a job lead tomorrow.

FINDING WORK

So far we've identified three specific methods for locating freelance work. Connect with advertising and public relations agencies that already have client bases and become part of their pool of talent (which can certainly help expand your own personal client base); contact the communications arm of the individual companies on your own; and hone in on a specific area. It might be a subject you've written on frequently or you may have a medium in which you have worked frequently. In either case, you'll make the most headway the fastest if you zero in on your area and stick with it. Nowhere is this technique more necessary and more useful and advantageous than in the word markets. When you write for a magazine or a newspaper, your voice tends to be distinct and you are awarded a byline to distinguish your accomplishment. But in word markets, the *information* is *key*; language is first and foremost utilitarian.

If you know the "hows" of a particular methodology, you can pretty much plug in whatever information is applicable. For example, in writing direct mail pieces, there is a basic structure that is generally followed. You can't deviate too much from that structure or the piece ceases to function as a direct mail piece. If you know how to do direct mail, you can do it again and add this expertise to your résumé.

All this talk of utilitarian language and formats for different media doesn't mean there is no place for originality in writing for word markets. On the contrary, a quality initial concept for a campaign or project is probably the only difference between an adequate direct mail packager who's done it a dozen times and the first-timer who has a creative spark. In fact, one advertising copywriter said, "You don't have to be a really good writer (in this field). You need to be a good thinker and a good conceptualizer."

Content and form, plus creativity, are the elements that contribute to all communications projects. It's up to you to isolate your own strongest knowledge areas and examine closely your professional accomplishments and experiences, as well as your interests and personal enthusiasms. You can shuffle these elements like cards and come up with endless combinations. Some opportunities will find you, by serendipity. You may go after others in an aggressive or more laid-back style, whichever suits your personality. It's wise to aim high, find a practical middle ground, and have a secure fallback position. That is, locate a way to have a secure and regular partial income, at least; set aside a certain amount of time in your work schedule to vigorously pursue new freelance assignments in your domain; and never lose sight of your dream assignment.

WORD MARKET LISTINGS

In the reference section of your library, look for the following:

Standard Directory of Advertising Agencies
(also called the "Red Book")

Encyclopedia of Associations
(This excellent sourcebook lists by category all kinds of organizations. For

example: trade business, commercial; agricultural and commodities; legal, government, public administration and military; scientific, engineering and technical; health and medical; public affairs; fraternal, ethnic, religious; hobby and vocational; patriotic, athletic and sports; labor unions, chamber of commerce; fan clubs. The main volumes do not list geographically, but a separate volume does give a geographical cross-index. It's likely that your local branch will not have this, but the main library may. If the main library doesn't either, inquire about your library's extension services. Perhaps they can get this directory for you on a loan from another institution.

There are a number of "job shopper" directories for technical writers. A good many of the jobs listed are related to military contracts, but more and more commercial jobs of a technical nature are being included.)

CO Publications, Inc.
P.O. Box 79000
Kirkland WA 98083
(206)823-2222

This company publishes a weekly mailing of jobs listed, a periodic magazine, and a state-by-state directory that lists companies who use contractors regularly.

National Technical Employment Service (NTES)
P.O. Box 217
Scottsboro AL 35768
(205)259-1828

This service publishes a weekly newspaper called "Hot Flash," which gives jobs listings for contract employees nationwide. It includes information like a company's fax number, so you can fax your résumé immediately. The $55/ year subscription rate also includes a quarterly directory of companies as well as a "shopper index" that will publish summaries of contractors seeking employment in this field.

PD News
P.O. Box 399
Cedar Park TX 78613-9987
(512)250-8127

Many specialized "word markets" have their own books, periodicals and professional organizations (some of which have their own job networking organizations). Below are examples of two — for others, the best method is to ask a person working in that area for the names of relevant organizations. The library can be helpful too.

Greeting Card Creative Network
Suite 615
1350 New York Ave.

Washington DC 20005
(202)393-1780

Public Relations Journal
33 Irving
New York NY 10003

These two listings are periodicals aimed at people in the direct mail industry.

Direct Marketing
Hoke Communications
224 7th St.
Garden City NY 11530

Who's Mailing What
P.O. Box 8180
Stanford CT 06905

PROMOTING YOURSELF

Suddenly you're an author and if previously your prayers were "If only I could finish this book" or "If I only I could get it published," now your cries are "If only it would sell!" or "If only people *knew* about it!" Your friends and colleagues all know, but is your book reaching the wider reading public for which it was intended?

In this section, we focus on some of the things you can do to promote your book, and in some cases, yourself. For some authors, your book and your profession are intertwined: say you're in the real estate business and you give seminars or teach a class on buying your first house. Now you've distilled the information from your popular local classes into a book you hope to promote nationally. Naturally, good book sales may bring new offers to teach or speak—after all, now that you have a book, your "expertise" is official—and wherever you appear from now on becomes an ideal opportunity to promote your book. Promotion opportunities include a table of books for sale outside the lecture hall to a bookstore signing (probably only right after the book comes out) and perhaps some local media attention, including newspaper reviews, feature articles and radio interviews.

The scenario I just described includes all the elements for a smooth and comprehensive promotional campaign: a targeted audience, a hardworking author willing to do the advance legwork and make the most of a natural opportunity, and the snowball effect of rippling interest. If the entire operation is a success, you'll be armed that much more when you approach book buyers and media contacts in the next city.

But not every author fits the formula so perfectly. Some authors may need to work a little harder or dig a little deeper to unearth their audience and motivate that audience to buy the book. Some books are just harder to sell than others: There may be many other books on the same subject, or the subject itself may be one the public has resistance to.

If it's fiction—especially fiction that is self-published—you will not want to delude yourself about bestseller status. A great many novels by even the major publishers die an early death on the bookstore shelves. There are outlets for specialized fiction—romance, mystery, science fiction—and there is a very focused audience for literary fiction as well (see Promotion Listings for some of the organizations that can offer more information in these areas). But for the most part the reward of writing fiction is frequently the publication of the work itself; the pride that comes with recognition, acceptance and reputation among one's peers; and finally whatever sales can be mustered through independent bookstores, local, publicity and—if you're thorough, lucky and talented—distribution through one of the small press distribution networks.

But for nonfiction, almost anything can happen. And it doesn't "just happen." There are countless stories of nonfiction works that are self-published or published by a smaller press on a tiny budget that suddenly seemed to burst through to the public's awareness. Sometimes an author just seems to hit a nerve or be on the first wave of a new trend, but more often it is due to a lot of hard work and creative effort on the author's part. Assess your book realistically—who is it written for? How can you let those people know about it?

"Nonfiction doesn't sell well in bookstores," says Dan Poynter, head of Para Publishing which specializes in books that help publishers and authors sell more books. Poynter is also an author, having written and marketed a line of his books on skydiving, and he has used the technique of targeted promotion with great success.

"Skydivers and parachute engineers don't go into bookstores," he says. "But I know what magazines they read, what organizations they join, what conventions they go to." Although you may not agree that skydivers avoid bookstores, Poynter's point is well taken. Whatever it is that you're writing about, give it some concerted thought and you'll realize that "you already know where your customers are."

If you are a self-published author, you will have to do all your own promotion unless you hire someone to do it for you (see the Publicists section). If your publisher is a smaller or "independent" press (which can range from a shoestring operation that publishes one or two books a year to one that publishes a half dozen or so titles a year) you can do quite a bit to supplement their efforts. These publishers are probably going to take care of distribution and sending the most important review copies quite effectively, but you should work closely with them to make sure they know "where your customers are"; it is very likely that you'll have more information on this subject than the publisher. Finally, if you've published a book with a major publisher, don't make the mistake of thinking that they've got it completely covered. There is still quite a bit you can do, especially after the first few months when the money and time allotted to your book by their publicity department has run out and their attention has turned to newer books.

Probably the most important points to keep in mind are the following:

One — media attention (print reviews, radio and television appearances) is important, but if the book doesn't have the proper distribution either through bookstores or through telephone ordering, any efforts you make to put yourself or your book in the public eye will be completely wasted. You must be sure your books are in the stores and/or libraries or can be otherwise easily obtained; if your publisher is not doing this, you can handle it on your own, but there is only so much you can do by yourself. This will be discussed in more detail in the section on Distribution.

Two — to make the most efficient use of your personal time, energy and financial resources, target your audience whenever possible. There are a number of resources, directories and listings that can help you compile a list of associations, trade shows and conventions where *your* audience gathers and help you tap into the periodicals, newsletters and other publications they read. You may very well have some information at your fingertips, or at least in your own files, that your publisher didn't think to check out. Again, find out what your publisher is willing to do — and let your contact in the publicity department know what *you* are willing to do. Often, the publicity staff's efforts increase in direct proportion to your demonstrated commitment.

Poynter offers a great deal of advice on penetrating the "nontraditional markets," which he contends is "where all the fun is" in book promotion.

"It's all about going where people congregate. If you're selling a book on scuba diving, you deal with 'dive' shops. If it's a book on parachuting, you deal with parachuting associations, you deal with their members, with catalog houses that sell parachutes, with parachute clubs and parachute schools. There are (parachute) magazines ... Concentrate your efforts where you know you can find the people."

Whether you're placing an ad, asking for a review or getting a brief mention in a specialized publication, you're putting into motion the keys for effective word-of-mouth publicity. But don't stop there, especially if your book is on a less esoteric subject, perhaps even of wide possible general interest.

Poynter believes strongly in sending out review copies. "Most publishers will send out 25 or 30," he says. But "book reviews are the least expensive and the most effective promotions you can do for your book." For those whose commitment to self-promotion includes a certain amount of financial investment, a little can go a long way if you spend it wisely. You may think a full-page ad in a national publication will reach a lot of people, but it's more likely a lot of people will turn the page very quickly and your extravagant shout into the marketplace will fall on deaf ears. Poynter recommends that the author "blast 300 to 500 of the books out to all the appropriate magazines" with a well-written news release, declaring that "a great many are going to get reviewed."

His logic is that at $2.50 per package—the approximate cost of sending out one review copy and accompanying materials—you can send out 400 books and "you've only invested $1,000. How much advertising can you buy for $1,000?"

Reviews are worth much more, he contends, because "people *believe* editorial copy; they don't believe advertising copy." So, "don't spend your money on advertising. Put your creativity [and money and time] into review copies and news releases and trying to achieve editorial copy."

Jeff Herman, a onetime New York book publicist and currently a literary agent, says that "if the author is up front about (his) commitment (to do promotion of his own), the publisher will usually cooperate by giving you all the review copies. They love it, in most cases; they're stupid if they don't."

Poynter reminds authors that a publisher normally budgets a certain amount of money on the book ("and it may not be very much"). He strongly recommends that "you should be there with a program and suggest *where* that money is going to be spent. Otherwise, they'll just go and blow it."

BOOK REVIEWS AND EDITORIAL COPY

TRADE PUBLICATIONS

Be sure you communicate clearly with your publisher so you don't duplicate one another's efforts. The in-house publicist probably will send review copies (frequently prepublication galleys) to the major review publications, especially trade publications. *Publishers Weekly* is, of course, the most influential and widely respected, but there are a number of publications like it—smaller, sometimes more specialized, of varying degrees of influence—that are read by bookstore and library buyers. These publications are the first and most important outlet for publicizing your book because they will heavily influence what books become available to the buying public through the largest bookstores in every city.

If you are a self-published author, you must start with these publications, even before you develop your specialty mailing lists. The time to begin thinking about your marketing plan is not *after* your book comes out, but *before*.

If you can send galleys (or, because galleys are expensive, copies of the galleys), you will be perceived as much more thorough and professional. Sending a published book to a book trade publication is a case of doing too little too late.

A very useful guidebook for this task—and a wealth of additional information—is the *Book Publishing Resource Guide*, by John Kremer (Ad-Lib Publications). This guide, and the *Literary Market Place* (R.R. Bowker) — available at libraries — should give you plenty of specific places to send your galleys or review copies.

In Kremer's book, look under the heading "Magazines for Booksellers, Librarians, and Publishers"; in *LMP*, you'll find listings under "Books and Magazines for the Trade." Some of the best known are *Booklist* and *Kirkus*. Some have a special focus such as reference books, young adult books, small press or science. Many distributors also publish reviews of the books they carry. It is likely that the mainstream trade publications will not be receptive to self-published authors, but you can give it a try if you are convinced you've got something with wide appeal. There are plenty of alternative and small press trade publications that are geared toward these books, and the buyers who are most interested, however.

MAGAZINE AND NEWSPAPER REVIEWS

After the trade publications are taken care of, the next important group is book reviewers in general magazine and newspaper publications. Many of these are also listed in *LMP* and Kremer's book; you might also check the *Gale Directory of Publications* and the newspaper listings. Call to double-check or find out the name of the book editor so you can send your book directly to that person. (Book review editors will be listed in the *Gale Directory* as well.) Again, be sure you are not duplicating the efforts of your publisher, but by all means make sure these reviewers get a copy of your book.

The *Book Publishing Resource Guide* lists 400 book reviewers of large and small magazines, with information about any special focus — for example, mysteries, science fiction, nursing, music, engineering, books by Pennsylvania authors, careers, psychology, law books and genealogy. The geographical index in the periodical guide will help you locate regional publications in your area, as well as appropriate publications likely to be interested in the subject of your book. Poynter also publishes book promotion mailing lists you can rent. The lists come complete with pre-addressed peel-and-stick labels; cost is approximately 8¢ to 10¢ per label plus shipping and handling. Some examples: 500 computer magazines and newsletters, 285 sports magazines, 88 aviation newsletters, 30 hang gliding magazines, 205 education magazines, and so on. The *Encyclopedia of Associations* is equally useful here (see Word Market Listings). Make phone calls to find out who reviews books, and don't neglect your own alumni publications when selecting controlled-circulation publications. If you target closely enough, you can almost guarantee to, in Poynter's words, "achieve editorial copy."

As an example, Galynn Nordstrom, editor of *Recreation, Sports, and Leisure* — a magazine that goes to people who manage recreational facilities — says, "We run (reviews) on most of (the books) we get, if they're appropriate."

Casey Hill, editor of *New Pages*, a Michigan trade publication that focuses on alternative publications and small presses, particularly books with a political/environmental theme, also says, "What we get and what we will review are pretty close." That doesn't mean they review whatever they get: It says *most* of the time "someone has matched up what *New Pages* is about and sends an appropriate book." If they receive something outside their range of interest, Hill guesses that the author probably "hasn't taken the time to (do the) research."

You can send a copy of the published book to a specialty magazine such as *Recreation, Sports, and Leisure* later in the game to pick up extra sales, but when you're contacting trade publications or newspaper reviewers, the earlier you send — preferably galleys before publication — the better your chances are of getting attention. When considering newspapers, emphasize the word "news" in your mind. Book review editors usually get galleys in March to assign to a reviewer with an April deadline and schedule it to appear sometime in May. They prefer that the book not be two months old when their review comes out, so you've got to think ahead, too.

George Myers, Jr., book review editor at the *Columbus* (OH) *Dispatch*, says his paper regularly covers the small and independent presses, particularly when it's an Ohio author. Authors should look at local and regional markets for reviews ("A newspaper has to cover its own backyard first"), he says, and also tap into newsworthiness whenever possible ("A smart author knows what's newsworthy. And [if it is newsworthy], we'll always take a second look at [a book].")

FEATURES

Myers also points out that book reviews are not the only way to draw attention to your book: Feature articles are equally, and sometimes more, effective.

"In our Lifestyles pages," he says, "probably 20% of the copy is book-driven. Actually, you're better off getting a feature sometimes than a book review."

Maria Simpson, associate editor of the Trade News department of *Publishers Weekly*, a features section that recounts behind-the-scenes stories of a new book's publication, concurs: "Some things are better than a review!"

Your local paper is a good place to start angling for feature copy. "(Local papers) will usually do a little write-up on you," says Ken Follette, marketing manager of Sigo Press in Boston. "Send that around to a larger paper, and you can build publicity that way." John Kremer takes this scaffolding strategy one step further: "If you want to get good national publicity from newspapers, one of the most·effective ways is working with the major city local newspaper [in your town]. Work with a reporter there to get a good feature article on you and your book, preferably primarily on your book. Once the feature article comes out, encourage (the reporter) to put it over the newswire. If it goes over the AP or UPI newswire it's not uncommon for 100 or 200 or 300 newspapers to pick it up — and it's one of the most effective and efficient ways to get national publicity. I know people who do it that way all the time. If (the reporter) has done a good story, it is to (his) benefit to get it on the newswire. A good reporter is going to want to see his or her story published nationally — it's good for (his) career."

You can also, says Kremer, go directly to your local AP or UPI bureau (it's listed in the phone book) and point out the story. "They may have done it already but it doesn't hurt to remind them."

Send books not just to book editors but to the various feature editors at the newspapers, adds Kremer. "If you have a cookbook, send it to the food editor." Travel book, travel editor. Business book, business editor.

And so on. Send a news release that is tailored to inspire a feature story.

"Come up with an issue," suggests Poynter, "something that is vital to this readership. If that issue is a problem, and you can answer the question or solve the problem, then way down in your release you tell them that more information is available in your book—(this) makes for a very interesting piece." This method will probably get better results than sending a release that announces the publication of your book with all the specifics right up top; editors get dozens of these releases in a day. They need to know right away why they should pay special attention to *your* book.

Keep in mind at all times that attention to distribution is as important as getting those reviews. Don't make it hard for the reader whose interest you have piqued to find your book (see Distribution section).

TELEVISION AND RADIO

If Johnny Carson should happen to mention your book on the "Tonight" show, you may just have it made. If Phil or Geraldo or Oprah invites you as a guest, you may also have hit pay dirt for book sales. Though these three are the most oft-mentioned and probably best known of the talk show hosts, they do book authors regularly, and not just famous names. Nor are they the only ones who do so. Frequently you may land a guest spot on a show to talk not about your book per se, but about whatever it is that you are an expert on, whatever it is that you wrote about—because it's timely or relevant or relates to something going on in the news. In such cases, your book will almost always get a plug anyway—if not by the host, you can certainly find a way to mention it ("As I discuss in my book, *Daring Adventures for the Midlife-Bored . . .*"

"Good Morning, America," for example (and other shows similar in structure), produces numerous interviews and special interest segments. The show has a fashion segment producer, a money segment producer, and segment producers for the following additional topics: science, fitness, medicine, consumer news, law, entertainment, gardening, politics, film and music, plus other special projects producers.

Lifetime Cable Network has several talk shows on the air, and many of the other cable television stations do as well. Television is no longer just the "Big Three" networks anymore: the rise of cable has expanded programming needs across the board, and the viewing public's apparent insatiable interest in people and information make it possible—and even likely—that you can find a way to promote yourself, and your book, on television.

The lists of shows and names of people to contact are fairly easy to gather. There are listings in *Literary Market Place* (LMP), and Kremer's Ad-Lib Publications publishes a report on "The Top 200 National TV News, Talk, and Magazine Shows" which is updated every six months (see Promotion Listings).

Rather than doing a massive mailing recommended for print—where just a few printed lines are a good bet if you target well, and can go a long way toward boosting sales—it's a good idea to do firsthand research for television promotion to narrow down your selections.

Spend a week watching television. Look in the television guides and locate anything that might possibly be construed as a talk show, or anything that might find a place for you as a guest. If you find a show you want to be on, become familiar with the format and visualize yourself in the hot seat.

"What writers should do," recommends Pocket Books' publicist John Akesian, "is watch a week of everything (relevant) on TV and (ask yourself) how would I fit into this?"

Alex Wagner, public affairs director for Lifetime Cable Network (home of "Attitudes," "The Jane Wallace Show," and other "magazine" shows), expands on this theme: "The first rule of thumb (is to) know the show. Know who the hosts are. Learn what kind of questions they ask. Figure out the format by watching the show."

Do authors unaccustomed to appearing on television need to prepare in any way? Should they get video coaching from a professional?

"The only (time) that would be valuable," says Wagner emphatically, "is (if the) writer is a claustrophobic paranoid. We're talking about basic communication skills and basic human interest stories."

The question, according to Wagner, is not how dynamic you will be on TV, but whether or not the viewing public cares about what you have to say, or at least whether some specifically targeted audience does, and whether you can find the shows out there that cater to those interests.

Akesian thinks there is, however, a "type that will not do well on TV, period" and he recommends that authors do "a realistic assessment" of how they themselves will fare. Poynter also downplays the success of television sales in terms of actual book sales, saying, "Unless you are extremely 'mediagenic' or you've come up with something that is really different or startling, it won't pay." He cites, in particular, the "cost of wear and tear on your body."

Kremer, on the other hand, is quite optimistic on this point. On the phenomenon of "getting on Oprah," Kremer says: "They're looking for somebody who knows what (he) is talking about. They're looking for the expert, or people who have had the actual experience of whatever they're covering. You may send them something and it may be six months or a year before you hear back from them because what they do is hold on to (your material) until they're ready to do a show on that subject. It helps to remind them periodically—even if they didn't respond the first time— after three or four months that 'I'm available anytime.' I know one author who did that for a year—and a year after her initial contact with them got a call on Tuesday saying 'Can you be here Thursday?' They flew her in, put her up in a fancy hotel, (rented) a limo (etc.)."

Radio is, in the words of more than a few "mavens" in the book business, "hungrier" than television—and the chances of being able to promote yourself through this medium are excellent.

The main advantage is radio interviews are frequently done (live or taped) over the telephone, which means you can do it without that "wear and tear on your body" and you can hit many radio stations without ever leaving your home or office. Kremer's Ad-Lib Publications also publishes a report that lists 890 radio stations that do book/author programming, including details of time, host, subject interests, and so on (see Promotion Listings).

"I know people who have sold thousands and thousands of books through radio interviews," says Kremer, "averaging from five to 10 to 25 books every time they do an interview."

John Akesian says that radio in the smaller markets, particularly, is a good vehicle for authors. "We get desperate calls from radio stations all the time, 'We need an author, any author,'" he says. These stations "have a lot of time to fill" but they are usually looking for how-to books.

"You've got to be teaching someone something," says Akesian, cautioning, "A person may know all about their subject but (they have to know) what interests other people."

Mary Jo Meier, a producer at Cincinnati radio station WLW, says that on the controversial call-in talk shows she produces, she will occasionally do an author interview—generally, 15 or 20 minutes straight with the author. Then she opens up the phone lines to listeners who call in.

Meier is mainly interested in books that are getting national attention, or are "real controversial," but she is receptive to both official publishing house publicists and authors who are trying to promote themselves.

How does an author get her positive attention? She offers some tips: "The most effective thing is just a cover letter saying, as briefly as possible, what the book is about [and because she gets so much material she confirms that "less is more": you don't need a fancy media kit for radio]. Every producer I've ever met resents when an author or publishing company sends a list of publishing questions. If the host sees a press packet with that in it, they think 'the heck with them, they don't think I can do my show,' so that is something I recommend you *don't* do."

Although radio interviews are generally done on the phone, if you are traveling to another city, it could be advantageous to do a live interview in the studio. While it's not worthwhile to make a special trip for a radio interview, if you're going somewhere anyway—for business or plea-sure—certainly a little advance work can go a long way in securing some publicity for your book.

Kremer says most radio stations have a "stable of people that they can call on at almost anytime—people they've had on before that they've liked." He recommends, therefore, that if you do a radio interview, "write a follow-up letter saying basically 'I was really happy to do your show, I think it went really well, I'd be happy to do another.' If they liked you, if there was a good response," they're likely to invite you back.

BOOKSTORES AND DISTRIBUTION

Along with editorial mailings and radio television bookings, you'll want to make sure that copies of your book are available to people after they hear and read about it.

If you're publishing with a major publisher, you can probably rely on their national distribution abilities. They have all the machinery in place to ship books—usually through a major distributor or wholesaler, like Baker & Taylor or Ingram—to the main retail outlets. But it never hurts to double-check specific stores, or outlets in specific locations, in advance of a publicity tour.

"You should not assume the book is in every bookstore," says Jeff Herman. "The bookstore might carry three copies and they'll get sold out—and it will be three weeks before another shipment comes in."

If you're going to do a local radio show, for example, it might be wise to alert the local stores *in advance* so they can stock up. (Bookstores always have the option of returning unsold copies to the publisher, though it creates extra work for them. But they'll order books if they expect to sell them.)

Another option—and this is particularly useful for smaller presses or self-published authors—is to have an address or a toll-free number where people can call or write to order books directly from you—or your distrib-utor/wholesaler depending on what avenue you've chosen for order full-fillment. One advantage to this method is that it taps into impulse buy-ers—the person who calls immediately after hearing about your book. Not too many people literally rush right out to a store to make a book purchase but if they can "act now" with a phone call, they may just do so. Make it easy for them.

This is as good a place as any to explain the distinction between what a distributor does and what a wholesaler (also referred to as a "jobber") does. In truth, though there *is* a difference, the terms are sometimes used interchangeably by people in the book business, and there are often areas of overlap, so be sure to get complete and specific information from any company you may deal with about *exactly* what they do and do not do. Never assume anything.

For your purposes, distributors market the books they carry and so they select books based on what they think they can sell. They publish their own catalogs or directories, even including reviews at times. These are, of course, not reviews in the strict sense since they are designed to promote the book, but frequently these capsule reviews can make the difference with an unknown quantity and end up boosting sales for the author. Distributors often specialize: There are library distributors, small press distributors, as well as distributors that carry New Age titles or other specialty areas.

The wholesaler is strictly there for fulfillment of orders. He is a middle ground between the publisher and the stores or customers and he waits for the publisher to create the demand. You can contract with a local wholesaler, though. If your sales realistically are going to be fairly small, it may be just as easy for a bookstore or individual to order the book directly from you or your publisher. It's always a good idea, for such titles, to include an ordering address in the book itself.

LMP gives fairly comprehensive coverage of distributors and whole-salers. You can also find listings in Kremer's book or your local Yellow Pages. Jenny Owen, a Dallas publicist, claims that "there is a distributor for everyone." If you are fairly certain you have a book with good sales potential, distribution can make all the difference, especially in conjunction with good self-promotion. (See Promotion Listings for names of some distributors and wholesalers.)

You can send a review copy of your book with a letter or flyer or news release to a distributor just as you would to a reviewer and ask them to consider distributing your book.

If you're a self-published author, Ken Follette, marketing director of Sigo Press in Boston, recommends you join a marketing association such as Publishers Marketing Association on the West Coast, which will take your book along to "all the important trade shows." If you're publishing, say, a New Age title, join the New Age Publishing and Retailing Alliance (NAPRA). ("They have wonderful newsletters and wonderful gatherings.") Attending trade shows can be a big help, too—says Follette—especially for locating a distributor that is a good "match." Though, he says, "the national (trade shows) are almost *too* big for most people," the regional ones (which, Follette says, usually cost around $10 to attend) are worthwhile—particularly for independent authors not affiliated with major publishers. He cites the New England Booksellers Association in October as one such gathering; some others include New York's annual Small Press Book Fair, but these gatherings occur all over the country. *LMP* and Kremer's book both offer listings.

Advises Follette: "You can pick up everybody's catalog and you can see who their distributors are and what kind of books they sell. And you can talk to people, you can meet reviewers, you can meet the publishers themselves and tell them you have no distribution. Maybe they can help you." Though Follette may sound unduly optimistic about the nature of competition in the business marketplace—even though they're *books*, we're still talking about business—still, he's right about one thing: Never underestimate the power of "working the room."

One distributor that deals with a lot of self-published authors is Quality Books, a library distributor just outside Chicago. Amy Mescalino, director of product development, says of the company's operation: "The majority of our line is self-published or small publishers with only 10 titles or so—mostly how-to books, only nonfiction, adults and children's books."

Quality Books has sales representatives call on libraries and Mescalino says the numbers of books they sell can vary widely.

"We have some publishers (who) are very specialized and who are very happy when we sell 50 of their titles. We have others (for whom) we can sell thousands and thousands of one title," says Mescalino. She also points out that the majority of books they sell—including those that go to specialized and academic libraries—are trade paperbacks. "You don't necessarily need a hardcover for library (sales)," she explains.

There are some constraints, however. The book needs to be "professionally proofread and edited, and have a nice cover on it." While Quality Books does not require a four-color cover or an ISBN (a number assigned a book for cataloging and ordering purposes), she says these features are generally important for the trade, and authors who hope to benefit by bookstore sales are well advised to think about them.

The book should be well organized and have a table of contents, Mescalino continues. "The more professional it looks the better (it is) for us. We can't sell any more books that are not typeset. Eight years ago we got books that were literally done on a typewriter and with a mimeograph machine."

Authors who contact Quality Books will be sent their basic literature that explains how they operate, a book information form, and a distribution-to-libraries agreement (the contract). Once you fill in the basic information and return the forms, along with the book you've sent, a six-person selection committee reviews it. The selection committee works closely with the sales and marketing teams who know what the libraries are looking for, whether or not it's a title they can expect to do well with, and so on. Libraries are generally looking for books that will fill gaps in their collections.

As far as the logistics of book shipment and fees paid, Mescalino says, "We don't try and take their whole stock; we work on a consignment basis." You may be asked to send 100 books. You'll be paid when your books are sold, minus the percentage taken by the distributor.

Mescalino offers some advice to authors seeking a distributor of any kind: "Get some references. Find out how they're promoting the book—some just mail a catalog, (some have) sales reps out there showing the actual covers of books during sales calls. (Ask) what else the distributor requires—some do ask for additional complimentary copies of the book, or ask you to advertise in their publication—and that all adds to the cost."

Some distributors such as Independent Publishers Group in Chicago will not take on one-book publishers or authors as a matter of policy. They will take on small publishers but not individual titles. Like a number of distributors, IPG also requires an exclusive agreement from a publisher.

"We're looking for companies that will supply us with several titles every six months or year," says Mark Suchomel, vice president of sales and marketing. "There aren't too many (distributors) out there who will deal with one-book publishers," he adds, naming Publishers Group West as one who will do so. "There are also reasonable wholesalers that will—like Ingram Book Company—but they do not create the demand, though they fill the orders. But it will be up to the publisher [or author] to get (the books) into the bookstore initially."

Most important, according to Mescalino: "Work out a marketing strategy before the book comes off the press. Though there are many backlist titles that do very well for a while, you really need to promote a book when it's new. I get lots of calls from people who suddenly find themselves with 5,000 books in their basement or their garage and they don't know what to do with them. They never knew what to do with (those books): They wrote the book, published it, and had no idea how to sell those copies which they got back from the printer."

On the local level, you can, of course, walk your book around to the stores in your city, establishing yourself if you're not already known locally. It can't be stressed enough that this may be a case of too little too late; you should begin your promotion before your book is published. But there is still some value in the human touch, especially in the case of a self-published or short print run book. Some bookstores will take books from self-published authors on a consignment basis. Some will also work with you to set up autograph sessions—especially if it can be timed to coincide with a local radio interview, if you've had local press coverage or have done readings. But there is some difference of opinion as to how effective these really are.

John Kremer, on autograph sessions: "It's worthwhile doing it because if it works locally—and it really works well—maybe (you) can talk (your) publisher into doing more somewhere else." On the other hand, he says, "If it doesn't work well locally, it's not going to work anywhere else," so it can be a good testing ground of where to put your energy and resources.

"Obviously, the local people are going to be interested in you if you're a local person and you do it right," says Kremer.

Dan Poynter, however, on the same subject: "Book signings at bookstores are usually dreadful. You can make it work, but you have to do a little promotion. Running a little ad in the newspaper isn't going to do it. Do a mailing to all your friends and relatives. You've got to turn the bodies out."

David Sisk, a buyer for Bookstop Stores, a chain of 24 bookstores mainly in Texas, Florida and California, says that signings work best "as a follow-up to radio interviews" and it's "definitely most effective for (bookstores) to coordinate a signing with local media promotion." Echoing many others on this subject, he offers the opinion that "radio is probably one of the better ways to promote books."

PUBLICISTS

Advice about the use of publicists abounds, even among the publicists themselves. Jenny Owen, for example, warns prospective clients not to expect miracles.

"We're not going to sell a million books and get you reviewed in the *New York Times* or get you on the bestseller list," she says. "There are no guarantees. What I sell is intangible. But I have a pretty good track record—and the author has to take a gamble too."

A publicist might be a good idea for authors who really think they have an undiscovered gem, but who really don't want—or are too busy—to get involved in all the planning and legwork necessary to effectively promote even a very worthwhile book.

The main drawback to publicists is that they are quite expensive and they basically do for you the same things you can do for yourself with proper research and planning—though they frequently have more contacts in the book business and thus may be able to take some shortcuts, get some breaks, and do the job more quickly and effectively.

It's not uncommon for a publicist to charge anywhere from $1,000 to $3,000 as a monthly retainer for his or her services—and that will not include expenses such as postage and travel costs. It may take that first month for a publicist to read and become familiar enough with your book to write up all the requisite material—press releases, biography, fact sheet, media kit. So you will have shelled out quite a hefty sum before getting any return for your money.

You can find professional publicists listed in *LMP*, *The Writer's Yellow Pages*, and a selection in the *Book Publishing Resource Guide*. Some are listed as public relations and advertising agencies, which include authors among their clients, and some book publicists are specialists who work only with authors.

If you wish to explore this route, however, John Akesian recommends that you "find out what they've done. Have they done (publicity) for a book? Do they know the special rules that apply to doing a book? If they did publicity for a book, did that book sell?"

Agent Jeff Herman recommends the word-of-mouth approach: "Talk to other authors who have retained publicists and see who *they* recommend. Find out what campaigns the person has done recently, who his or her clients were. Talk to the clients. Look at the person's track record."

What about gimmicks that authors and publishers seem to come up with to grab attention from reviewers and buyers? Can't a publicist come up with gimmicks that will set you and your book apart from the crowd—perhaps like the author in Florida who promoted his novel about a magician by performing a magic act at selected bookstores?

By and large, professionals in the book business are skeptical of the value of such offbeat promotion. A magic act might be fun for the pedestrians in that mall, but it's not likely to sell more books.

"Initially, the idea of having a gimmick with a book was so unique that everyone reacted well to the idea," says Akesian. Now, he says, "gimmicks are increasingly a waste of time." Says one trade publication reviewer about the "gimmick" method of book promoting: "It doesn't get my attention at all."

PUBLIC SPEAKING

"Once you write a book, you should really think about all the possible profit centers," advises Dan Poynter. "If you like to do public speaking, join the National Speakers Association." This is an educational organization that Poynter says "has tried to elevate the whole speaking field" by running educational workshops, holding conventions and publishing newsletters, a magazine and audiotapes for its members (see Promotion Listings).

Please note that this organization does *not* do bookings—it is not a speakers bureau. But various speakers bureaus are listed in *LMP* and *BPRG*. These organizations set up paid speaking engagements for you and take a percentage of your fee for their services. They can be useful if you have something of serious interest to say to the business and corporate community—the major clients of speakers bureaus—and if you have some solid professional speaking experience. But most of them don't take amateurs: They won't take you on as a client just because you've written a book. Too many books have been published by this huge industry; being an author does not automatically confer any kind of status to CEOs and corporate heads.

"There is no shortage of speakers," said one representative of a national speakers bureau, claiming that most authors "will be sorely disappointed if they contact speakers bureaus." This assessment, he said, is the result of getting 20 unsolicited packages a day from people who want to speak, primarily so they can sell books.

His advice? "Develop a good presentation" and look for contacts locally—service clubs, community organizations, church and synagogue groups, PTAs, the Chamber of Commerce, and so on. You can come up with other more specialized groups the same way you targeted publications to which you sent review copies. Ask yourself two key questions: *Who* are the potential readers (or buyers) of your book and *where* do they gather?

Make sure you bring or ship plenty of books to display before, during and after your presentation. Arrange to have someone handle sales. Leave plenty of time for questions and answers. Your speaking presentation is bound to improve over time and you can fine-tune your talk by listening closely to the questions people ask most often. What seemed to spark the most interest in the audience? Next time, *begin* your talk with that focus.

Keep trying the speakers bureaus—not all are so formidable. Carol de Long at the American Program Bureau says authors should put together an information packet including the book, information about yourself, and an audio or videotape, if available. She says, "We'll look at it—and use it as a sales tool (as well)." Some speakers bureaus target several different markets, such as the college market or corporate market.

Ken Follette of Sigo Press says about promoting yourself, "If you're on your own, it's hard, but you can definitely do it. You have to think about how much time you want to spend (on it)."

And Alex Wagner of Lifetime Cable adds, "It doesn't matter what the name of the publishing house is. What matters is the title and the content of the book, and the willingness of the author to get out there and support the promotional efforts with dollars and with hard work. Be available, and be willing to give the hours. Be creative!"

PROMOTION LISTINGS

PUBLICATIONS
Literary Market Place
R.R. Bowker
121 Chanlon Road
New Providence NJ 07974

This bible of the book publishing industry is updated every year, but probably too expensive for most individuals to buy. It's available in library reference sections, however.

Book Publishing Resource Guide
by John Kremer
Ad-Lib Publications
51 N. Fifth St.
Fairfield IA 52556-3226
(515)472-6617
Toll free (for ordering): (800)669-0773
Fax: (515)472-3186

At $25, this book is a little more within reach — and it offers a wealth of information for anyone interested in promoting a book: information on distributors, wholesalers, fulfillment services, bookstore chains and independent booksellers, book clubs including special interest clubs, magazines that feature reviews for the book trade, reviewers at general, special interest, and business trade magazines, book fairs, author associations, and a bibliography of more than 500 additional books on the subject of book publishing.

Ad-Lib also publishes a number of books and special reports on book promotion, including the very useful *1001 Ways to Market Your Book*. Other products and services from Ad-Lib include various data files and newsletters on the subject.

Para Publishing
P.O. Box 4232-118
Santa Barbara CA 93140-4232
(805)968-7277

Toll free (for ordering): 1-800-PARAPUB
Fax: (805)968-1379

Some very useful *free* information from Para Publishing is worth sending
for: newsletters, special reports, and so on. Call or write; Dan Poynter will
put you on his mailing list and keep you there if you wish. His marketing
newsletter—automatic for a year if you order one of his books or products,
$9.95 for two years if you subscribe to it alone—has lots of useful news and
tips. Probably one of the most useful things he offers is the book promotion
mailing lists.

Both John Kremer and Dan Poynter have a wealth of information that can
set you on the right track. Both have personable office staff, are very willing
to help you isolate what it is that you need or want, and both have plenty of
well-produced brochures and sample material that will give you a very good
idea of just what they offer before you order anything that costs money. Both
are well worth exploring.

RELATED PUBLICATIONS
The Publicity Manual
by Kate Kelly
Visibility Enterprises
11 Rockwood Rd.
Larchmont NY 10538
(914)834-0602

The Writer's Guide to Self-Promotion and Publicity
by Elane Feldman
Writer's Digest Books
1507 Dana Ave.
Cincinnati OH 45207
(800)666-0963

BOOK PROMOTION AND MARKETING
Success Strategies to Increase Your Sales
(six hours of tapes with a workbook)
by Tom and Marilyn Ross
Communication Creativity
P.O. Box 909
Buena Vista CO 81211
(719)395-8659

Oxbridge Directory of Newsletters
Suite 301
150 5th Ave.
New York NY 10011
(212)741-0231

This directory of approximately 17,000 newsletters will help you target those specific to the industry or topic covered by your book.

Pocket Media Guide
Media Distribution Services/PRA Group
Dept. P
307 W. 36th St.
New York NY 10018

Lists addresses and phone numbers for more than 700 consumer, trade and technical publications, newspapers, TV and radio stations.

PUBLISHERS ASSOCIATIONS
Publishers Marketing Association
2401 Pacific Coast Hwy. #102
Hermosa Beach CA 90254
(213)372-2732

This is a 1,300-member national association of book publishers that at least one marketing director of a small press suggests is useful for smaller to medium publishers. Call for information to see if it's appropriate to your needs. Specializes in trade nonfiction.

COSMEP
P.O. Box 420703
San Francisco CA 94142-0703
(415)922-9490

Another 1,500-member national association of fiction and nonfiction book publishers.

New Age Publishing and Retailing Alliance
P.O. Box 9
East Sound WA 98245
(206)376-2702

This organization, formed just a few years ago, already has a very good reputation in the book trade. They have more than 200 members and they focus on New Age publishers and bookstores.

TRADE PUBLICATIONS
The following two publications do prepublication reviews for booksellers and librarians.

Publishers Weekly
249 W. 17th St.
New York NY 10011-5301
(212)463-6780

Kirkus Reviews
200 Park Ave. S. #1118
New York NY 10003-1543
(212)777-4554

The following two publications do prepublication reviews of general interest books for librarians only.

Booklist
American Library Association
50 E. Huron
Chicago IL 60611-2795
(312)944-6780

Library Journal
249 W. 17th St.
New York NY 10011-5301
(212)463-6819

TV/RADIO

Radio-TV Interview Report
Bradley Communications Corp.
135 E. Plumstead Ave.
Landsdowne PA 19050
(215)259-1070

The report is used by talk show producers, book reviewers and feature editors. Ads can be placed by those interested in getting a message to these groups.

The Top 200 National TV News, Talk, and Magazine Shows; Radio Phone Interview Shows: How to Do an Interview Tour From Home
Each of these books is $30 and can be ordered from Ad-Lib Publications, address above.

WHOLESALERS
Both of these major wholesalers have east and west distribution centers and numerous offices. Be sure to ask for the office closest to your area.

Baker & Taylor
P.O. Box 6920
652 E. Main

Bridgewater NJ 08807-0920
(201)685-3011
(800)526-3825

Ingram Book Company
1125 Heil Quaker Blvd.
LaVergne TN 37086
(615)793-5000
(800)937-8000

OTHERS
Publishers Weekly *magazine*
compiles a handy source of wholesalers each year in late October.

Inland Book Company
P.O. Box 120261
140 Commerce St.
East Haven CT 06512
(203)467-4257
(800)243-0138

Focus: general interest; small press; alternative

Bookpeople
2929 Fifth St.
Berkeley CA 94710-2776
(415)549-3030

Focus: wholesalers small press to bookstores and libraries

New Leaf Distribution
5425 Tulane Dr. SW
Atlanta GA 30336-2336
(404)691-6996
(800)326-2665

Focus: New Age; holistic health; New Age music

DISTRIBUTORS
Quality Books
918 Sherwood Dr.
Lake Bluff IL 60044-2204
(708)295-2010
Fax: (708)295-1556

Distributes to libraries only.

Bookslinger
2402 University Ave. W., #507
St. Paul MN 55114
(612)649-0271

This distributor focuses on books of the following subjects: art, children's books, gay/lesbian, multi-cultural literature, sociology, women's issues, contemporary novels, folklore, literary novels, small press. Distributes to bookstores and libraries.

Moving Books
P.O. Box 20037
948 S. Doris St.
Seattle WA 98108
(206)762-1750

Subjects: health, self-help, addictions, New Age titles. Distributes to bookstores.

Publishers Group West
P.O. Box 8843
4065 Hollis St.
Emeryville CA 94608
(415)658-3453

Subjects: Business, consumer issues, cooking, hobbies, family, health, house, New Age, philosophy, travel, general interest. Distributes to bookstores, schools and libraries.

SPEAKERS BUREAUS
Extensive lists of speakers bureaus can be found in *Literary Market Place* and *Book Publishing Resource Guide.*

American Program Bureau
9 Galen St.
Watertown MA 02172
(617)926-0600

Focus: General interest

Toastmasters International
2200 N. Grand Ave.
Santa Ana CA 92711

Chapter 6

WRITING AND SELLING IN CANADA

The scope of the preceding sections of this book might easily boggle the mind of the average person. But not, we would assume, of any successful writer, nor probably even of most aspiring writers.

Writing is work—that has been made quite clear in the material you have read up to now. But it is the nicest work you can find around—if you are intent on writing. That's probably why there are so many of us writing or wanting to write.

What you have read up to this point is pertinent, in general, to a writer living, working or selling anywhere in the world. We emphasize "in general" because there are regional differences—differences in markets, research resources, laws, restrictions and so on.

In the North American context, some of the greatest differences exist where one might least expect them. After all, the bulk of this continent, at least from the point of view of geography though not population, rests within two huge countries that sit north of the Rio Grande River and the Gulf of Mexico. The United States (fourth largest country in the world, in terms of geographic size) and Canada (second largest country in the world) share a common heritage, a common language and, in great part, a common network of communications. It should be noted here—in terms of the marketplace—that the population of the U.S. is 10 times larger than that of Canada.

But the sameness is not totally pervasive. In fact the differences are sometimes greater than the sameness. And that can be a surprise to a large percentage of Americans—and perhaps a similar number of Canadians. For the American writer seeking to sell into the Canadian market, there are as many differences, not quickly perceived on the surface, as there are for the Canadian writer looking to sell into the American market.

And strange as it may seem to some, especially Canadians, this exists in fiction (and by extension, drama) as well as in nonfiction. Poetry, music and other less strictured of the artistic disciplines don't present as many problems for the writer.

It's easy to understand why nonfiction can present differences. If you are writing on a political topic, for example, there could be much to explain to a reader across the border—in either direction—because the two systems of democratic government vary considerably. And if your novel has a political theme, the same problems may well exist. However, what the Canadian writer of fiction discovers quickly is that American publishers will often reject work because of a Canadian setting or an essentially Canadian theme. "No one will understand where Moose Jaw, Saskatchewan, is," one American publisher told a highly talented best-selling Canadian novelist not too long ago. "In fact, they won't even be able to pronounce Saskatchewan!" This rarely proves to be a problem for a British novel or one to be translated from a European language, and these novels often have settings far more obscure to the reader than a novel set in Montreal or Toronto, let alone Moose Jaw.

Nonetheless, this cultural bias (if that's what it is) has begun to dissipate for such writers as Robertson Davies, Margaret Atwood, Alice Munro, Mordecai Richler and countless others. Perhaps the day will come when a writer in Canada will be able to reach an audience in the U.S. without any biases other than the dictum that good, entertaining writing finds an audience while clumsy, dull writing doesn't.

What you are provided with in this section are the differences that exist on one side of the border as contrasted to the other, differences that a writer needs to know about. That information is as valuable to the American writer seeking to write for and sell into the Canadian market, as the information available in the previous sections is valuable to the Canadian writer seeking to write for the market in the U.S.A.

More important, however, this section is compiled for the writer in Canada or in the U.S. who is writing for the sizable market available in Canada. The structure of this section follows the structure of the earlier material in the book. It avoids the sometimes complex subject of vocabulary (Canadians call a tract of land set aside for Indians a "reserve," not a "reservation," for example). Nor does it refer to the differences in spelling (Canadians write "cheques" on their bank accounts, not "checks") but uses the U.S. spelling from the previous chapters.

All prices are in Canadian dollars unless otherwise noted; U.S. authors should check the latest exchange rate before ordering material. And please note that our style is to run postal codes one space after the province while it's traditional in typing an envelope to have two spaces to avoid confusing the alphanumeric code with the province abbreviation.

What you will find here is information specific to the Canadian market and to Canadian source materials—where, and if, information specific to, or concomitant with, what you have already learned is vital or useful to your needs as a writer seeking to sell into the market in Canada.

LIVING AS A WRITER

INCOME SOURCES

Opportunities for freelancing in Canada are not as numerous, obviously, as they are south of the border — but they exist in numbers that are just about adequate for those writers who actively seek assignments. Various writer's organizations regularly update listings in their respective newsletters — and some, such as the Canadian Authors Association and the Periodical Writers Association, provide information about regional opportunities as well as in the newsletters of their branches and chapters. *Canadian Author & Bookman* also carries a markets section in each issue.

As for freelance editing, the Freelance Editors' Association maintains an up-to-date databank both of members whose interests and specialties are readily available and of potential clients.

SETTING UP SHOP

The basic needs for going into business are similiar in Canada to what they are in the U.S. You may find that getting a bank willing to help finance you in starting a small business is not easy or even likely. Banking in Canada is carried on by fewer than a dozen national banks and not the many local or statewide banks found in the U.S.

While Canadians are comfortably covered by a national health scheme, the need for disability insurance still exists. A number of the national writers' organizations and some of the provincial writers' guilds have signed on with major insurance companies and provide disability protection for their members.

RECORDS AND ACCOUNTS

Writers with freelance experience who have resided in both Canada and the U.S., at different times, have found that there seems to be more appreciation of the entrepreneurial aspects of freelancing within the IRS than one finds generally within Revenue Canada. In the U.S. you are likely to find at least one agent in most large urban centers who knows what a freelance writer does and who can be sympathetic to the trials and tribulations of earning a living at a keyboard that isn't hooked up for musical output.

Nevertheless, if you keep records well — and accurately — you have a better chance of a civil discussion with the civil servant (if that isn't an oxymoron) assigned to your tax audit. The advice given earlier is excellent and, in the main, applies to the writer in Canada. There are retirement plans (with different names and acronyms) and other ways of getting the best break on your tax return — but essentially, with the help of a knowledgeable accountant, you should be able to stretch your dollars to cover most "taxing" contingencies.

A good number of writers who earn a living (or at least the bulk of it) from the sale of their writing, have found that setting up a small corporation is worth the expense and the other small requirements of operating a formalized business. For one thing, filing your taxes at the corporate rate is far less expensive than filing as an individual.

In Canada, as in the U.S., if you are engaged in earning money from self-employment activities, you have to make a quarterly return on your estimated taxes. This applies if:

- Your net federal tax for the past year, including surtax, is more than $1,000;
- Your net federal tax for the coming year, including surtax, is more than $1,000; and
- You will have income tax deducted at source from less than three-quarters of your net income for the coming year.

These quarterly returns are due by the 15th of March, June, September and December. The rules may change in any given year, and there are penalties if you don't file and pay as you go — a very important reason for getting yourself a competent accountant.

AVOIDING PROBLEMS

Among the things you should consider in full-time freelancing are, of course, saving receipts for purchases and other related papers. But the one piece of paper too many writers totally disregard is the cursed rejection slip.

True, some writers like to keep these missives to paper the walls of their workrooms (or bathrooms), others to fill a scrapbook. The wise ones file them carefully against the day that a Revenue Canada auditor wants proof that you're a serious writer.

Yes, those rejection slips, along with copies of all the query letters and other correspondence you have had with editors, and records of long-distance phone calls, copies of all manuscripts — as well as the receipts you already have been saving — should be preserved for a reasonable number of years (some accountants suggest six or seven). You'll want these in the event some curious tax department employee decides to ask questions long after you've forgotten the tax return you filed and the hard-earned dollars you sent the government.

It's a good idea to get a date stamp so you can stamp all the undated correspondence (especially memos) that might otherwise look suspicious in an audit.

As far as what receipts to keep, you must realize there are countless items you purchase for daily use in running a freelance business, items you take for granted and probably forget to keep account of.

Do you remember to ask the post office clerk for a receipt when you buy stamps or send a special delivery letter or a package? Do you record, and get receipts for, purchases of books and periodicals you use for research? Do you record your magazine subscription and newspaper delivery payments, as well as payments to the lawyer, researcher, typist, etc.? Do you attend, and keep records of payment for, professional development seminars, fees to writers' associations for memberships, meetings and conferences?

And, of course, if you face a tax audit, have you a solid record of your writing successes? Not only does this entail keeping your portfolio, but you should also save clippings of any articles that refer to your accomplishments. If you've decided to write for some non-paying periodicals, you can't show that the free copies they sent you added anything to your financial income, but a copy of your writing output in these journals is as impressive to the tax auditor as any for which you did receive payment.

You'll have to keep up with the tax laws if you don't use an accountant. They change almost annually, it seems. The Revenue Canada District Office in your area (it's listed in your phone book) should be able to help you with the most recent bulletins published by the department, which apply to small businesses and the self-employed.

LAW AND THE WRITER

BOOK CONTRACTS
The Writers' Union of Canada publishes two pamphlets on basic contract terms: *Help Yourself to a Better Contract* and *Tradebook Contracts*. Prices and ordering information can be found later in this chapter under Additional Resources. Essentially, the details are similar to the Authors Guild model contract, but there is special emphasis on the Canadian market as separate from the English-language market elsewhere in the world.

It is important for Canadian writers (and other English and French language authors) to understand that the market in Canada is sufficiently large to warrant separate publication rather than having the Canadian sales territory granted to a publisher in the U.S., U.K. or France as a subsidiary source of income. For the writer this method means more earnings because royalties will be paid to the author by the Canadian publisher rather than shared with the originating publisher. Sales also are usually greater for books published by Canadian publishers than books shipped into Canada and sold on an agency basis.

MAGAZINE CONTRACTS

The Periodical Writers Association of Canada also provides a model contract appended to the association's membership directory. Write to PWAC at the address listed in Additional Resources.

RESOURCES

Many of the problems writers face are legal ones—problems with a legal basis or aspect, problems that may have legal solutions. Acquiring legal rights or defending them are survival skills which are costly. To provide assistance to writers—and artists in all disciplines—Artists' Legal Advice Services has been formed in Toronto to offer legal assistance and educational services to artists of all disciplines. The service is free to all artists and writers; funding is provided by the Ontario Legal Aid Plan.

The lawyers on duty have expertise in issues that affect the artist's confidentiality. If your problem cannot be dealt with immediately, you will be advised about how to obtain further legal services.

An appointment is essential; do not drop in unannounced. To make an appointment, telephone (416)360-0772 between 9 a.m. and 5 p.m., Monday to Friday. The ALAS office is located at Suite 310, 80 Spadina Ave., Toronto ON M5V 2J3. There is a clinic held every Thursday evening from 5:30-7:30 p.m. at that address.

Several unique sources of income are available to Canadian writers. These are grants available from various governmental bodies for works in progress and public readings, etc.; payments to writers whose books are held in libraries (Public Lending Right); and payments to writers whose work is photocopied for various purposes (reprographic rights).

We will not discuss a tax that went into effect at the beginning of 1991. Known as GST (for Goods and Services Tax), it is the equivalent of VAT (Value Added Tax) now current in a few countries around the world. Suffice it to say that writers are required to add 7% to their invoices to publishers and, of course, will be paying that tax on materials they buy for their own use as writers. Remitting the tax to the government involves a sometimes-complicated formula that will probably prove time-consuming. Writers who have not already done so should inquire from their local Revenue Canada Excise Office as to whether, and how, they are involved. Registration forms are available at local post offices.

GRANTS

A major program of grants is administered by the Canada Council, a body created by the Canadian Parliament in 1957 to promote and foster the arts in Canada. The council's programs provide assistance in all the arts, and its Writing and Publishing Section has a wide variety of support for writing in various genres — fiction, children's literature, poetry, drama and nonfiction (biographies, studies, essays and criticism).

The council supports writers engaged in writing projects, provides awards and literary prizes, assists Canadian-owned publishing houses and periodicals, supports and collaborates in efforts to promote and improve the distribution of Canadian books, and administers other programs to assist writers.

Five types of grants are available to individual writers. The largest of these is to a maximum of $32,000. "This program is designed to allow free time for personal artistic activity to writers who have made a nationally or internationally recognized contribution to their discipline through a number of years and who are still active in their profession," says Gordon Platt, Writing Program coordinator at the council. The grant allows the writer to work on a novel, a collection of short stories or poems, a stage play or a work of children's literature over a period of between four and 12 months.

A second grant program provides writers with the opportunity to do personal creative work or improve their skills and provides for living expenses up to a maximum of $18,000, also for the same period of time as the larger grants.

Grants for nonfiction writers cover living expenses, production and travel costs up to $18,000 for periods up to four months. These are for writing projects that include biographies, studies, essays and criticism.

A grant of up to $4,000 is available to help writers pursue creative work or to work on a specific project. This program provides a living allowance if the applicants arrange to devote the major part of their time to their program.

Travel grants not exceeding $2,800 for round-trip airfare plus $100 a day are intended to enable writers to make trips of a maximum of five days on occasions important to their professional careers.

To assist writers in projects that "venture into new territory in the arts and culture," a program called Explorations is available to individuals and groups with "innovative projects that may introduce new approaches to creative expression, cross disciplines, or which fulfill specific needs in the development of the arts," according to Joyce Ziemans, the council's executive director. The maximum available is $16,000.

There are two programs that provide funds for public readings by authors. One is for readings within Canada, while the second provides for readings in the United States. In the first program, organizations may apply to have the Canada Council sponsor readings by "approved" Canadian writers for which the writer gets $200 plus travel expenses to a maximum of $400. The U.S. readings program pays the writer a $200 fee and pays travel costs. The American sponsor is limited to three such readings a year and must pay the Council $100 (U.S.) per writer to help defray travel costs. The host also pays for meals, lodging and publicity.

Two writer-in-residence programs enable writers to give consulting services to those who seek help with their writings. The first, a so-called short-term program, allows an eligible writer to spend four to 10 days in a community to be available for discussions, interviews, public readings, speeches and manuscript readings. The council pays $125 of the prescribed $200-per-day fee plus travel expenses. The sponsor pays the remaining $75, plus meals, lodging and publicity costs. The second program allows for writers to provide individual consulting services and participate in workshops at post-secondary educational institutions and other public organizations such as libraries. The writers in this program *must* be free to spend time on their own writing. The council pays 50% of the writer's stipend and the host organization pays the rest.

Other programs include a writer-in-residence program that takes a Canadian writer to Scotland for a year, and a series of literary prizes.

LISTINGS

Detailed information on deadlines and program criteria are included in a kit, *Programs in Writing and Publishing*, available from the council, which also accepts collect phone calls from writers.

The Canada Council
Writing and Publishing Section
350 Albert St.
P.O. Box 1047
Ottawa ON K1P 5V8
(613)598-4334 or (613)237-3400

There are grants available from some provinces. For specific information in your province write or call:

Alberta Culture, Film & Literary Arts
12th Floor, CN Tower
10004 - 104 Avenue
Edmonton AB T5J 0K5
(403)427-2554

British Columbia Department of Municipal Affairs, Recreation and
   Culture
Cultural Service Bureau
6th Floor, 800 Johnson St.
Victoria BC V8V 1X4
(604)387-7912

Manitoba Arts Council
123 - 555 Main St.
Winnipeg MB R3B 1C3
(204)944-2237

Newfoundland and Labrador Arts Council
P.O. Box 5011
St. John's NF A1C 5V3
(709)726-2212

Nova Scotia Department of Culture
P.O. Box 864
Halifax NS B3J 2V2
(902)424-5929

Ontario Arts Council
500 - 151 Bloor St. West
Toronto ON M5S 1T6
(416)961-1660
or (800)387-0058 (toll free)

PEI Council of the Arts
P.O. Box 2234
Charlottetown PEI C1A 8B9
(902)892-8788

Ministère des Affaires Culturelles
225 est Grande Allée
Québec PQ G1R 5R5
(416)643-8900

Saskatchewan Arts Board
2550 Broad St.
Regina SK S4P 3V7
(800)667-7526 (toll free in Saskatchewan)
or (306)787-4056

A number of municipal governments also maintain grants programs. A call to your local city hall's information desk should direct you to the appropriate department to learn if such programs exist and what they are.

PUBLIC LENDING RIGHT

The Public Lending Right Commission, which consists of authors, librarians and publishers, was established in 1986 — after decades of lobbying by writers' groups, starting with the Canadian Authors Association in 1946 and continued in more recent years by The Writers' Union. The commission administers a program of payments to Canadian authors for books of theirs that are eligible for the program and are cataloged in libraries across the country.

Payments are determined by sampling the holdings of a representative number of libraries. The more libraries in which an eligible title is found, the larger the PLR payment. The number of copies found in a library is not important; it is the title's presence in a library's catalog that determines the payment.

The available budget determines both the dollar value of each title held in a sampled library as well as the maximum that an author can earn. Compensation most recently was $42 for each title found in each of the libraries checked (though it has been less in the past). The maximum an author can earn currently is $4,200 — no matter how many titles are registered in an author's name, or in how many libraries his or her books are found. Checks are sent to eligible authors each spring.

An author who has not registered in the program has to apply for an Author Registration Sheet. These are obtainable from the Public Lending Right Commission, at P.O. Box 1047, 350 Albert St., Ottawa ON K1P 5V8. If you wish to phone the commission, the number is (613)598-4378, and the PLR fax number is (613)598-4390. The PLR office does *not* accept collect calls. Along with the registration sheet you will receive a Title Data Sheet. You will need to submit one title Data Sheet for each book you seek to register, so make photocopies of that form for as many books as you intend to register. It is important to complete the sheets in every respect. "It is shocking to learn that writers sometimes can't read and don't follow instructions," says Gwen Hoover, executive secretary of the commission. "This causes delays and can result in the loss of your payments for a year." The only question that need not be answered is that of a pseudonym, but only if that happens not to be applicable. For each title registered, you must send a photocopy of both the title page and the table of contents page. If the work does not have a contents page, you must make this fact known to the commission.

The PLR program is applicable if you are a Canadian citizen (whether living in Canada or abroad) or are a permanent resident in the country. Your name must appear on the title page or, for contributors to an anthology, in the table of contents. However, you are not eligible if your work was created for an employer in the course of your employment.

It should be noted, too, that "a claim cannot be made on behalf of a deceased author by the estate or survivors," warns Hoover. Nor do the shares of ineligible or deceased authors accrue to the eligible or surviving authors, or to contributors in the case of anthologies, or to books that qualify for payments to editors, translators and illustrators or photographers; you may only claim your own percentage share in such cases.

Every time you register a new title you must also submit a photocopy of the title page and the table of contents as you did the first time you registered.

What isn't eligible for PLR?

A title is not eligible if it is:

- wholly or mainly a musical score;
- a newspaper, magazine or periodical;
- a calendar, agenda, coloring book or game;
- a directory, index, compilation, bibliography, dictionary, atlas, encyclopedia or genealogy;
- the catalog of an exhibition or the published proceedings of a conference, seminar or symposium;
- a work containing fewer than 48 pages, or a children's work containing fewer than 24 pages;
- a report, study, survey, analysis or program evaluation prepared for or published by a governmental or para-governmental organization, institution or corporation;
- an instructional or self-help book or manual (including books that describe "how-to" techniques, skills or games, travel guides and cookbooks);
- an unpublished work (i.e. dissertations or theses in manuscript form, etc.);
- a textbook or book designed primarily for an educational market.

There is a change likely to be made in the criteria regarding instructional and self-help books which will increase the number of books eligible, but that decision had not been made when this book went to press, according to David Homel, currently president of the executive committee.

It is important to know that works may only be registered once, regardless of how many editions have been published. Translations, however, are considered individual works and should be applied for separately.

For specific eligibility criteria regarding authors, editors, translators, contributors to anthologies, illustrators and photographers, write to the commission to ask for their pamphlet *How the PLR System Works*.

THE REPROGRAPHY COLLECTIVE

The Canadian Reprography Collective—known popularly as Can-Copy—represents the interests of writers when their published works are photocopied by individuals or organizations for various purposes. The collective, established in 1988, "negotiates contracts with various governmental bodies, businesses and library systems so that records can be kept of photocopying," says Edith Yeomans, the collective's executive director. Writers who register with the collective are eligible for payments when their works are photocopied.

Canadian Reprography Collective
M1 - 379 Adelaide St. West
Toronto ON M5V 1S5
(416)366-4768

A COMMUNITY OF WRITERS

AUTHOR ASSOCIATIONS

In addition to a number of major national groups in various disciplines, there are writers' clubs in almost every community in the country. To find one in your community, ask your local bookshop or library if they can help. You also might find notices of meetings published in the "What's On" column of your local newspaper.

The largest and oldest major group in the country is the Canadian Authors Association. Founded in 1921, the CAA currently has branches in 18 centers from Atlantic to Pacific. Dedicated to the concept of "Writers Helping Writers," its membership consists of about 70% professional writers. The remaining 30% (associates) either have insufficient published material to meet the criteria to be full members, or are still in the process of learning about the craft. The principal programs in the branches involve workshop groups in various writing disciplines. At the national level, the CAA publishes a variety of publications for the benefit of writers and beginners, and maintains an active awards program that is highly regarded by the arts and publishing communities. In the last quarter-century it has sired a variety of other writers' groups that have specialized interests.

ACTRA Writers' Guild (Alliance of Canadian Cinema, Television and Radio Artists)
5th Floor
2239 Yonge St.
Toronto ON M4S 2B5
(416)489-1311

Canadian Authors Association
275 Slater St., #500
Ottawa ON K1P 5H9

Canadian Farm Writers Federation
% Karen Davidson
Country Guide
350 Main St. East
Milton ON L9T 1P6

Canadian Science Writers Association
24 Ryerson Ave.
Toronto ON M5T 2P3
(416)592-3327

CANSCAIP (Canadian Society of Children's Authors, Illustrators and Performers)
P.O. Box 280, Station L
Toronto ON M6E 4Z2
(416)654-0903

Crime Writers of Canada
202 Keetwatin Ave.
Toronto ON M4P 1Z8

Federation of British Columbia Writers
P.O. Box 2206, Main Post Office
Vancouver BC V6B 3W2
(604)683-2057

Island Writers' Association
P.O. Box 1204
Charlottetown PEI C1A 7M8
(902)675-2454

League of Canadian Poets
24 Ryerson Ave.
Toronto ON M5T 2P3
(416)363-5047

Manitoba Writers' Guild
3rd Floor
374 Donald St.
Winnipeg MB R3B 2J2

NEWSbusiness (National Editors & Writers Society for Business Media)
113 - 23 Thorncliffe Park Dr.
Toronto ON M4H 1H7

Periodical Writers Association of Canada
24 Ryerson Ave.
Toronto ON M5T 2P3
(416)868-6913

Playwrights Union of Canada
2nd Floor
54 Wolseley St.
Toronto ON M5T 1A5
(416)974-0201

Romance Writers of America, Ontario Chapter
% Chris Grover
904 - 115 Main St.
Hamilton ON L8N 1G5

Saskatchewan Writers Guild
2049 Lorne St.
P.O. Box 3986
Regina SK S4P 3R9
(306)757-6310

Writers' Alliance of Newfoundland and Labrador
P.O. Box 1133
St. John's NF A1C 5M5
(709)739-5215

Writers' Federation of New Brunswick
P.O. Box 37, Station A
Fredericton NB E3B 4Y2

Writers' Federation of Nova Scotia
1809 Barrington St., Ste 901
Halifax NS B3J 3K8
(902)423-8116

Writers' Guild of Alberta
10523 - 100th Ave.
Edmonton AB T5J 0A8
(403)426-5892

The Writers' Union of Canada
24 Ryerson Ave.
Toronto ON M5T 2P3
(416)868-6914

COLONIES, RESIDENCIES AND RETREATS

There are a few places that writers in Canada can go to get away from the regular routine of daily life — to write, commune with other writers, as well as nature, and partake of the opportunities that such retreats provide. Among them are:

Canadian Young Authors Camp

A seven-day summer program that provides a unique opportunity for young writers to develop their talents. The camp offers one-on-one sessions with professional authors. There are also three-day intensive seminars for fiction, poetry and picture books. For information, write to Suite 1204, 5795 Yonge St., Willowdale ON M2M 4J3 or telephone (416)730-8357.

Delta Marsh Writers' Retreat

This program is sponsored by the Manitoba Writers' Guild. At this writing, plans for the future are uncertain. The first retreat was held in September, 1990, at Delta Marsh, Manitoba, and a second retreat is planned for the fall of 1991. But as we went to press, details were not firm. The retreat is open only to members of the guild. If you qualify, call (204)942-6134 for information.

Ganaraska Writers' Colony

A summer gathering in eastern Ontario, this operation could supply no details as we went to press. They suggest that interested writers contact them at RR #1, Bailieboro, Ontario KOL 1B0.

Sage Hills Writing Experience
This retreat is located 75 kilometres north of Saskatoon, Saskatchewan, and is operated in late summer. for more information, call Steven Smith at (306)665-6166.

Saskatchewan Writers Colonies
These colonies (which now include retreats for artists in all disciplines) are run by the Saskatchewan Writers' Guild. Subsidies are available for writers from provincial culture departments in Alberta, Manitoba, British Columbia and Ontario as well as from the Canada Council. Information can be obtained by writing to P.O. Box 3986, Regina, Saskatchewan S4P 3R9 or phoning (306)757-6310.

WestWord Retreat for Women
This retreat is run by the Canadian International College in conjunction with its summer school in North Vancouver, British Columbia, and is held for two weeks in August. Information can be obtained from Gloria Greenfield at (604)872-9014.

CONFERENCES AND WORKSHOPS

Ad Astra Convention
P.O. Box 7276, Station
Toronto ON M5W 1X9

Ad Astra, a society of science fiction and fantasy writers, holds an annual convention every June.

Banff Writing Workshops
Banff Centre School of Fine Arts
P.O. Box 1020
Banff AB T0L 0C0

Workshops are held each spring and summer.

Canadian Authors Association Annual Conference
275 Slater St., #500
Ottawa ON K1P 5H9

A four-day program each June that is jam-packed with workshops in all genres. The conference is held in a different city each year; the 1991 conference is in Ottawa. Future conferences are planned for southwestern Ontario, and Vancouver, British Columbia. Open to non-members.

Canadian Authors Association Manitoba Branch Workshops
202-180 Market Ave.E.
Winnipeg MB R3B 0P7

This CAA Branch runs highly acclaimed and successful workshops and blue-pencil sessions on an on-going basis. Open to non-members.

Children's Writing Workshops
CANSCAIP
P.O.Box 280, Station L
Toronto ON M6E 4Z2

CANSCAIP, the Canadian Society of Children's Authors, Illustrators, and Performers, a group of professionals in the field of children's culture, is probably the best able to run workshops in writing for this genre. Information is available by telephone at (416)654-0903.

Festival of the Written Arts
P.O. Box 2299
Sechelt BC V0N 3A0

A four-day progrm in August featuring guest speakers representing all genres. Write, or phone (604)885-9631, for information regarding future events.

Kingston School of Writing
P.O. Box 1061
Kingston ON K7L 4Y5

A summer workshop open to all writers who desire to improve their craft, regardless of age or experience. Write, or phone Bob Hinderley or Kathryn Morris at (613)548-1556.

Ottawa Independent Writers
School of Continuing Education
Carleton University
301 Administration Building
Ottawa ON K1S 5B6

An annual conference is conducted with workshops in various genres.

Red Deer College
Creative Writing Workshops
Red Deer AB T4N 5H5

The creative writing workshops and a "writers on campus" program are available each summer. Write, or call (403)342-3300.

Ross MacDonald Mystery Writing Weekend
CAA Waterloo-Wellington Branch
104-121 Avenyue Rd.
Toronto ON M5R 2G3

The Waterloo-Wellington Branch of the Canadian Authors Association operates this workshop from time to time. Write, or phone (406)629-8084 for information.

Ryerson Polytechnical Institute
350 Victoria St.
Toronto ON M5B 2K3

Workshops, as well as credit courses, are offered in various genres. Write, or telephone (416)979-5129.

Toronto Trek Convention
P.O. Box 187
65 Front St. West
Toronto ON M5J 1E6

A summer program allowing writers of science fiction and fantasy to meet and have their work criticized by professionals. Write, or phone (416)925-6241 for further information.

University of Toronto Writer's Workshop
School of Continuing Education
158 St. George St.
Toronto ON M56S 2V8

A summer workshop whose instructors are prominent writers. Write, or telephone Anne Montagnes at (416)978-2400 for information.

Upper Canada Writers Workshop
St. Lawrence College Saint-Laurent
King and Portsmouth Streets
Kingston ON K7L 5A6

Open to emerging and experienced writers, with special programs designed for high school students. The workshops are held in July and are designed to stimulate, refine and diversify each participant's writing ability through group instrution and individual consultation.

Writewords Studio
196 Elm St.
Winnipeg MB R3M 3J2

Established with the assistance of the Manitoba Branch of the Canadian

Authors Association, this group can be reached by telephone at (204)488-0511 for more information.

RESEARCHING IT

Perhaps the best source for writers in Canada doing research is *Finding Canadian Facts Fast*, compiled by Stephen Overbury (Methuen). Overbury is a professional researcher who has taught the techniques of his trade to hundreds of would-be researchers in many walks of life.

Among the volumes you will find handy from time to time are such books as *Dictionary of Canadian Biography* (University of Toronto Press) covering, in the first 12 volumes produced to date, the years 1000 (yes, 1000) to 1900; *Canadians All* (Gage) with eight volumes so far; and *Book of Canadian Winners and Heroes* by Brenna and Jeremy Brown (Prentice-Hall).

Canadian News Facts (MPL Communications), *Canadian News Index*, as well as *Canadian Periodical Index* dating back to 1938, *Canadian Magazine Index* which began operations in 1984, and *Canadian Business Index*, listing some 72,000 articles annually carried in more than 200 business periodicals, all provide excellent factual data for the writer.

LIBRARIES

Virtually all of the more than 3,000 public libraries in Canada are linked, either through formal or informal networks. This means that you can usually manage to get a copy of almost any book you may need for your research. Your librarian can tell you about interlibrary loans and how you can arrange to borrow a book that may not otherwise be available.

And before you go off searching for books that may not exist, or seek to find what books may have been published in a particular discipline, consult *Canadian Books in Print*, published by the University of Toronto Press.

SPECIAL LIBRARIES

If you've searched the public library system and the academic libraries without success, your librarian may refer you to a special library. These are private libraries that serve a particular organization's special needs. They prefer to work through a librarian rather than directly with you simply because the special librarian knows what books are held in the public system. They are unable to afford to serve outside sources unless there is no alternative available.

It has been estimated that there are perhaps 2,000 special libraries in Canada, and some of them are treasure troves in that they are more than a century old. The *Canadian Library Handbook* lists the special libraries and you should look for a copy of that volume in your own library.

THE NATIONAL LIBRARY OF CANADA

The National Library of Canada has collections and offers services that can be of great benefit to the writer-researcher. Established in 1953, the National Library is in midtown Ottawa within walking distance of the Parliament Buildings. One of its prime functions is to collect copies of everything published in Canada. The National Archives, discussed below, is housed in the same building.

A gift of some 300,000 titles from the Library of Parliament laid the foundation of the National Library collection. Under the terms of the National Library Act, two copies of each book and serial printed and published in Canada that is priced at less than $50 — or one copy if the price is more than $50 — must be deposited with the library. In addition to printed materials, sound recordings with a Canadian connection (Canadian content, composer, artists, conductor, etc.) and educational kits are also subject to the deposit provisions.

Along with the deposited material, a completed information form has to be submitted. These forms enable the National Library catalogers to ensure a complete and accurate entry for each title in *Canadiana*, the national bibliography available in your local library.

As well as works published in Canada, the library attempts to acquire one copy of all materials published abroad that are by Canadian authors or are about Canada.

In addition to collecting published materials, the Canadian Acquisitions Division and Legal Deposit Office maintains clipping files on Canadian authors. Newspaper clippings of reviews, book jackets and author information forms requested from publishers are maintained in vertical files. Access is normally restricted to researchers in the National Library and to authors in accordance with the Privacy Act.

The National Library has a huge union catalog that lists some 15 million books in the social sciences and humanities that are available in about 300 libraries in the country. Similar union listings of social science and science periodicals are kept at the Canada Institute for Scientific and Technical Information in Ottawa.

While the National Library will answer questions directly from the public, it can often tell you which libraries in the country have the book you are looking for. You can then arrange with your own library for an interlibrary loan.

Among the many publications issued by the National Library's own publishing program, you may find especially useful *Research Collections in Canadian Libraries*.

ARCHIVES

The National Archives of Canada in Ottawa are a virtual treasure trove of material — especially when you may have found gaps in other research sources. This institution is responsible for acquiring from any source all significant archival material of every kind, nature and description relating to all aspects of Canadian life and to the development of the country. It is also responsible for providing suitable research services and facilities to make this material available to the public.

The Archives Branch of the NAC is composed of the Manuscript Division, the Federal Archives Division, the Machine Readable Archives Division, the National Map Collection, the Picture Division, the National Photography Collection, and the National Film, Television and Sound Archives. Other branches include the Conservation and Technical Services Branch which provides reproductions for the public of all materials held in the NAC.

The NAC is located at 395 Wellington St., Ottawa ON K1A 0N3, in the same building that houses the National Library. For information about the archives, call (613)995-5138.

Other archival sources include the Public Archives of Nova Scotia, the Archives of Ontario, the Prince Edward Island Department of Education Public Archives, Les Archives nationales du Québec (Quebec National Archives), and the Saskatchewan Archives Board.

The Nova Scotia institution was founded in 1857 and provides a plethora of records as well as photos, maps and architectural collections. It also has a film and sound department. You can write to the Provincial Archivist at 6016 University Ave., Halifax NS B3H 1W4, or telephone (902)424-6060.

The Ontario archives were established in 1903 and have a vast collection of early newspapers, government documents, historical manuscripts as well as other potentially useful material for the writer. Located at 77 Grenville St., Toronto ON M7A 2R9, it can be reached by telephone at (416)965-4039.

The PEI archives are located at 100 Richmond St., Charlottetown PEI C1A 7K7 and can be reached by telephone at (902)368-4290.

The Quebec institution is at 1210 avenue du Séminaire, P.O. Box

10450, Ste-Foy PQ G1V 4N1. The telephone number is (418)644-1069. There is a branch of the Quebec archives in Montreal at 1945 rue Mullins, Montreal PQ H3K 1N9 where the telephone number is (514)873-3064.

The Saskatchewan archival collection was established in 1945 and contains a large collection of the private papers of politicians and community leaders, as well as records of churches, cooperatives, voluntary associations, businesses, unions and political parties. It is located at 3303 Hillsdale St., Regina SK S4S 6W9 and can be reached by telephone at (306)787-4068.

The Association of Canadian Archivists has published a *Directory of Canadian Records and Manuscript Repositories* that might also prove useful.

DATABASES

While most of the major computer services are American-based (and they do offer Canadian material), there are Canadian services available to the writer who has a computer and knows how to tap into the services available on-line.

You might want to refer to *COIN: A Directory of Computerized Information in Canada* published by the Alberta Information Retrieval Association. Also useful is *Omni Online Database Directory* by Mike Edelhart and Owen Davies, an American book published by Macmillan in 1983 and distributed in Canada by Maxwell Macmillan.

Among the many services available, you may find that Info Globe is quite useful for Canadian material in that it offers a list of articles and the full text of stories published in *The Globe and Mail* from Nov. 14, 1977, to the present. For information on accessing the services of Info Globe by modem, there are toll-free lines. In Ontario the number is (800)268-8043. Elsewhere in Canada the number is (800)268-9128. In the U.S., callers can use Info Globe's regular phone service at (416)585-5250.

GOVERNMENT PUBLICATIONS

The federal government through the Canadian Government Publishing Centre, a department of Supply and Services Canada, Ottawa ON K1A 0S9, is responsible for the publication of thousands of pamphlets, books and other materials. The only complete catalog available is on microfiche. Printed catalogs are issued quarterly at $15.20, but only cover the previous three months.

To determine if there are government publications you would find useful for your own research, check with your librarian. Most libraries across the country subscribe to the microfiche service and this will provide constant updated lists of everything available, including free publications.

All of the provinces have publishing programs as well. The same advice applies inasmuch as each of the 10 provincial governments prepare catalogs in a different fashion and a library check will provide the information you need more quickly and at less expense.

One of the best sources of information in the country on an ongoing basis is Statistics Canada. This federal department (known familiarly as StatsCan) produces more than 600 publications annually in such fields as economics and demographics. As a result StatsCan interprets and publishes information on Canada's social and economic life that can prove extremely useful to the work of the writer.

In addition to producing the population census, the department prepares a labor force survey that keeps track of the country's employment situation, the consumer price index revealing changes in prices over time, and many business and economic surveys providing details on the country's economy.

Most of the information is readily available, not only through various publications but also through CANSIM, the public computer system. Thus the writer is able to gain information on everything from the census to Canadian culture.

You will probably find StatsCan's *Market Research Handbook* a useful volume.

StatsCan also utilizes a geocartographic system that translates numbers into visual images such as maps and charts. Information is accessible toll-free through regional offices. Going from Atlantic to Pacific, here are the numbers to call—first if you live in the area, and second if you live outside the area and require information from that region:

Newfoundland and Labrador
Local: 772-4073
Toll free: (800)563-4255

Maritime provinces
Local: 426-5331
Toll free: (800)565-7192

Quebec (except the National Capital Region)
Local: 283-5725
Toll free: (800)361-2831

Ontario (except the National Capital Region)
Local: 973-6586
Toll free: (800)263-1136

National Capital Region
Local: 951-8116

Manitoba
Local: 983-4020

Saskatchewan
Local: 780-5405
Toll free: (800)667-7164

Alberta and Northwest Territories
Local: 495-3026
Toll free (to Alberta): (800)282-3907
(to Northwest Territories, call collect): 1-403-495-3028

Southern Alberta (Calgary)
Local: 292-6717
Toll free: (800)472-9708

British Columbia and the Yukon
Local: 666-3691
Toll free (to B.C.): (800)663-1551
Toll free (to Yukon): Zenith 08913

The major publication available from Statistics Canada is *The Canada Year Book*, a standard reference for more than 120 years. It is available at most bookstores. It can be ordered by mail for $58.85 (shipping, handling and GST) going to Canadian addresses. For orders to the U.S. and other countries, the price is $70 in U.S. funds; this price includes shipping and handling costs. Checks or money orders should be made payable to the Receiver General of Canada, and should be mailed to Publications Sales, Statistics Canada, Ottawa ON K1A 0T6.

PERMISSIONS AND COPYRIGHT

Getting permission to quote from other writers is, as you read earlier, "a mysterious and muddied area"—that quote is permissible under the "Fair Use" provisions of the U.S. Copyright Law. In Canada, however, while quoting those few words is also permissible under the equivalent section of the *Copyright Act*, there is less flexibility in the Canadian law regarding the use of other people's words than there is in the U.S. statute.

The pertinent section of the Canadian law that governs the use of material whose copyright is owned by another writer is called "Fair Dealing." The two concepts—Fair Use and Fair Dealing—are vastly different. The Canadian law provides that it is not an infringement of copyright "to deal fairly" with any work provided that use is for one of five enumerated purposes: private study, research, criticism, review or newspaper summary. In contrast to the American law, in the Canadian statute fair dealing is not an exception under which a user obtains an advance statutory authorization to do things that are exclusively the right of the copyright owner.

When the Canadian Parliament worked through the 1980s on major revisions to the *Copyright Act*, which had been in place since 1924, almost everyone testifying before the government committee studying the problems of copyright agreed that the Fair Dealing section of the 1924 Act had worked well. No change was made. Meanwhile, says Marilyn Kay of the Canadian Copyright Institute, "work continues to revise the old act but there is no Parliamentary schedule giving anyone a clue as to when the second set of revisions will be debated, or even whether there may yet be a third set of revisions."

Canada has for decades been a signatory to the Berne Convention which provides copyright protection to the works of Canadian writers in the international field. This explains why for so many years—despite U.S. adherence to the Universal Copyright Convention under which the copyright notice embodied the © symbol—publishers in the United States arranged to have their books "published simultaneously" by a Canadian publisher. Now that the U.S. has signed the Berne agreements, this protective move is no longer necessary.

One important point that creative artists in the U.S. gain in having the country belong to the Berne group is that the writer's "moral rights" are protected. This means that no user of copyrighted material can make substantive changes in the original without the copyright holder's permission. An intriguing court case in Canada some years back involved a sculptor who created a flock of Canada geese in flight. These carved birds were suspended from the top of the atrium in a major shopping mall. At Christmas the following year the proprietors of the mall decided to "deck" the birds with winter scarves. The sculptor sued, claiming violation of his moral rights. He won the case.

The moral rights clause protects a novelist's work, for example, from being mutilated in a movie, TV or stage adaptation—unless the writer permits the revised version.

In Canada authors and their heirs have always retained copyright for life plus 50 years—a term introduced into the U.S. law in the late 1970s. Under Canadian law, writers and other artists possess an automatic copyright whether the work is published or not. Canadian copyright law does not require writers to register copyright, only to provide proof that they are owners of the work.

To register copyright in Canada, ask for the appropriate forms from Copyright and Industrial Design, Phase One, Place du Portage, 5th Floor, 50 Victoria St., Hull PQ K1A 0C9.

TRADEMARKS

Trademarks are not ordinary words. They are proper names that identify products of a business and distinguish them from products of other similar businesses. The life of legal protection for trademarks varies from country to country. That means that a trademark can lose its protection in one country but not in its neighbor.

A classic example is the trademark registered by the Bayer pharmaceutical company of Germany. They marketed pills composed of acetylsalicylic acid under the trademarked name, Aspirin. Eventually, after World War I, other pharmaceutical companies in the United States began to use the name and the German company was not given adequate protection against the trademark violation. The name became used generically so that now in the U.S. anyone can market aspirin (without the capital A). In Canada, however, the trademark was zealously protected so that only the Bayer brand is Aspirin (with the capital A), and other drug companies market the product as ASA (the acronym for the drug's chemical name).

The list of trademarks still protected is a mile long. It includes such words, used casually in everyday language, as Vaseline, Jell-O, Deepfreeze, Band-Aid, Jeep, Dictaphone, Mixmaster, Windbreaker—and so many more that it boggles the mind. As a writer, you should be as careful with a corporation's trademark as you would want them to be with your copyright. Many of the trademark words are identified in dictionaries—so if you want to be sure not to violate another person's property, the least you can do is spell the trademark word with an initial capital letter.

For specific information on trademarks that are registered in Canada, the Canadian government publishes a weekly periodical, *Trade Marks Journal*, that you might find of interest.

INFORMATION ACCESS

The *Access to Information Act* has been in operation in Canada since July, 1983. It allows Canadians to peruse federal documents—with certain exceptions. The exceptions are intended to provide protection for particular kinds of information, the release of which would cause "an identifiable harm" or would be contrary to the law. These exemptions protect, for example, information about national security or trade secrets. Also excluded is material directly connected with the operation of the federal Cabinet — such as Cabinet documents and minutes of records of decision. The act cannot give you access to records that are outside the control of the federal government, such as records maintained by provincial or municipal governments or by private institutions such as banks or credit bureaus.

To get access to the records you want, you need to refer to a copy of the *Access Register* which is available in public libraries and government information offices in major population centers as well as in some 2,000 postal stations in rural areas. You will also need to get an Access Request Form at the same location.

The *Register* and Request Form contain detailed instructions on how to identify, as far as possible, the information you are looking for, how to get assistance — if necessary — and how to apply for access. If you are not able to consult an *Access Register* or fill out a form you may write directly to the appropriate government institution clearly stating that you are requesting information under the *Access to Information Act.*

If you want to make personal contact with the Access Coordinator in the government institution involved, you will find the name, address and telephone number of all the coordinators in the *Access Register*. The coordinator will assist you to identify the records you wish to see, at no charge. If you ask for assistance by letter, include as much information as you can to identify the records you are looking for and be sure that you provide sufficient information to enable an official to send you a reply.

There is an application fee of $5 that must be submitted with your request. You also have to pay for time in excess of five hours spent in processing your request, as well as for copying and computer processing time. If the costs are considerable, you will be notified before they are incurred, and you may be asked to make a deposit.

The government institution has 30 days to respond to your request. If the request is for a large number of records, or is complicated, the institution can extend the time limit, but it must inform you that it has done so.

If you are not satisfied with the material you get, the government has established the Office of the Information Commissioner which will deal with your complaint. You have the right to complain to the commissioner if you believe you were wrongly denied access to information, or if the response took too long or cost too much. If, after complaining to the Information Commissioner, you are still unable to get access to the information, you may then take the case to the Federal Court.

You should be aware of the fact that the *Access to Information Act* prohibits disclosure of records that contain personal information unless the person to whom it relates has consented to disclosure, or the information is already publicly available, or the disclosure is in accordance with conditions set out in the *Privacy Act*.

RESOURCES

OUT-OF-PRINT/RARE BOOKS

If you can't find an antiquarian bookstore in your area, write to the Antiquarian Booksellers Association of Canada, P.O. Box 863, Station F, Toronto ON M4Y 2N7 for assistance. But you should first check to see if your library has a copy of the *Canadian Antiquarian Book Sellers Directory* published by Brandon University Press. You will also find local listings in the Yellow Pages under "Book Dealers—Used and Rare." There are also a number of book search operators who track down out-of-print titles. You will usually find small ads for such dealers in many of the book-related periodicals mentioned later in the Selling It section.

PRODUCING AND POLISHING IT

If you are looking for an editor to help you with the final polish on your manuscript, you may want to contact the Freelance Editors' Association of Canada (FEAC) at 35 Spadina Rd., Toronto ON M5R 2T1. They can be reached by phone at (416)366-7417. Services from this organization of professional editors include a referral hotline, which consists of members who are available to read your work, offer editorial services and give assistance in rewriting manuscripts.

You may also find editors who advertise in the classified sections of the trade magazines listed later. Some literary agents will provide a reading service, but understand that this does not commit the agent to represent you.

An excellent—but expensive—service is available from a highly respected editor and published novelist who only works with three or four writers at a time. This service is supplied by George Glay who, in addition to having had a number of bestselling books to his own credit, has been a literary agent in New York, editor-in-chief of Macfadden-Bartell and editorial director of Award Books (both in New York), and editorial manager for Harlequin Books at its world headquarters in Toronto.

Glay works by correspondence in an intense one-on-one association with only a few writers at a time — and he gives up to a full year of attention to each writer. He works in all fiction genres. Recent publication by his students has been in the fields of mystery, science fiction, romance, historicals and mid-list novels. His fee is $2,500 for the one-year association, paid in monthly installments, plus an override of 10% of all money earned by the book. Only seriously interested writers should follow up on this lead which can be done by writing to him for more information at Suite 1809, 80 St. Clair East, Toronto ON M4T 1N6.

TRANSLATORS

If you are looking for someone to do a translation of your work, or are yourself a translator looking for employment, contact the Literary Translators Association at Suite 510, 1030 rue Cherrier, Montreal PQ H2L 1A7.

INDEXING

To market your skills as an indexer, contact the Indexing and Abstracting Society of Canada at P.O. Box 744, Station F, Toronto ON M4Y 2N6, about membership requirements.

COLLABORATION

One of the most important aspects of making a collaboration agreement in Canada is that of credit — on the title page. Because of the public lending right (PLR) program and the reprography collective (CanCopy), referred to earlier, writers who are "credited" formally for a work are entitled to income from the use of their books in libraries and for use by photocopying.

GRAMMAR SERVICES

Are you the type for *who* the bell tolls? Then maybe a Grammar Hotline is what you need.

While some 60 hotlines are currently available in North America for the writer seeking an answer to a grammatical problem, only two are in Canada. But long-distance tolls may be less expensive to a hotline south of the border than to one of the Canadian services, so you may want to consider getting your help from one of the U.S. operations.

The Canadian Writer's Guide, listed in the Selling It section, names 31 hotlines in the United States that might be geographically less expensive. Or you can send a self-addressed stamped envelope (#10) to Grammar Hotline Directory, Tidewater Community College Writing Center, 1700 College Crescent, Virginia Beach VA 23456, and they will send you a copy of their latest directory.

Remember to use a U.S. postage stamp on your return envelope or get an International Reply Coupon from your local post office. If you prefer to use U.S. postage, write to Communications Unltd. at P.O. Box 55014, Fairview Mall P.O., Willowdale ON M2J 5B9 and send $7 in U.S. funds or $8 in Canadian funds along with a stamped return envelope. This will bring you 10 U.S. stamps in appropriate denominations and a chart outlining U.S. first class postal rates to Canada.

CANADIAN GRAMMAR HOTLINES

Grant MacEwan Community College
Edmonton AB T5J 2P2
(403)450-4666

This service is conducted by Karl Homann. The phones are staffed Monday to Friday, from 10 a.m. to noon and from 12:30 p.m. to 2 p.m., Mountain Time.

University of New Brunswick
Fredericton NB E3B 5A3
(506)453-4666 or 453-3631

The service here has variable hours due to a lack of funding from the university. It is run by A.M. Kinloch.

The states closest to the Canadian border in which grammar services are available are, from west to east, California, Colorado, Kansas, Missouri, Wisconsin, Illinois, Indiana, Michigan, Ohio, Pennsylvania, New York and Massachusetts.

ARTISTS AND PHOTOGRAPHERS

The prime published source of illustrators and photographers in Canada is *Creative Source* published by Wilcord Publications Limited, Suite 100, 511 King St. W., Toronto ON M5V 2Z4. Wilcord can be reached by telephone in Montreal at (514)849-5812, in Toronto at (416)599-5797 and in Vancouver at (604)688-6819. The book is distributed in Canada by

Firefly Books. Distribution in the U.S. is handled by Watson Guptill, where it is called *Canadian Creative Source*.

The big, oversize volume lists hundreds of illustrators and photographers from coast to coast, shows samples of their work and indicates in which of 16 styles they create—from abstract to technical.

Another source of photographers is the *Canadian Directory of Professional Photography*, an annual published by The Professional Photographers of Canada and distributed by Craig Kelman Associates at Suite 17, 399 Berry St., Winnipeg MB R3J 1N6. Their phone number is (204)885-7798.

In addition, the Professional Photographers of Canada Inc., at 1215 Penticton Ave., Penticton BC V2A 2N3 is the parent body of seven provincial member associations. The PPC can be reached by phone at (604)493-4322. The member associations are:

Alberta Professional Photographers Association
16136 - 110B Ave.
Edmonton AB T5P 4E6

Professional Photographers Association of B.C.
1215 Penticton Ave.
Penticton BC V2A 2N3
(605)492-0202

Professional Photographers Association of Manitoba
704 Watt St.
Winnipeg MB R2K 2S7
(204)661-2463

Maritime Professional Photographers Association
221 Reade St.
Moncton NB E1C 6S7

Professional Photographers of Ontario Inc.
4501 Eglinton Ave.
Toronto ON M9C 5K6
(416)620-1203

Les Photographes professionnels du Québec
C.P. 1068
Sorel PQ J3P 7L4
(514)743-7385

Saskatchewan Professional Photographers Association Inc.
P.O. Box 1295
Battleford SK S0M 0E0
(306)937-3800

SELF-PUBLISHING

More and more Canadian authors are turning to self-publishing since the advent of the desktop publishing revolution – often without an awareness of the problems they have set up for themselves *after* their books are printed and delivered to be stored in a basement or in the garage. Of course, there are success stories that one can point to, but inevitably the authors have outgoing personalities and can *sell* those books just as capably – or even more – as they were able to write them. If you are prepared to make the effort to sell your books, here are a few of the elements of getting them into the marketplace that you should know.

Once you have finished books, you have to establish a marketing plan, including self-promotion. You have to be able to get around to bookstores in as far-reaching an area as possible, and you have to beat the drums with radio and TV talk shows (principally at the local level) and try to get yourself interviewed by the print and electronic media.

If the book "takes off," there is always the possibility that a trade publisher will contact you and seek to undertake commercial publication. That will mean broader distribution but, of course, smaller profits. Getting royalties, on a per-book basis, is never as much as getting all the profits – but that's a decision you have to make for yourself.

The first step you take after having written the book, and having it edited, copyedited, set into type and then proofread (even if you did the typesetting yourself with a desktop facility), is to find a printer and, possibly, a binder if the printing house you use doesn't do binding.

The Book Trade in Canada, mentioned later in Word Markets, lists all kinds of services in this area. Having made your deal, you'll want to find sales representatives and/or wholesalers who might be interested in trying to get your book into bookstores. You will find a listing of both in *Canadian Publishers Directory*, published semi-annually by *Quill & Quire*. This directory is not likely to be found on the shelves of your local library, but check at the reference desk. Most libraries subscribe to the journal and get the *Directory* free with their subscription.

You will probably want to carry an ISBN (that is, an International Standard Book Number) in your book. To get ISBN information write to the Canadian ISBN Agency at the National Library of Canada, 395 Wellington St., Ottawa ON K1A 0N4, or telephone them at (819)997-9565.

If you intend to approach bookstores to carry your book, you'll want to consult the list available in *The Book Trade in Canada*. They are arranged by province to ease your task.

To help you in your promotion, you should look at:

- *Five Fast Steps to Low-Cost Publicity* by Barbara Florio Graham, which is available in bookstores and might be in your local library, too. The book is distributed by Opal Services, 2156 Dublin Ave., Ottawa ON K2C 0X6, but if your bookstore can't supply a copy, you can write to Simon Teakettle Ink — enclosing $18 to cover postage, handling and GST — at 200 Charles St., Gatineau PQ J8P 3X4.

- Another useful handbook that gives the Canadian angle to self-publishing is *The Canadian Self-Publishing Handbook*, by Laura M. Gateman (Spinning Wheel Publishing). If your bookstore can't get you a copy, write to the publisher (a self-publishing operation) at R.R. 1, Chesley ON N0G 1L0.

You might also want to try to advertise your book to a mailing list of some 5,000 bookbuyers that is available once a year. This service has been developed by the Canadian Authors Association. For information as to when the next catalog is going to press and what the current price is per listing, address your inquiry to:

Authors' Bookshelf Catalogue
Suite 104
121 Avenue Rd.
Toronto ON M5R 2G3

ADDITIONAL RESOURCES

(Prices quoted may change but include postage, handling and GST unless otherwise specified.)

From The Canadian Children's Book Centre:
35 Spadina Ave.
Toronto ON M5R 2S9
Writing for Children Kit
$12.95 (plus $3.25 for handling and $1.13 GST)

From League of Canadian Poets:
24 Ryerson Ave.
Toronto ON M5T 2P3
Poetry Markets for Canadians
$15.51

From Periodical Writers Association of Canada:
24 Ryerson Ave.
Toronto ON M5T 2P3

Words For Sale
A how-to book on "breaking in" to the Canadian market. $17.07

The Write Way
A discussion of problems writers have with editors. $6.42

Magazine Markets and Fees
Editorial requirements and fee schedules for 250 Canadian periodicals.
  $17.12

From The Writer's Union of Canada:
24 Ryerson Ave.
Toronto ON M5T 2P3

Anthology Rates and Contracts
Discusses contributions, rates and a suggested contract. $4

Author-Editor
Describes the author-editor relationship, with a list of do's and don'ts. $4

Authors and Archives
A guide to marketing your archival material. $2

Author's Wills
Why and how writers' wills are different. $2

Awards, Competitions & Grants
A descriptive list of what's available to Canadian writers. $4

Help Yourself to a Better Contract
A checklist of favorable book-contract provisions. $6.50

Libel: A Handbook for Canadian Publishers, Editors and Writers $3

Tradebook Contract
A list of reasonable minimum terms, and a model royalty statement. $4

Writer and Literary Agent
Guidelines governing the relationship; includes a list of Canadian agents.
  $3.50

Writers' Guide to Canadian Publishers $5.50

Writer's Income Tax Guide $3

From Public Focus:
500 - 489 College St.
Toronto ON M6G 1A5

Environmental Resource Directory
A two-year subscription including three biannual updates. $37.45

From Saskatchewan Writers Guild:
2049 Lorne St.
P.O. Box 3986
Regina SK S4P 3R9

Saskatchewan Literary Arts Handbook
Useful for Canadian writers from coast to coast. $10.70

From Seniors Secretariat:
Health and Welfare Canada
Ottawa ON K1A 0K9

Seniors' Guide to Federal Programs and Services
A wealth of information for the writer covering the seniors' scene. Free.

From Canadian Authors Association
275 Slater St., #500
Ottawa ON K1P 5H9

Careers in Journalism
A primer for secondary school guidance counselors. $22

From Cherry Tree Press
P.O. Box 5113, Station B
Victoria BC V8R 6N3

Writer's Mini Kit
Tips and guidelines for beginning writers. $12.80

SELLING IT

NEWSPAPERS

There are several sources listing newspapers in Canada. All the reference volumes group the newspapers by province, but they vary in what information they give. Some give only addresses. Others list the names of specific editors, as well as mailing addresses, telephone numbers and, more often than not, fax numbers.

Canada's largest newspaper is *The Toronto Star*. It publishes seven days a week and offers many special sections, especially in the Saturday or Sunday editions. There are, for example, sections dedicated to home and gardening, cars, entertainment, travel, sports, business, careers, lifestyles, insights, people and fashion. Each of these sections is open to material from freelance writers, according to John Honderich, editor of the *Star*.

The Globe and Mail (also published out of Toronto) calls itself "Canada's National Newspaper" and is printed in various cities across the country by satellite transmission every day except Sunday. As a national newspaper, it specifically stresses the business scene and carries a daily section called "Report on Business" that occasionally uses non-staff-written material, says Publisher Roy Megarry.

The Globe and Mail also publishes a variety of magazines, some on a monthly basis, others less frequently. These include three city magazines, *Montreal*, *Toronto*, and a third published out of Vancouver called *West*, as well as magazines on travel (*Destinations*), and fashion (*Domino*), which buy material from freelance writers.

The daily edition is also a market for the freelance writer and seems to have a wider scope of interests in that it has several "opinion" pages that frequently take contributions from freelance writers. The Saturday edition is a larger offering with special sections on travel, sports, entertainment and, of course, business. A recent cutback in the size of the sports staff may open up some opportunities for writers in this area.

The Globe has just produced a new stylebook which might prove useful for the writer seeking to sell to that market. It is available for $24.95 (Canadian orders must add $1.75 for Goods and Services Tax). Orders should be sent to Style Book Sales, Marketing Department, 444 Front St. W., Toronto ON M5V 2S9.

The daily newspapers in Ottawa (the nation's capital), Halifax, Montreal, Winnipeg, Regina, Saskatoon, Calgary, Edmonton, Vancouver and Victoria serving, as they do, the larger population centers of the country, are also possible freelance markets.

In many respects the travel article seems to have the broadest appeal — the subject matter can be most eclectic as well as having the widest possibility of serving more than one market. Two national business papers also provide opportunities for the freelance writer. *The Financial Post* publishes daily and has a weekly edition, while the *Financial Times* is published weekly.

NEWSPAPER LISTINGS

CARD
(Canadian Advertising Rates and Data)
Maclean Hunter Publications

777 Bay St.
Toronto ON M5W 1A7

Because this monthly is used widely by advertising agencies, there probably isn't a single newspaper or periodical in the country that isn't listed—and they make sure they keep getting listed by returning corrected proof copy of their listing *every month!* That makes *CARD* a very useful publication for the freelance writer to have access to. Your library more than likely subscribes— it costs $384 a year, or $175 for a single issue if you're thinking of buying one for your own reference shelf. It carries lists of business publications, community newspapers, dailies, ethnic newspapers and periodicals, farm periodicals, religious magazines and newspapers, scholarly journals, "shoppers" (the give-away weeklies that are loaded with advertising, but do carry editorial), weekend newspapers (there are only two English-language ones in Canada), and even university and school papers. Radio and television stations are, of course, listed—and so are the advertising agencies with listings of their personnel. The addresses are complete—and very up to date, considering that they are checked each month.

Canadian Almanac and Directory
Copp Clark Pitman Ltd.
2775 Matheson Blvd. East
Mississauga ON L4W 4P7

An old standby, this annual carries reams of useful material—though its listing of newspapers and periodicals is slim; there is usually only one line devoted to each with the simplest of addresses. It is worth having on your reference shelf but, depending upon the type of writing you do, it could be this volume or the two-volume work listed next.

The Corpus Almanac and Canadian Sourcebook
Corpus Information Services
Southam Communications Limited
1450 Don Mills Rd.
Don Mills ON M3B 2X7

This directory is available in the reference section of most libraries. It is published in two volumes. In Volume I you will find a list of English, French and bilingual newspapers published in Canada (about one-quarter of the population speaks French as a first language), as well as a list of periodicals covering the ethnic-minority communities. All the listings are of publications that are issued minimally once a month and consist only of address, phone and fax numbers. The ethnic press listing ranges across some 40 languages from Arabic to Urdu, and covers the Black and native communities as well. The weeklies listed in the Corpus volume include only a few of the "alternative" newspapers published in Canada.

Matthew's List
Corpus Information Services
Southam Communications Limited
1450 Don Mills Rd.
Don Mills ON M3B 2X7

This is an expensive reference volume, but it can be found at many libraries. It provides names, contact information, and program producers of Canadian radio and television stations and editors of newspapers. It is published three times a year and if you want to subscribe, the *List* costs $150 for a one-year subscription.

A selected list of Canadian dailies:

Calgary Herald
215 - 16th St. S.E.
Calgary AB T2P 0W8

Chronicle-Herald
1650 Argyle St.
Halifax NS B3J 2T2

Edmonton Journal
P.O. Box 2421
Edmonton AB T5J 2S6

The Gazette
250 St-Antoine St. West
Montreal PQ H2Y 3R7

The Globe and Mail
444 Front St. West
Toronto ON M5V 2S9

Guardian & Patriot
165 Prince St.
Charlottetown PEI C1A 4R8

The Hamilton Spectator
44 Frid St.
Hamilton ON L8N 3G3

The Leader-Post
1964 Park St.
Regina SK S4P 3G4

The London Free Press
P.O. Box 2280
London ON N6A 4G1

The Ottawa Citizen
1101 Baxter Road, P.O. Box 5020
Ottawa ON K2C 3M4

The Star-Phoenix
240 5th Ave. North
Saskatoon SK S7K 2P1

Telegram
P.O. Box 5970
St. John's NF A1C 5X7

Telegraph-Journal
210 Crown St., P.O. Box 2350
Saint John NB E2L 3V8

The Toronto Star
1 Yonge St.
Toronto ON M5E 1E6

The Vancouver Sun/Province
2250 Granville St.
Vancouver BC V6H 3G2

The Victoria Times-Colonist
2621 Douglas St., Box 33
Victoria BC V8W 2N4

Winnipeg Free Press
300 Carlton St.
Winnipeg MB R3C 3C1

Among the alternative press offerings are one national paper, *The Independent*, which is interested in news and opinion from all parts of the country. It is published from 15 King St., Elmira ON N3B 2R1.

Other alternative newspapers exist mainly in Toronto, and include such offerings as *NOW*, but its content is very local in interest and seems to stress the entertainment scene in the main. Most of the major Canadian cities, however, have alternative newspapers that come and go — and they, again, tend to be extremely local in their outlook, with an entertainment bent.

There are no longer any weekly magazine sections in the newspapers of the country. However, some of the dailies do occasionally produce a "magazine" section depending, it seems, on the economy and whether advertising dollars can be found to support such efforts. The most recent magazine to close shop had been included with the Saturday edition of *The Toronto Star*. In its place, the Saturday Entertainment section has been enlarged.

SYNDICATES

Syndication in Canada is not a major source of income for the freelance writer looking for new markets. There is only one major syndicate, affiliated with *The Toronto Star*. They are not interested in seeing material over the transom. "This, however, does not preclude our expressing interest in something we may see in print," says Jim Cherrier, manager of the Toronto Star Syndicate.

The second largest syndicate, run by the Southam newspaper chain, is more likely to take a look at ideas from freelance writers.

The others may be worth approaching. Being smaller, they are usually open to the possibility of coming up with the next world-beater.

A great source for the freelance writer is to get hold of a copy of the *Annual Directory of Syndicated Services* published by *Editor & Publisher* at 11 West 19th St., New York NY 10011. It has an office in Canada at 148 King Rd. E., King ON L0G 1K0 which might be able to help you acquire a copy.

This annual not only lists all the U.S. syndicates but also lists a few in the U.K. and elsewhere in the world.

CANADIAN SYNDICATES

Asterisk Features
P.O. Box 250
Nanoose Bay BC V0R 2R0

Canada Wide Feature Service Limited
P.O. Box 345, Station A
Toronto ON M5W 1C2

Christian Features Inc.
126 Metcalfe St. East
Strathroy ON N7G 1P3

HFM Literary Enterprises, Inc.
P.O. Box 307
Edmonton AB T5J 2J7

Miller Features Syndicate, Inc.
1100 - 180 Bloor St. West
Toronto ON M5S 2V6

Southam Syndicate
20 York Mills Rd.
North York ON M2P 2C2

Toronto Star Syndicate
1 Front St.
Toronto ON M5E 1E6

TELEVISION

With cutbacks in government assistance to the arts continuing unabated into 1991, and the economy generally in a tight situation, the high cost of production—especially in the field of television—means that every project is being gone over with the proverbial fine-toothed comb. Nonetheless, new work continues to be produced and writers continue to find markets—if they are persistent and have something unique to offer.

The Canadian Broadcasting Corporation, the country's largest network in both mediums, suffered a huge budgetary—and staff—cutback at the end of 1990 but it continues to consider outstanding ideas, particularly in the one-hour and 90-minute TV categories. Global Television Network is prepared to support productions that have been initiated independently—particularly shows with series potential.

Other TV possibilities include the independent CTV network, through its flag station CFTO-TV, as well as CFMT-TV, which may consider short freelance contributions, and CITY-TV which is prepared to look at series concepts (five to 20 episodes) and feature-length films.

Another possibility is the education network, TV Ontario, which does programming in various areas such as children's, educational, part-time learning and adult.

CARD carries listings for all the networks, regular and cable, as well as all the TV stations in the country.

LISTINGS

CBC Television Script Services
P.O. Box 500, Station A
Toronto ON M5W 1E6

CFTO-TV Project Development Department
P.O. Box 9
Scarborough ON M4A 2M9

Global Television Network Project Development Department
81 Barber Greene Rd.
Don Mills ON M3C 2A2

CITY-TV
99 Queen St. East
Toronto ON M5C 2M1

CFMT-TV
545 Lakeshore Blvd.
Toronto ON M5V 1A3

TV Ontario
2180 Yonge St.
P.O. Box 200, Station Q
Toronto ON M4T 2T1

Cable television is providing new markets on a small scale as the networks of cable-distributed programming seek to offer alternative types of entertainment and educational programs on the channels they control. The largest of the cable operators are Rogers and Maclean Hunter. But there are smaller companies across the country and a quick check of the programming on your local cable channel will give you a fair idea of the kind of material your cable distributor might be interested in pursuing. You can get the cable company's address in your local telephone book and the switchboard operator can probably tell you who's in charge of programming.

FILMMAKING

The National Film Board of Canada (NFB) was founded in 1939 to produce, promote and distribute films in the national interest. NFB provides assistance to and works with independent filmmakers, encouraging innovative themes or approaches to filmmaking. About 100 original films are produced annually, and more than 4,000 have been produced since the board's inception. NFB has maintained a high profile at international film festivals and has won almost 2,000 awards, including many Oscars.

In recent years, the board has placed increased emphasis on research and development into film and video technology and has established training programs for young filmmakers. They operate a cross-Canada film library service and produce film catalogs.

Operational headquarters of the board is in Montreal and the mailing address is P.O. Box 6100, Station A, Montreal PQ H3C 3H5. For general inquiries the phone number is (514)283-9000. There are six regional centers and three offices abroad.

REGIONAL CENTERS

1571 Argyle St.
Halifax NS B3J 2B2

102 - 200 Dorchester West
Montreal PQ H2Z 1X4

1 Lombard St.
Toronto ON M5C 1J6

245 Main St.
Winnipeg MB R3C 1A7

10031 - 103rd Avenue
Edmonton AB T5J 0G9

1161 West Georgia St.
Vancouver BC V6E 3G4

OFFICES ABROAD

16th Floor
1251 Avenue of the Americas
New York NY 10021

1 Grosvenor Sq.
London, England W1X 0AB

15 rue de Berri
Paris 75008 France

RADIO

There are some outlets for radio writing, even in the face of cutbacks throughout the industry early in the 1990s. Experienced writer/broadcasters of commentary continue to find markets for their work, as do writers of documentaries. Radio drama has special needs and Canadian Broadcasting Corporation, particularly, has a variety of programs that are always on the lookout for good radio drama. CBC Script Services at the ubiquitous CBC mailing address (P.O. Box 500, Station A, Toronto ON M5W 1E6) will send guidelines for both radio and TV dramatic scripts. Address your queries for guidelines to Script Services. For contributions to variety programming, direct your inquiries to "Radio Variety"; and for radio plays, address the query to "Radio Drama" – all at the above address.

Aside from the listings in *CARD* other radio markets include:

CHFI-FM *(which does occasional lifestyle features)*
10th Floor
25 Adelaide St. East
Toronto ON M5C 1H3

CJRT-FM *(which welcomes ideas for "Open College")*
297 Victoria St.
Toronto ON M2B 1W1

WORD MARKETS

There are many magazine and corporate markets in Canada. The advice given previously about these markets covers the territory admirably for the Canadian market as it does for the U.S. market.

In the corporate field, the obvious sources of clients are listings in the telephone Yellow Pages. Looking under "Associations," for example, leads to hundreds of organizations that use freelance writers from time to time. And a quick look through the Yellow Pages – if you've never done so before – will provide you with endless leads: from accountants to zoos, with hundreds of possibilities in between, including such categories as hospitals, advertising agencies, insurance companies, art galleries and photographers.

An excellent volume to check is *Sources* in which hundreds of businesses as well as associations buy space to list their public relations contacts. The volume is used by the news media and magazines whenever they need a source to quote or have information to gather. But for the freelance writer, that same PR source can prove to be a useful contact to get leads on writing jobs that need to be done for the organization listed.

The Better Business Bureau in your city (or the largest city near you) probably publishes its own *Directory and Consumer Guide*, ranging from accommodations to wreckers. And the telephone company publishes an *800 Service Directory*, which lists companies and organizations across the country ranging from abattoirs to yogurt manufacturers – and you can telephone any of them toll free!

In addition, there are reference volumes in most libraries that will open your eyes as to the possibilities that exist. A handful include *The Canadian Book of Corporate Management* (Dun & Bradstreet), *The Financial Post Directory of Directors* (Maclean Hunter), *Who's Who is Canadian Business* and *Who's Who in Canadian Finance* (both Trans-Canada Press), five directories published by the federal department of Industry, Science and Technology – *Directory of Canadian Consulting Engineers*, *Directory of Canadian Trading Houses*, *Directory of Computer Software and Services*, *Directory of Architects*, and *Directory of Management Consultants*.

The Directory of Associations (MicroMedia) and *The Blue Book of Canadian Business* (Canadian Newspaper Services International Ltd.), are great sources of leads for the writer interested in the lucrative corporate markets.

Sources
Suite 402
9 St. Nicholas St.
Toronto ON M4Y 1W5

BOOK REVIEWS AND EDITORIAL COPY

TRADE PUBLICATIONS

The book trade in Canada is covered by a number of publications, one of them on the national level – *Quill & Quire* – and several on a regional basis. In addition *Books In Canada*, while mainly a book review monthly, also carries news of the industry.

MAGAZINE AND NEWSPAPER BOOK REVIEWS

There are a number of periodicals that regularly carry book reviews. While they are not specifically identified that way, the long list of periodicals (divided by category) carried in *The Canadian Writer's Guide* (Fitzhenry & Whiteside) is the most useful source of magazines that should be checked as possible users of items relating to books (and possibly even to reviews).

The newspapers referred to earlier in this section are probably the best bets to getting a book reviewed, though depending on the subject matter of your book, you may find many of the newspapers listed in *CARD*, *Matthew's* or the *Corpus Almanac* will entertain the possibility of reviewing books that fit their audiences. A query letter with a stamped, addressed return postcard will let you know quickly whether it is worth sending them material.

TELEVISION AND RADIO

The one major national television news show in Canada that can have an impact on book sales is CTV's "Canada AM." It does author interviews fairly frequently and every publisher's publicity department undoubtedly tries to get each of their authors onto that early morning exposure slot. Also on television are a number of shows in various locales across the country and if you are not aware of them, you should consult your local TV listings and check out the talk shows that welcome authors as guests.

On radio, CBC's "Morningside" with author/host Peter Gzowski is the one cross-country show that every publisher tries to sell to. But, in this medium there are many talk and phone-in shows on the local level that you should check out yourself—shows that most publishers' PR departments know about. By stressing the local angle, you might be able to interest the program in doing something on your book.

BOOKSTORES AND DISTRIBUTION

Checking out local bookstores is a worthwhile activity. If you are not entirely aware of all the bookstores in your area, your library should have a copy of *The Book Trade in Canada*. It carries an extensive listing of bookstores across the country.

The Book Trade in Canada
Ampersand Communications Services Inc.
2766 Sheffield Rd.
Ottawa ON K1B 3V9

This is the Canadian equivalent (in a small way) of *Literary Market Place* (LMP) in the U.S. It is an annual, though publication has not been too regular—yet it does appear with updated material about every 12 to 16 months. If it isn't in your local library, it can be purchased by mail.

The Canadian Writer's Guide
Fitzhenry & Whiteside
195 Allstate Parkway
Markham ON L3R 4T8

The "official handbook of the Canadian Authors Association," this guide will be reissued in its 11th edition in the summer of 1991. The volume currently consists of more than 100 chapters aimed at helping writers—both professional and emerging — in every possible way on just about every aspect of the writing game. It also has a large markets section that lists up-to-date details of more than 1,000 magazines published in the country, as well as more than 300 book publishers and their needs. Like all guides of this kind, it suffers from the vagaries of the publishing business. Almost before it is off press, some publishers have gone out of business, others have changed philosophical direction and still others have moved. Nonetheless this large volume is the best value for money — a statement that can be attested to by the fact that both the ninth and 10th editions reached bestseller proportions in bookstore sales.

The Canadian Writer's Market
McClelland & Stewart
481 University Ave.
Toronto ON M5G 2E9

This slim volume is in its ninth edition and is mainly a listing of periodical and book publishers. It attempts to give the names of the current editors, but as with addresses and editorial directions, these change frequently and you should double-check before sending material.

Writers' Guide to Canadian Magazines
Writer's Publishing Group
671F Market Hill
Vancouver BC V5Z 4B5

A newcomer to the publishing reference scene that suffers even more than the previously mentioned publications from changes in data. It was published in 1988 and the publisher is no longer at the phone number given in the book and does not reply to mail sent to the address listed. Whether a new edition will appear is moot. The editors state that their survey questionnaire sent to 1,241 magazines only elicited a 20% response. Nonetheless, if your library carries a copy, or if you can still find a copy at your local bookstore, it may prove useful to you in a particular area and is worth checking.

Canadian Author
Suite 500
275 Slater St.
Ottawa ON K1P 549

This quarterly magazine, founded in 1919, in addition to carrying useful craft articles and author interviews (as well as fiction and poetry) has a regular markets feature that updates the current scene in both the magazine and book fields in Canada. It also reviews books about writing and publishing. Interestingly, it has a large circulation — both to individual subscribers and libraries — in the U.S. and overseas.

PUBLISHERS ASSOCIATIONS

Association of Book Publishers of British Columbia
1622 West 7th Ave.
Vancouver BC V6J 1S5
(604)734-1611

Association of Canadian Publishers
260 King St. East
Toronto ON M5A 1K3
(416)361-1408

Association of Canadian University Presses
% Pontifical Institute of Mediaeval Studies
59 Queen's Park Crescent
Toronto ON M5S 2C4
(416)926-7143

Association of Manitoba Book Publishers
406 - 100 Arthur St.
Winnipeg MB R3B 1H3
(204)947-3335

Atlantic Publishers Association
4th Floor
1741 Barrington St.
Halifax NS B3J 2A4
(902)420-0711

Book Publishers Association of Alberta
10523 - 100th Ave.
Edmonton AB T5J 0A8
(403)424-5060

Canadian Book Publishers' Council
203 - 250 Merton St.
Toronto ON M4Y 1S2
(416)322-7011

Christian Booksellers Association
1574 Lincoln Rd.
Windsor ON N8Y 2J4
(519)254-8692

Literary Press Group
260 King St. East
Toronto ON M5A 1K3
(416)361-1408

Western Book Reps
P.O. Box 69718, Station K
Vancouver BC V5K 4Y7

TRADE PUBLICATIONS

The following publications carry prepublication reviews and are read by booksellers and librarians:

B.C. BookWorld
940 Station St.
Vancouver BC V6A 2X4
(604)684-2470

Books In Canada
Canadian Review of Books Limited
432 - 366 Adelaide St. East
Toronto ON M5A 3X9
(416)363-5426

Canadian Author
275 Slater St., #500
Ottawa ON K1P 5H9

CA&B reviews poetry books in its Canadian Poetry section, and books on the craft or business of writing.

Canadian Bookseller
Canadian Booksellers Association
301 Donlands Ave.
Toronto ON M4J 3R8
(416)467-7939

Prairie Book World
710 Beresford Ave.
Winnipeg MB R3L 1K1
(204)475-9160

Quill & Quire
4th Floor
70 The Esplanade
Toronto ON M5E 1R2
(416)360-0044

Associations and Organizations

Business-Related Resources

Books, Periodicals and Directories

Databases, Bulletin Boards and Vendors

More Great Books for Writers

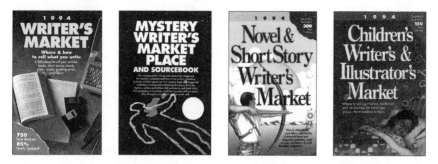

Writer's Market — updated annually to bring you the latest information on the publishing industry from top professionals in the field. You'll also find 4,000 listings of buyers who are looking for your work, how much they pay, how to submit, etc. *#10339/1008 pages/$26.95, hardcover*

Mystery Writer's Market Place and Sourcebook — Takes you inside the mystery field offering listings of 115 mystery book and magazine publishers, writing and marketing tips from top mystery writers and editors, and a look at what's happening in the current mystery market. *#10380/312 pages/$17.95*

Novel & Short Story Writer's Market — get your short stories and novels published with these complete, updated listings of 1,900 fiction publishers. And, expert tips from successful writers and editors help you target your work to the right buyers. *#10361/662 pages/$19.95, paperback*

Children's Writer's & Illustrator's Market — updated each year, includes 600 comprehensive listings of book and magazine publishers; along with helpful articles by experts to help you make it in this lucrative market. *#10362/352 pages/$19.95, paperback*

Guide to Literary Agents & Art/Photo Reps — answers the most-often asked questions about reps, and offers a listing of over 480 literary agents or artists' and photographers' agents. *#10363/240 pages/$18.95, paperback*

How to Write Irresistible Query Letters — covers how to slant your story, use research shortcuts, hook an editor with a tantalizing lead, and sell yourself as the expert for the job. *#10146/144 pages/$10.95, paperback*

How to Write a Book Proposal — a step-by-step guide that helps you check the salabilty of your book ideas, offers inside tips and addresses to help you get additional help, and a complete sample proposal. *#10173/132 pages/$11.95, paperback*

Writer's Digest Guide to Manuscript Formats — an easy-to-follow guide to all types of manuscript formats preparation and presentation — from books and articles to poems and plays. *#10025/198 pages/$18.95, hardcover*

Use the order form below (photocopy acceptable) and save when you order two or more books!

- -